Rethinking Third Cinema

This innovative and timely anthology addresses established notions about Third Cinema theory and its impact on the cinematic practices of developing and postcolonial nations. Emerging from the activism of Che Guevara and Frantz Fanon, the Third Cinema movement called for a politicized tri-continental approach to film-making in Africa, Asia, and Latin America which would foreground issues of social justice, class division, ethnicity, and national identity.

The films that best represented the movement, including those from such internationally respected directors as Ousmane Sembène, Satyajit Ray, Fernando Solanas, Tomás Gutierrez Alea, and Nelson Pereira dos Santos, are among the most culturally significant and politically sophisticated texts of the 1960s and 1970s. Yet despite the popularity and critical attention enjoyed by its acknowledged masterpieces, Third Cinema and its critical framework – notably the only major body of film theory that did not originate in a specifically Euro-American context – appear to have lost their momentum.

Rethinking Third Cinema returns Third Cinema and its theory to the critical spotlight. The contributors address the most difficult questions Third Cinema posed and continues to pose in an age of globalization, suggesting new methodologies and redirections of existing ones, whilst rereading the phenomenon of film-making in a fast-vanishing "Third World". Ranging over terrain that encompasses the majority of the world's cinemas, they offer case studies within and beyond the national cinemas of Brazil, Egypt, Indonesia, Argentina, China, Iran, Ghana, and India.

Anthony R. Guneratne teaches film, media, and visual culture at Florida Atlantic University and is presently a visiting scholar in Harvard University's Department of English. He is author of *Cinehistory: The Representation of Reality in Documentary and Narrative Cinema* (2004).

Wimal Dissanayake is a Visiting Professor in Cultural Studies at the University of Hong Kong. He is the author of *Melodrama and Asian Cinema* (1993), *New Chinese Cinema* (1998), and *Colonialism and Nationalism in Asian Cinema* (1994).

Rethinking Third Cinema

Edited by Anthony R. Guneratne
and Wimal Dissanayake

Routledge
Taylor & Francis Group

NEW YORK AND LONDON

First published 2003
by Routledge
29 West 35th Street, New York, NY 10001

Simultaneously published in the UK
by Routledge
11 New Fetter Lane, London EC4P 4EE

Routledge is an imprint of the Taylor & Francis Group

Typeset in Galliard by
HWA Text and Data Management, Tunbridge Wells
Printed and bound in Great Britain by
MPG Books Ltd, Bodmin, Cornwall.

Library of Congress Cataloging in Publication Data
A catalog record for this book has been requested

British Library Cataloguing in Publication Data
A catalogue record for this book is available from the British Library

ISBN 0–415–21353–3 (hbk)
ISBN 0–415–21354–1 (pbk)

Contents

Contributors

Sumita S. Chakravarty is a member of the core faculty of New School University and Chair of Cultural Studies at Lang College. She has contributed chapters to several anthologies on the cinemas of the Third World and her books include *National Identity in Indian Popular Cinema, 1947–1987* and the anthology *The Enemy Within: The Films of Mrinal Sen*. Her present research centers on media and globalization.

Rey Chow is Andrew W. Mellon Professor of the Humanities at Brown University where she teaches Comparative Literature, Modern Culture and Media Studies. Among her books are *Writing Diaspora: Tactics of Intervention in Contemporary Cultural Studies* and *Primitive Passions: Visuality, Sexuality, Ethnography, and Contemporary Chinese Cinema*, as well as the forthcoming *The Protestant Ethnic and the Spirit of Capitalism*.

Wimal Dissanayake is Visiting Professor of Comparative Literature and Cultural Studies at the University of Hong Kong. He has written or edited over a dozen works on Indian and other Asian cinemas and media phenomena, among which are *Colonialism and Nationalism in Asian Cinema*, *Global/Local: Cultural Production and the Transnational Imaginary*, *New Chinese Cinema*, *A Profile of Sri Lankan Cinema* and *Sights of Contestation*.

Marvin D'Lugo is author of over one hundred articles, books and book chapters on Spanish and Latin American cinema, is Professor of Spanish and Screen Studies at Clark University. Among his books are *The Films of Carlos Saura* and *Guide to the Cinema of Spain*. He is currently completing a number of articles on Argentinian cinema and a book on *The Transnational Imaginary in Spanish-Language Cinema*.

Anthony R. Guneratne teaches film, media and cultural studies at Florida Atlantic University. He has published articles on film history and historiography, on the interrelation of different media, on Indian and Singaporean cinema, and on manifestations of postcoloniality in literature and film. He is author of the forthcoming *Cinehistory: The Representation of Reality in Documentary and Narrative Cinema*.

Hamid Naficy is the Nina J. Cullinan Professor of Art and Art History and of Film and Media Studies at Rice University. He has published extensively on national, transnational, exilic and diasporic cinemas. Among his recent books are *An Accented Cinema: Exilic and Diasporic Filmmaking* and *Home, Exile, Homeland: Film, Media and the Politics of Place*. A book on *Cinema and National Identity: A Social History of Iranian Cinema* is forthcoming.

Krishna Sen teaches on various issues pertaining to contemporary Indonesian culture at Curtin University of Technology (Australia). She has written a number of articles on Indonesian cinema and society, as well as on related topics. Her books in the field include *Indonesian Cinema: Framing the New Order* and (with co-author David Hill) *Media, Culture and Politics in Indonesia*.

Ella Shohat is Professor of Art and Public Policy, Middle Eastern Studies and Comparative Literature at New York University. In addition to serving on the boards of the journals *Social Text* and *Public Culture*, she has published a variety of books of feminist and postcolonial issues including *Talking Visions: Multicultural Feminism in a Transcultural Age* and, with Robert Stam, the multi-award winning *Unthinking Eurocentrism: Multiculturalism and the Media*.

Robert Stam is University Professor of Cinema Studies at New York University. The author of numerous works on Third Cinema theory and Third World films, his most recent books include *Film Theory: An Introduction*, *Tropical Multiculturalism: A Comparative History of Race in Brazilian Cinema and Culture*, and (with Ella Shohat) *Multiculturalism, Postcoloniality and Transnational Media*.

N. Frank Ukadike is a member of the Department of Communication and the Program in African Diaspora Studies at Tulane University. He has edited a special issue of the journal *Iris* on African filmmaking and has published a book on *Black African Cinema*. He was the recipient of a Rockefeller Foundation Grant for his forthcoming *A Questioning Cinema: Conversations with African Filmmakers*.

Acknowledgments

In compiling these acknowledgments I feel rather like one of those orchestral conductors who, having waved his arms about and forced others to make the music, turns to the audience at the end of the performance to receive their approbation. In this instance the feeling is exacerbated by the vague sensation that I am still enmeshed in a rather Felliniesque fantasy.

The true credit for this undertaking really belongs to the brass, the strings, the woodwinds and, yes, even the tricky percussion section, who have given this work its symphonic scope. The contributors to this volume do not need me to point at them to direct the applause, for they, more than any other writers on film presently at work, have shaped the scholarly terrain that is the subject of this anthology.

None of these efforts would have been heard, however, were it not for our Concert Master, Rebecca Barden. If there were such a thing as an Academy Award for Best Acquisitions Editor surely she deserves one, for during the lengthy adagios and hectic allegros of this manuscript she has had to play, variously, the ambassador, the hostage negotiator, the supplicant, the tyrant and the nurse. Although at the time I first presented the project to her my experience of editing consisted of a few journal issues, her support for the fledgling project was immediate and has never wavered. Without her suggestions and frequent ministrations, as well as those of her long-suffering assistants, Alistair Daniel and Kate Ahl, I would have thrown up my hands and thrown in the baton months ago.

In this regard I have others to thank also. It was over lunch in Los Angeles many moons (or considering the warmth of the day, perhaps suns) ago that Bob Stam and Ella Shohat got into a heated argument over the shape *Rethinking Third Cinema* should take. I had merely asked whether they would like to contribute. For the first time I knew that the project really mattered. Not long afterwards I brought my early efforts to Wimal Dissanayake who, like Rebecca, has been both guide and critic throughout the gestation of the project.

Conductor though I may be in one guise, I am also compelled to play the role of soloist here and sing the praises of many on behalf of all the contributors. As for my own debts, no amount of thanks would suffice for the attention granted to me by the directors of the New Indian Cinema, particularly the hours devoted to me by Girish Karnad, Girish Kasaravalli and Adoor Gopalkrishnan, the last of whom even granted me the privilege of mourning Gandhi in his *Kathapurushan*. It is they who provided me with the short concluding narrative that I offer in the introduction as a case study, allowing one productive outpouring of Third Cinema to stand for a legion. I am one of many who would not have been able to experience at first hand India's contributions to the world's cultural richness and heterophony were it not for the generosity and patronage of the late Dr B.V. Rao, one of the country's greatest benefactors and philanthropists; nor could I have completed my researches in India without the help and expertise of the film archivists and government agencies in Pune, Bombay and Trivendrum or proceeded to make sense of them without the reference librarians at Harvard, without the helpful advice of Karen Dalton at Harvard's W.E.B. DuBois Institute, and without many an heroic emergency triage by David Frasier, whose encompassing knowledge of film studies has spread far beyond his desk at Indiana University. My gratitude is no less to the guardians who have watched over my (regrettably Rake-like) progress over the years: Harry Geduld who has played the role of Socrates in various dialogues concerning this and other work and who has, I suspect, been more than once at the point of self-administration of hemlock; Douglas Hofstadter, who allowed me to begin work on *Rethinking Third Cinema* as a Visiting Scholar at the Center for Research on Concepts and Cognition at Indiana University; Carlo Ginsburg and Guido Fink who opened my eyes to history at the University of Bologna; and Stephen Greenblatt, another teacher from my Berkeley days, who invited me as a visitor to Harvard's English Department where I received the final revisions of the contributors and, at long last, found the time to assemble them into a coherent order. Were it not for that thirteenth of the alphabet that contains G and H, I doubt I would ever have been able to write at all, let alone attempt to reframe Third Cinema theory with the aid of our contributors' profound insights.

Last, but not least, I must thank my overworked assistant Denis Warburton, who has oft reminded me that postcoloniality is no license for neocolonialism, and that he is more Ariel than Caliban. His stacks of wood were the typed and retyped letters on these pages. He now has his freedom and Prospero has his book.

With my charms all o'erthrown some thanks I cannot legitimately give. Even the most cursory reading of the contributions will confirm the depth of research that informs every one of these pages. To acknowledge with any degree of adequacy all of the archivists and librarians in the institutions where the contributors labored and each of the latter's sources of inspiration would double the length of this manuscript and thus I have allowed them to offer their thanks in their own words, in the brief notes to their chapters. It is not just the filmmakers, festival directors, philanthropists and spectators, but they, too, who give life to alternative cinemas.

Harvard University
10 December 2000

Introduction
Rethinking Third Cinema

Anthony R. Guneratne

The function of any introduction is to justify the purpose and necessity of the project it prefaces and, usually, to find cunning ways of apologizing for excesses of length, brevity, stimulation or tediousness. I have no need to do so here for what you have is an anthology of some of the most original and deeply-researched writing of acclaimed historians and theorists of film, a *summa*, if you will, of the best that contemporary scholarship has to offer in terms of reevaluations of Third Cinema and its consequences both to film theory and subsequent filmmaking practice. It is comprehensive without lapsing into garrulous all-inclusiveness, concise without being gnomic or abstruse. Unlike many another volume devoted to film theory, the introduction and the contents of *Rethinking Third Cinema* are deliberately aimed at a broad constituency, not only of students and scholars who are at home in the metropolises of theoretical discourse, but also those from the wider cultural and intellectual terrain which Third Cinema theory embraced.

As a theory the latter made over-arching, even messianic, claims and purported to speak for a vast socio-geographical region that even then (in the early 1960s) already produced the majority of the world's films. Yet it has suffered the contradictory fate of never being treated seriously as a theory while at the same time becoming – especially when indolently pressed into service in classrooms as a mechanism of generalization – the measure of all the cinemas of an increasingly ephemeral Third World now teetering on the brink of being globalized away. Thus, even at a guarded and sometimes hostile distance from those commercially-orientated postcolonial cinemas it stigmatized as immature relics of imperialism and Neocolonialism, Third Cinema theory addressed the largest of all constituencies of filmmakers and the widest subject area within the purview of film studies. Its neglect among film theorists coincides with what has been, until recently, a corresponding (and even more scandalous) neglect within film studies in general of the cinemas of non-industrialized countries, as Robert Stam, unique among authors of introductions to film theory both in devoting a section to Third Cinema theory and differentiating it from the broader concerns of postcolonial film theories, points out.[1]

Stam is only one of a gathering of stellar film scholars who have brought an astonishing array of interests and breadth of knowledge to this volume, but even these polymaths have not encompassed every nook and cranny of Third Cinema. In my introduction I propose both to provide a general background to the arguments that are refined, tested or challenged in these pages and to underline some of the key facets of Third Cinema which these authors, with perhaps an occasional excess of optimism, assume will be familiar to their readers. What I hope emerges from our collective endeavors is not only a clearer understanding of the legitimacy of Third Cinema theory as theory, but also a richer appreciation of its limitations, its sometimes astonishing achievements when applied constructively to the practice of filmmaking, and its deeply consequential impact in providing both the foundations of subsequent theoretical models and the inspiration for counter-models and alternative approaches. Like most socially oriented and historically particular theoretical frameworks Third Cinema theory enjoyed an evanescent heyday; yet it continues to live in some unforgettable films that it inspired and in the imperishable and as-yet-unfulfilled vision of universal equality and justice that it embraced.

The condescension of posterity?

Of all film movements, including those instigated by the angry young women and men of the French New Wave and New German Cinema, Third Cinema remains the one most closely allied to the theoretical expositions and precepts of its first practitioners. Yet even when examples of Third Cinema are imported into Euro-American classrooms, it is seldom with reference to Third Cinema theory. The discipline of Film Studies, no less than the medium from which it derives, has been shaped by social forces and intellectual currents of a turbulent century, and the marginality of the *petit histoire* of Third Cinema in its grander progress is less a tale of neglect than one of considered omission or deliberate exclusion. Even a cursory survey of the correlation between film history and theories of cinema makes this self-evident.

Consider, for instance, a study of French cinema that fails to treat André Bazin's theories of Realism or a history of Soviet cinema that bypasses Formalist theory. For most film scholars such omissions would be certain signs of amateurishness or dilettantism. Film theory is, as I have suggested elsewhere,[2] as old as the cinema itself, and having emerged from the same constellation of social and cultural conditions which gave rise to the new medium, has remained inseparably linked to its subsequent historical development.

Moreover, the impact of theories originating beyond the purview of film studies per se, though perhaps less obvious and direct than Sergei Eisenstein's influence on film editing or Bazin's on the aesthetic preoccupations of the *Nouvelle Vague*, has nevertheless also been considerable. Jacques Lacan, perhaps the most famous psychoanalyst of his generation, is reputed to have shown Buñuel's *El* (1952) and *Belle de Jour* (1967) in lieu of lectures on "paranoia" and "female masochism"[3] and he, in turn, has played a crucial role not only in the emergence of a theory of the gaze in narrative cinema but also in the influential recent analyses of Hitchcock undertaken by Slavoj Zizek.[4] Moreover, Lacan's reading of Freud and Christian Metz's reading of Peirce and Saussure provided the foundations of the anti-classical filmmaking practice advocated by Laura Mulvey and Peter Wollen.

Marxist thought, too, had a prolonged and fecund engagement with film-making practice even before it served as a unifying force in the revolutionary struggles against Neocolonialism that inspired Third Cinema. It is no secret that Surrealist filmmakers such as Dalí, Buñuel, Unik and Franju had an uneasy relationship with orthodox Communism,[5] but each of them derived inspiration from personal interpretations of socialist doctrines. Despite the many crises of Socialism and its virtual eradication in the United States as a political move-ment during the McCarthy era, elsewhere it spawned film practices of note, particularly in the cinema of the Senegalese Ousmane Sembène (the universally acknowledged inspiration for African *auteur* filmmaking), in that of the Bengali Ritwik Ghatak who has come to be acknowledged as one of India's major directors and the inspiration for later filmmakers like the Brechtian Saeed Mirza, and those of a host of Latin American filmmakers.[6] Many of the latter had, in fact, been inspired like their European contemporaries by festival showings of Italian Neorealist films, particularly Vittorio De Sica's 1948 *The Bicycle Thieves*, which had already been embraced as the quintessence of socialist filmmaking by critics as diverse in orientation as Bazin and Guido Aristarco. In the generation after Bazin, those he influenced through his writings, notably Jean-Luc Godard and Chris Marker, as well as the great semiotician and inter-preter of Antonio Gramsci among Italian filmmakers, Pier Paolo Pasolini, have made notable cinematic contributions to post-Althusserian Marxist philosophy at the same historical moment as, and to some extent in solidarity with, the proponents of Third Cinema and ongoing liberational struggles on many continents.[7]

It is no coincidence that one of the most cogent critiques of Bazin's inter-pretation of *The Bicycle Thieves* is Kristin Thompson's in *Breaking the Glass Armor*, a work that in some ways stands as the manifesto of Neoformalist theory. Thompson argues that the film's ideology is far from self-evident and that many of its "realist" effects are the products of extreme artifice,[8] both consequential claims when we consider the transformation this film wrought on the Indian Satyajit Ray, the Brazilian Nelson Pereira dos Santos, the Argentine Fernando Birri, the Sri Lankan Lester James Peries and other film-makers who inspired and helped forge a Third Cinema. Although Third Cinema theory indisputably arose in Latin America in response to world-wide liberation struggles and decolonization movements, its various manifestos of the 1960s, "An Aesthetic of Hunger" (Glauber Rocha, Brazil), "Towards a Third Cinema" (Fernando Solanas and Octavio Getino, Argentina), "For an Imperfect Cinema" (Julio García Espinosa, Cuba), "Problems of Form and Content in Revolutionary Cinema" (Jorge Sanjinés, Bolivia), were influenced by a huge range of historical specificities ranging from Brazil's socially-conscious Cinema Nôvo and the Cuban Revolution to the genocide of Fourth World populations and Peronist Socialism.[9] But they had in common that same tri-continental call to arms against social injustice and post-imperial exploitation as those of the inspirational activist-theorists of the preceding generation, Ho Chi Minh, Frantz Fanon, Che Guevara and Amilcar Cabral.

One would expect, therefore, that with such a pedigree and so explicit a political allegiance Third Cinema theory would be among those fiercely contested in *Post-theory*, an anthology edited by David Bordwell and Noel Carroll who are as vigorously opposed to such "Grand Theories" as psycho-analysis and Marxism as they are sympathetic to Neoformalism and "cognitive" theory. Yet here, as so often in film studies, Third Cinema theory does not appear to merit even a dishonorable mention.[10] Not surprisingly, when Bordwell turned to writing what has become one of the most notable studies of a non-Western film industry, *Planet Hong Kong*,[11] he made only the barest of allusions to the postcolonial discourses which once dominated criticism of Hong Kong films and no mention at all of Third Cinema theory.

If this trend were unique to a single seminally influential critic with an admitted suspicion of most theoretical positions, Third Cinema theory might still be on safe ground. Yet Bordwell is by no means alone in denying grandeur to Third Cinema theory. At a time when the Eurocentric model of film history and film studies has given way to a spate of publications and university courses on non-Western national cinemas and the award-winning *auteurs* of the various film movements of the moment (Edward Yang and Hou Hsiao-Hsien in the case of the New Cinema in Taiwan; Zhang Yimou and Chen Kaige in the case of Fifth Generation Chinese filmmaking; Abbas Kiarostami and Mohsen Makhmalbaf in the case of the New Iranian Cinema, and so on), Third Cinema and the theory that undergirds it are very much in danger of achieving the "condescension of posterity" which Mike Wayne, for one, fears might befall them.[12] Certainly, when there is no reference to Third Cinema theory in a recently published work purporting to address "social justice in world cinema," nor – to take an example in a relevant national cinema – in the most com-prehensive recent collection of essays devoted to Mexican cinema (which nevertheless does treat issues of American-Mexican cultural interaction as found in the genre of the "border film" as well as the neocolonial role Hollywood cinema has played during the entire history of Mexican film production), at the very least posterity's disregard seems assured.[13]

Taken collectively the contributions to this volume encompass so wide a range of epistemologies that they may well demonstrate that even the exaggerated concern to court posterity's favor is no more than a Eurocentric preoccupation, perhaps even a vestigial remnant of the self-justificatory imperialist historicism of the nineteenth century. Indeed, it is probably no mere coincidence that part of the project of Third Cinema was to challenge this Hegelian notion of a "philosophy of history" that distinguished the then regnant epoch of "the German world" from its predecessors, what the anthropologist Claude Lévi-Strauss characterized in another context as the Western obsession with diachronicity.[14] That such a challenge could be accomplished triumphantly in answer to and beyond the historical horizons of the Occident is acknowledged, for instance, in the fine and all-too-brief chapter of *Cinematic Uses of the Past* which Marcia Landy devotes to Sembène's use of memory as the true record of the past and his mythic-folkloric contestation of imperialist tellings of history in *Xala* (1974), *Ceddo* (1976) and, especially, the more recent *Le Camp de Thioraye* (1989) and *Guelwaar* (1992).[15] In *Xala*, for instance, the gender disparities inherent to the practice of polygamy are satirized through the uneasy clash of two competing histories, the urban modernism bequeathed by the pseudo-progressive colonizing west and the atavistic pre-colonial inheritances that remain embedded in a corrupting political environment

Yet she could just as well have cited some of the films that emerged in the Latin American cradle of Third Cinema, films which took direct aim at the Eurocentric erasure of the distinction (which so preoccupies Jacques Derrida, amongst others) between history and reality. One might even reverse her argument to suggest that, setting aside the anomalous *Citizen Kane* (1940) or *Rashomon* (1951), First World cinema has remained largely innocent of postmodern challenges to what Lyotard has stigmatized as the *grand récit*, the legitimating myth, of Western history. Latin American filmmakers, more practiced than their still-colonized African and Asian brethren in standing at an analytical remove from the ideologies of Neocolonialism, understood well that the history of the West is also the erasure of the reality of the West's others. Hence, nowhere else but in the final (so-called "cannibal-tropicalist")[16] phase of Brazilian Cinema Nôvo would one be likely to encounter a film such as Nelson Pereira dos Santos's *How Tasty Was My Little Frenchman* (1971), in which the point of view of naked "savages" overwhelms the artifices of over-dressed History to such an extent that as a priestly historian reads from his manuscript we can witness his logocentric falsification of the events he historicizes. (This technique is later quoted, for instance, by Hector Babenco at the conclusion of his internationalist – and yet historically specific – film, *The Kiss of the Spider Woman* [1985].) Indeed, one could even argue that the contestation of the historical bedrock of Eurocentric imperialist self-justification was to become the foundational premise of post-revolutionary Cuban Third Cinema which, in addition to Tomás Gutiérrez Alea's celebrated epics of ordinary life, also produced two of the most rigorous (if in more ways than one Imperfect) challenges to modes of representation inherited from Europe. Humberto Solas's *Lucia* (1968) draws symbolic parallels between different forms of oppression experienced by women – here represented by a single protagonist, Lucia – in three widely separated historical epochs, the reverse of D.W. Griffith's strategy in *Intolerance* (1916) of intercutting seemingly unrelated stories from four historical epochs to illustrate a single theme. Both historical certainty and textual veracity are challenged by Sergio Giral's *El Otro Francisco* (1975) in which a celebrated nineteenth-century sentimental novel (decrying slavery) undergoes an anti-adaptation that through a contest-atory, mock-documentary voice-over narration and discordant generic mixing, refutes the historical ideology of its source.

This is not to say that other "Third World" cinematic challenges to orthodox historiography have not been as subtle or as successful. Few analyses of the waxing and waning of an empire have been as suggestive as Satyajit Ray's philosophical *The Chessplayers* (1977) or psychological *Home and the World* (the latter, one of his last major works and released in 1984, also lends itself to a variety of analytical approaches, as Sumita Chakravarty's contribution illustrates). That the present is not only shaped but often ruptured by the past has received unique expression in the films of the Taiwanese Hou Hsiao-Hsien, in whose long takes the now and the then are juxtaposed and infect each other. Then again, perhaps it is because history has followed Fredric Jameson's formulation and hurt so much in the Third World that the concerns of classical film theory — Munsterberg's gestalt psychology as much as Bazin's ontological concerns — have been foregrounded in fifth-generation Chinese filmmaking and the post-revolutionary cinema of Iran. Chen Kaige's allegorical portmanteaus, particularly the magisterial *Farewell my Concubine* (1993) and the subject of Rey Chow's chapter, *Temptress Moon* (1996), while remaining anguished rejections of demands for cultural conformity still so pervasive that even his abundantly gifted lead actor, Leslie Cheung (1956–2003) could not survive them, nevertheless resist the temptations of overt historicization and foreground individual consciousness in depicting China's coming to terms with historical ruptures. Just as China's painterly tradition of the monumental landscape contrasts in scale with the Persian miniature, the controversial films of post-war Iran (whose reception is treated with amusing candor in these pages by Hamid Naficy) often dramatise historical events on a microscopic scale rather than on the epic canvas favored by Fifth Generation directors. Thus, Makhmalbaf might turn the camera on himself when squabbling with an actor attempting to play his "younger" self (as in the 1996 *A Moment of Innocence*), while for his part Kiarostami might even have a false Makhmalbaf and the "real" one act in vertiginous simultaneity in a film such as *Close-up* (1990). Few First World cinemas could boast of a similar conceptual rigor in contesting the grandest *grand récit* of them all.

It is not the concern of our present project, however, to engage in futile historiomachy with the intent of winning a few more pages for Third Cinema in books on film history or film theory; rather, we hope to create a blueprint for the future rather than redrawing the boundaries of the past. We strive, in fact, to recontextualize the project of Third Cinema by reassessing its origins, its goals, its accomplishments, its insinuation into the other cinemas of the once and future Third World, and even the very theory which, for a brief but glittering moment, underwrote some of the most provocative films made anywhere in the world. If that theory itself invited, even demanded, contestation and challenge, then these contributions together explore the paths it opened (and sometimes failed to open) for filmmakers and film scholars.

An alternative to Eurocentric theory

Third Cinema theory is the only major branch of film theory that did not originate within a specifically Euro-American context. No other theory of cinema is so imbued with historical specificities, none so specific in its ideological orientation, and yet none so universal in its claims to represent the highest aspirations of a post-colonial world in the throes of resisting Neocolonialism. Yet, paradoxically, it is the discursive practice of the West which gave rise to the "Third World" that this theory addressed, a term popularized by its use at the 1955 Bandung Conference of Non-aligned Nations by the then leftist President Sukarno of Indonesia as a linguistic designation for the collective plight of those countries which had until very recent memory suffered through the dying spasms of the grand imperial projects of Europe. As Ella Shohat and Robert Stam have pointed out, the term was initially coined by the demographer Alfred Sauvy by way of analogy to the Third Estate of France; aptly so for while it appeared to stand for a political entity (the First World being those of industrialized, free-market systems, the Second being the recently consolidated socialist blocs and the Third a catch-all for what remained), it also acknowledged a social, political and economic hierarchy harking back to its derivation and the notion of an undifferentiated lumpen-proletariat.[17]

From the start the "Third World" had its problems. Michael Chanan notes that China, uncomfortable with the prospect of assimilation (on the basis of political orientation) to a Soviet bloc, preferred alignment with the Third World.[18] Amongst other anomalies this placed the thriving British Crown Colony of Hong Kong – soon to be a leading film "factory" after the founding of the world's most intensely productive studio, Movieland, in 1961, by the Singaporean Shaw brothers – in the curious position of boasting a First World economy, a pre-Third World system of colonial governance, and a decidedly Third World ethnic composition (for while ethnically Europeanate populations were to be found in Latin America and elsewhere in the Third World, no predominantly non-white population, even those of oil-glutted Brunei and Kuwait, enjoyed the distinction of being First World).

The perverse polymorphism of the Third World designation has resulted in a succession of definitional crises. Embraced by intellectuals, particularly those of Latin America and the Caribbean as the focus of a common cause, it is most frequently used as an adjective of contempt by Western news media in whose hands it serves to denote national backwardness, political corruption, dictatorship or indigent mendicancy at the feet of the World Bank, the International Monetary Fund or other organs of the First World's carefully calibrated charity. Still more confusing have been the ever-shifting boundaries of the designation itself. For the apartheid government of South Africa, for example, a First World trading relationship with Japan necessitated the racial categorization of Japanese businessmen as "honorary whites," a dubious honor denied the ethnically Chinese populations of mainland China and Southeast Asia. Meanwhile, China's ambiguous status within the Third World (once it emerged as the world's third superpower) was further underlined by the "middleman" status enjoyed by satellite economies as a result of China's economic isolation enforced by the First World, economies such as those of colonized Hong Kong, "renegade" Taiwan and anomalous Singapore.

It is thus noteworthy that there is little evidence of irony in the self-congratulatory title (*From Third World to First*) of the most recent book of Singapore's politically astute, even visionary national leader, Lee Kuan Yew, who emplots the progress of the island as involving as sudden a shift of gears (eliding Second World-ness altogether) as his own personal trajectory from Marxist, anti-colonial insurgent to the conservative poster boy of Western capitalism. No less an authority on world affairs than Henry Kissinger once more proffers his best foot when in his forward to the book he observes that "history shows that normally prudent, ordinary calculations can be overturned by extraordinary personalities" and that Singapore excelled and prevailed over its larger (predominantly Melanesian) neighbors through "superior intelligence, discipline, and ingenuity."[19] In fact, "the Singapore story" is rather more complex and less sanitary than such remarks, drawn from Washington's compendious dictionary of received political ideas, suggest; Hong Kong, now busily exporting its action-film virtuosos to Hollywood, might never have enjoyed its supremacy in its field had it not proved the beneficiary when on the eve of Singapore's independence from the Malayan Federation the island's major film producers, the Shaw Brothers, precipitately centralized their operations in Movieland and concentrated on Chinese-language film production thus relinquishing, save for a dwindling operation on the Malayan mainland, the unchallenged position they once enjoyed as the leading producers of Malay-language films (with predominantly Malay actors) for a Southeast Asian market. As Singapore's state-run industries thrived and the government exerted an increasing control over the island's media, its film industry declined into oblivion, to be replaced by government-run network television and censored commercial films until the recent revival of filmmaking under a newly revitalized Ministry of Culture.[20]

Yet the "biggest" definitional problem with regard to the Third World, both literally and figuratively, remains China. China's Shanghai studios were in the late 1930s and early 1940s among the most technologically sophisticated in Asia, but dwindled during the Japanese occupation and, once revived in Mao's period, were dominated by the dictates of his one-time actress-singer spouse. Hence the sudden emergence of an important group of film directors in the 1980s as the result of new levels of state support for filmmaking and the appointment of the adventurous Wu Tianming as the new studio head at Xi'an, astonished international audiences. Rey Chow, another of our contributors, has made the observation that the kind of Chinese cinema which then won favor among international festival juries and audiences bore the flavor of anthropologism, the film director taking the place of the "native informant" in revealing the secrets of a mythic Chinese history to the curious Western observer; simultaneously, to educated Chinese viewers the cultural translations attempted by filmmakers like Zhang Yimou rendered them traducers of an assumed Chinese ur-culture, ethnocentricities challenged by Gianni Vattimo and other philosophers of cultural exchange.[21] Furthermore, the apparent ease of translation of these films also attests to other, apparently incommensurate characteristics: studio-oriented production values that often surpass those of many First World cinemas, a folklorism characteristic of what Solanas and Getino, for instance, ascribed to *auteur*-driven Second Cinema, and oblique challenges to authority that enabled them to incur the apparent displeasure of the government and thus pass themselves off as examples of socially relevant Third Cinema. I will shortly address some of the definitional deficiencies of Third Cinema that have resulted in such paradoxes, but for the present it will suffice to note that the Chinese government enjoyed substantial returns in foreign capital from the success of a number of these films, and that the practice of proscribing a film and thus contributing to its popularity in a "liberal" First World, subsequently permitting its distribution within China once its initial release in Europe and the United States had run its course, might well illustrate a familiarity with market economics of which both Second and Third Worlds have been thought innocent.

Nevertheless, it cannot be the semantic crisis of the "Third World" alone that has resulted in the critical marginalization of Third Cinema. In their original manifesto on Third Cinema Solanas and Getino mention a number of film movements that would constitute Third Cinema within a Euro-American field of production including those in the US, Italy, France, Britain and Japan.[22] Despite the egalitarianism of this vision of trans-continental Third Cinema, the *de facto* challenge of institutional political authority resistant to each of these forms of Third Cinema was soon paralleled by a growing schism amongst the second wave of theorists of Third Cinema who were troubled by the distinction this position instituted between Third Cinema and Third World Cinema and by the implication embedded in this position of a homogenization of political challenges to institutional authority, disregarding any particularities of nation and culture (issues addressed by Julianne Burton in 1985, by Paul Willemen in a book chapter published in 1989 and subsequently through a variety of approaches by Wimal Dissanayake, another of our contributors).[23]

And still I would argue that it is not even this schism to which we can attribute the neglect of Third Cinema theory, for other theories (such as psycho-analysis) have survived challenges even to their most influential applications within film studies (witness, for instance, the debates over the theory of the gaze). Moreover, schisms are frequently the sign of the process of maturation of a theory rather than a sign of their collapse, as Jungians and Bakhtinians would hasten to point out. Rather, the fundamental causes of neglect have more to do with Eurocentric critical perspectives and philosophical impositions than with the internal disputes within Third Cinema theory. Perhaps the most salient of these factors is that film theory as a whole is not merely Eurocentric but almost exclusively Anglo-Francophone in outlook and in orientation. If Third Cinema's rendezvous with "posterity" was already compromised by the exclusionary practices of First World cinema and by its own critique of and challenge to Eurocentrism,[24] then it was further disadvantaged linguistically and ideologically in that its initial exposition took place far away from the metropolises of theoretical discourse.

A second, no less crucial aspect of its displacement from the center of theoretical debate has been the equally important critical attitude of "Third-worldism" that at once exoticizes and homogenizes the products of this imaginary terrain. The kinds of critical generalization made about Third World Cinema would be unthinkable for First World Cinema. Ignoring audiences in "Third World" societies, scholars working in developed countries have tended to project their own political agendas as moral and aesthetic requirements upon films from the "Third World" without, however, insisting on a similar requirement for First World Cinema. As Stam has observed, such critical imperialism requires the Third World filmmaker to assume the role of spokesperson, just as minority actors in Hollywood were once expected to be a credit to their race. Even erstwhile proponents of Third Cinema have, in this respect, succumbed to universalism and risked "installing a formula for correct cinema, but one which ignores the concrete conditions, needs and traditions of particular countries."[25]

The third and possibly most disadvantageous factor, although again one stemming primarily from Eurocentric critical prejudices, has been that from Rocha's 1965 statement onwards early Third Cinema theory did not produce a body of closely argued criticism but instead assumed the form of a disparate constellation of polemical manifestos of the kind generally associated with modernist avant-garde artistic practices such as Futurism, Surrealism, the French New Wave or the New German Cinema. Chanan points out that initially García Espinosa's "Imperfect Cinema" was less restrictive than the "Third Cinema" proposed by Solanas and Getino in accommodating Neorealist-inspired examples of Cinema Nôvo such as dos Santos's and those of the Argentine Birri. Moreover, the seemingly hermetic division of cinemas into those represented by big-budget commercial films (First Cinema), independent, *auteur* films (Second Cinema) and films made by militant collectives (Third Cinema), led to various misinterpretations such as the automatic assumption that First Cinema was necessarily a cinema of entertainment, the Second one of intellect and interiority, and the Third one of political radicalism. Chanan goes on to illustrate the successive modifications of these positions by the original authors to broaden their permitted canon of Third Cinema and to account for local differences because the "idealistic" erasure of national and regional differences proved untenable and, worse still, because the Second Cinema of the *auteurs* soon proved more visibly fruitful in contesting social inequality and Neocolonialism than the more restricted activities of militant collectives.[26] For Paul Willemen, on the other hand, these difficulties could be avoided were Third Cinema to be defined by the nature of the cinematic utterance itself, thus being equated to a particular cinematic *approach* whose masters, he avers, are dos Santos, Sembène and Ghatak, with a gallery of leading practitioners as stylistically varied as Soulemaniye Cissé, Haile Gerima, Kumar Shahani, Youssef Chahine, Edward Yang, Chen Kaige, Allen Fong, and even some then-contemporary French and British filmmakers.[27] Thus the ground of Third Cinema appears to undergo periodic perspectival shifts in apparent accordance with Getino's later revision of his original statement of Third Cinema to the effect that "the value of a theory is always dependent on the terrain in which the praxis is carried out."[28] In sum, in disregarding systematicity and emphasizing the practice of filmmaking as its central project, Third Cinema theory finessed, to its own disadvantage, the epistephilic and logocentric enterprise of Western theory. As theory it lacked the coherence that would have won it either the censures or the approval of Bordwell and Carroll.

To some extent this has remained true even after the watershed of Teshome Gabriel's 1982 *Third Cinema in the Third World*, which was for many Euro-American scholars their introduction to Third Cinema theory, being the first work in English to undertake a comprehensive exposition of Third Cinema theory in relation to the social and political situations it addressed.[29] Gabriel, perhaps in accordance with the militaristic style of the early manifestos, gave his propositions a polemical edge and was explicit in granting preference to "films with social relevance and innovative style and, above all, with political and ideological overtones." These films contribute to a universal "decoloniza-tion of the mind," thus engendering the development of "radical consciousness" which would in turn lead to "a revolutionary transformation of society." Following Solanas and Getino, Gabriel also requires that these films "develop a new film language with which to accomplish these tasks,"[30] echoes of which we find in Willemen's phenomenology of style.

This last, superficially illogical requirement – why would postcolonial audiences be more attuned or responsive to formal innovation than bourgeois Western cineastes? – can best be explained by Louis Althusser's notion of the ideological state apparatus: as a medium of communication, First World cinema, whose classical model, Hollywood cinema, demonstrably underwrote such imperialist enterprises as the Vietnam War (at least until the political tide turned), served as a mechanism of interpellation into the larger sphere of capitalist consumerism. Moreover, that continuous process of asymmetrical cultural transmission, that as Shohat and Stam have recently pointed out has been accelerated and exacerbated by globalization, has only amplified the far from localized (i.e. Euro-American) Hollywoodcentrism resulting from generations of hegemonic industrial practices and international market penetration.[31] Thus, a more precise definition of Gabriel's requirement would not insist on formal innovation per se, but rather on a filmmaking practice whose departures from the model offered by Hollywood underline its ideological rejection of the latter, for indeed Solanas and Getino argue that a cinema which imitates US industrial models "leads to the adoption of the ideological forms which gave rise to that language and no other."[32]

Challenges to Third Cinema

Equally central to Gabriel's argument is the notion of a parallel evolutionary development of national cinemas within formerly colonized territories. Elaborating on his early writing, Gabriel retrospectively detailed the extent to which he drew on Frantz Fanon's three-stage model of "the decolonization of the mind" in his reformulation of Third Cinema theory.[33] Paradoxically Fanon, himself a controversial and at times contradictory figure and one deeply critical of the majority of the orthodox Marxist revolutionary movements in the wake of the collapse of European imperialism,[34] might himself have felt some unease about the structural hierarchies Gabriel instituted. These Gabriel illustrated with a trinity of Venn diagrams, the first being three distinct phases of national film industries, the second being intersecting critical theories devoted to "text," "reception" and "production," and the third being a confluence of the previous two wherein a larger historical perspective subsumes earlier ones. Similar in appearance to Andrew Sarris's diagrams illustrating *auteur* perspectives, Gabriel's vision of Third Cinema also explicitly privileges certain kinds of filmmaking and the critical practices associated with them.

Some of the difficulties encountered in this model, including the rigorous demand that Third Cinema must be "part of a public service institution" and "owned by the nation and/or the government,"[35] thus presupposing active, presumably progressive state support in what could only be a Third World context, were taken up by critics soon after the appearance of *Third Cinema in the Third World*. The first notable challenge came from Julianne Burton in the pages of *Screen*, whose editors' devotion to polemical confrontations bore fruit well nigh instantly in the form of a particularly harsh response from Gabriel.

Burton begins with the premise that neither filmmakers nor theorists in the Third World enjoyed the luxury of reflection and theoretical elaboration, that their theories must perforce translate into practical application and that a negative consequence of this has been a dismissive suspicion of First World criticism and a "defensive attitude" leading to an ongoing "development of critical underdevelopment."[36] She goes on to argue that critics of Third World cinema who operate in a First World context (and undeniably metropolitan theorizing either took over or at the least overtook Third Cinema after the 1970s), "have been motivated by the contradictory impulse to win recognition for their object of study within the very institutions which serve to endorse and perpetuate dominant, colonizing, hierarchical cinematic discourses."[37] Throughout the 97 pages of *Third Cinema in the Third World*, contends Burton, Gabriel must thus cling to the idea of a Third World which for decades enjoyed a "unitary, autonomous, ideologically transparent cultural practice," a distortion of historical fact that leaves him "groping for a conclusive definition of 'Third

Cinema'." She goes on to point out the limitations of Gabriel's inductive approach to formulating such a definition, employing the very films he uses as examples of "the unity of Third World texts" to illustrate the failure of *Lucia* or Sara Gomez's *One Way or Another* (1977) to generate consensus among critics attuned to gender issues. Finally, she points to the work of Ismail Xavier, who is sensitive to a dialogical relationship between theoretical practice and concrete social situations, as a useful alternative to Gabriel's rejection of First World theorizing in being a *rapprochement* between the marginal and the mainstream which synthesizes textual and historical approaches.[38]

Gabriel's response was mortifying in likening Burton's suggestion that Third (World) Cinema differed only in degree and not in kind from other cinemas to what he perceived as the First World intellectual arrogance of Immanuel Wallerstein's "World System Theory" which subsumed Socialism within all forms of non-capitalism and denied the possibility of post-capitalism. For Gabriel Third World agency was no more marginal than First World agency, and the notion of *rapprochement* between such unequal positions is premature when the ideology of globalization has also been one of cultural homo-genization on terms defined by the First World. "Just as 'socialism' is not only non-capitalism but 'Socialism,' so also is Third World cinema not only non-spectacle but Third World cinema," insists Gabriel, for the otherness of Third (World) Cinema is "not only one of degree but also of kind": it is not a cinema purged of or innocent of complex signification but one with a semiotics of its own.[39] In his most cogent rebuttal Gabriel refutes the implication that mainstream critical theory should either assimilate or be accounted for by others since its superiority or importance is (as Buñuel observed about "great" writing) in direct proportion to the position of power from which it emanates. Had hegemonic power not determined the canon of great filmmakers, according to Gabriel, it would be dos Santos, Sembène, Alea, Mrinal Sen, Birri, Solanas, Miguel Littín, and the progressive directors based in the First World who would have been the actual luminaries of the era.[40] If one grants the latter point, however, it would suggest that transformations in critical opinion about films from the Third World are just as irrelevant to Third Cinema as accounting for the vagaries of metropolitan theoretical discourse. Yet, as Dissanayake suggests in these pages, in the case of an internationally influential, culturally penetrative phenomenon such as India's popular films, with their immense popularity throughout Africa, the former Soviet Union, China and Indonesia, the sea change that has occurred in criticism of marginal cinemas cannot be legitimately avoided or ignored by theorists of Third Cinema.

It is only in the context of the particular terrain covered by the exchange between Burton and Gabriel that appeared to shed at least as much heat as it did light (the wounded Burton more or less withdrew from the field of contest thereafter), and with the backdrop of the productive colloquies of the conference on Third Cinema under the aegis of the Edinburgh Film Festival of 1986, which occasioned *Questions of Third Cinema* kept in view, that we can properly apprehend the extent of the schism that had developed as exemplified by Willemen's extended critique of Gabriel's book and the latter's contributions to the anthology. In a sense Willemen attempts to distinguish between the propositions of the Latin American theorists of Third Cinema and what he suggests, rather cannily, is Gabriel's misapprehension and over-determination of them in the somewhat restrictive character of his model of Third Cinema. The principal issues that Willemen raises are these: (1) that unlike European "counter-cinema" which placed undue emphasis on stylistic countermeasures to classical narrative cinema, the theorists of Third Cinema appreciated "the historical variability of the necessary aesthetic strategies to be adopted," even to the extent of suggesting that there are "36 different kinds" of Third Cinema; (2) their insistence, in contrast to some of the early Formalist experiments in defamiliarization, on "lucidity" (i.e. intelligibility), thus suggesting something other than the mere rejection of Hollywood's model, a discursive repugnance to which Gabriel grants axiomatic authority; (3) that their theories suggest national and local variations (at least 36 of them!) while Gabriel's "committed internationalism" risks trapping him in contradictions arising from a premature homogenization of Third Cinema.[41]

Interestingly, Willemen's "corrections," while pointing to Gabriel's flaws, themselves institute certain unsustainable lacunae and contradictions. His insistence that the Edinburgh conference selected Third Cinema and "most emphatically not Third World cinema"[42] snatches at a theoretical scalpel to perform a simplifying lobotomy which neither Solanas and Getino nor Gabriel envisage when they permit filmmakers working without the Third World into the Third Cinema pantheon. Although subjective in their choices (as Willemen is in his), the First World-based directors whom they permit into their ranks are precisely those who address the very issues of First World dominance and Third World abjection which concern the more politically-sensitive Third World filmmaker.

The emphatic nature of Willemen's abjuration of Third World cinema is not unconnected with the obsessive crypto-*auteurist* listmaking in instituting canons of worthy films and filmmakers, a habit to which all the constituencies promulgating Third Cinema theories succumb. Even if Solanas, Sembène and dos Santos emerge as a Holy Trinity included on all such lists, the canon of true Third Cinema must, to use Gabriel's analogy, constitute a very small and select circle indeed. As Chanan illustrates, the slippage between Second and Third Cinema in those original statements enables Gabriel to cite as examples of Third Cinema many films that more comfortably fit into García Espinosa's category of Imperfect cinema than into Solanas's and Getino's Third Cinema.[43]

At this point I need not dwell on the inherent contradictions and ultimately damaging results in the tacit advocacy of an *auteur* cinema, for Marvin D'Lugo addresses this very issue in these pages, but I should point out that Gabriel may not have been the only target of Willemen's proscription of Third World cinema. In *Third World Filmmaking and the West*, published shortly after Edinburgh, Roy Armes proposed a far wider constituency of filmmaking practices that remained distinct from the cinemas of the West and, in their cultural particularity, distinct from each other. Armes's work suffers all the deficiencies one would expect from a non-specialist attempting to traverse most of the world's film industries in a single leap of faith: he over-generalizes regional cinema (although revised in later works, the "Middle East" is a category), makes numerous but hardly unexpected errors of fact as a result of attempting to cover too large a terrain, omits many an unrecorded cinema that has fallen through the cracks of both Third Cinema and mainstream Film History, and lapses into an even more stereotyped *auteurism* than his colleagues (is Glauber Rocha more worthy of inclusion among the six *auteurs* highlighted at the end, one wonders, than dos Santos because of his impressive showings at Cannes?). However, unlike Willemen Armes does make space for a consideration of such anomalous films as Gillo Pontecorvo's *The Battle of Algiers* (1966), an early and provocative example of transnational Third Cinema (as, for instance, is Mikhail Kalatozov's Cuban *I Am Cuba* [1964], fated to be eventually distributed in the US by the devoutly Second Cinema-ish Francis Coppola and Martin Scorsese). Thus, even in his analytical failures, Armes suggests that Third Cinema must consider the nuances of the historically-particular choices of filmmakers like the Algerian Mohamed Lakhdar-Hamina, whose films, in striving for aesthetically perfect lyricism, are the antithesis of *The Battle of Algiers*, or of Rui Guerra who in 1968 took refuge in the Imperfection of his native Mozambique in the face of the increasing commercialization of Brazilian Cinema Nôvo. The only solution to the bracketing of "World" in Third (World) Cinema is, perhaps, that of "circles of denotation" proposed by Shohat and Stam in which the core circle is occupied by Third Cinema in the Third World, the next by Third World films in general, the third by Third Cinema made outside the Third World and the fourth by diasporic hybrid films imbued with Third Cinema properties.[44]

On the other hand Stam is not averse to challenging another premise of Third Cinema's undeniable attachment to a conception of the Third World which "elides the presence of a Fourth World existing within all of the other worlds, comprising those peoples variously called 'indigenous,' 'tribal,' or 'first nations'," few of whom were allowed, until taking matters into their own hands in recent years, the opportunity of self-representation beyond auto-ethnographism even within the purview of Third Cinema.[45] Indeed, the urgency of Fourth World self-representation, as with the filmmaking activities of South America's Yanomamo, has become even more evident with recent revelations of the genocidal, capitalist machinations of the revered ethnographer, Napoleon Chagnon, whose use of his subjects for experiment and financial gain hearken back not only to the imperialist anthropologies and white sciences of the nineteenth century, but also to the Fascist ideologies which more recently shaped European history.[46]

Still another challenge to Willemen's notion of the Third World as a real but constantly shifting, historically contingent entity might be the insufficiency of the very insistence on "national" particularity which he demands at some length of Gabriel. As Krishna Sen points out in her contribution to our present endeavor, Willemen's dichotomization of Third World and Third Cinema relied on a negative definition (i.e. what the latter was not). As she elaborates, globalization has itself brought into focus the complex cultural negotiations involved not only in the constitution of the "national," but also of the local and the regional. Furthermore, the central thesis of Mike Wayne's recent reconsideration of political cinema points out that the effort spent in divorcing Third Cinema from the Third World led to an insufficient clarification of the distinction between First, Second and Third Cinema.[47] Wayne attempts, heroically, to argue for the continuing relevance of Third Cinema practices by attempting to purify the concept of Third Cinema, demonstrating its dialectical opposition to First Cinema and to Second Cinema through a patient comparison of thematically related films which he regards as representatives of each species.

From the outset it is fairly clear, however, that if Gabriel was in danger of a "premature homogenization" of the Third World, Wayne is similarly imperiled by the possibility of a belated homogenization of each of the three cinemas. In the case of First and Second Cinema the divide is, for the most part, clear enough, for the distinction Solanas and Getino (as well as Espinosa and the other early theorists) adhere to is essentially the same made by Truffaut, Godard and the other *Nouvelle Vague* critics of commercial, studio-orientated cinema. Yet, as Chanan had already observed, even the systematic Gabriel has to fall back on Espinosa's looser definition when trying to cross the bridge between Second Cinema and the Third. Unlike Wayne, therefore, Gabriel, Willemen and Chanan have resisted collapsing Third Cinema theory into the initial statement made by Solanas and Getino in that they successively grappled with one of the major blind spots of that manifesto, one that subsequently troubled Solanas and Getino and one that neither they nor their successors ever fully resolved despite laborious, conscientious and repeated effort. As the lists of Third Cinema greats provided by Gabriel, Willemen and, more subtly, Chanan attest, the torch of Third Cinema has more or less been passed from one *auteur* to another. Moreover, the only conclusive example of a then-contemporary filmmaker's direct engagement with the instability of the aesthetic distinctions between Second Cinema and Third Cinema and the ideological ones between Second World and Third World may well be that of Pasolini (in his 1970 *Notes for an African Oresteia*), one of Italy's most celebrated post-war *auteurs*.

Pasolini's film is in some ways far more conceptually complex and less easily dismissed as Third Cinema than Gillo Pontecorvo's slightly earlier *The Battle of Algiers* (1966), a film Wayne for some reason does not regard as "guerilla cinema," another category granted by Solanas and Getino. Instead, for him Pontecorvo's film is a "compromised textual formation, never quite managing to *transform* its First and Second Cinema elements and influences fully into the service of Third Cinema." It fails as Third Cinema because it incorporates only those elements of Fanon's political philosophy "that could most easily be integrated into *the language of First and Second Cinema* [my italics], thus excluding some of Fanon's more acute and radical ideas".[48]

In the process of making this "linguistic" distinction, however, Wayne inadvertently brings up another of Third Cinema's intractable problems. Referring to Ranjana Khanna's display of *The Battle of Algiers* as certain proof that Third Cinema is "incapable of engaging with gender politics in a way which calls into question male domination," he demonstrates that her argument stems from a misconception of First, Third and, especially, Second Cinema.[49] Wayne is correct, of course, to draw attention to a common methodological flaw, that of elevating a single, arbitrarily selected cinematic text to stand for the work of a film movement; but in doing so he sidesteps the issue Khanna raises so provocatively. This we can rephrase as Third Cinema's double marginalization of women both as filmmakers and political actants in that without access to as much power and as many resources as their male counterparts they have, with rare but significant exceptions, historically been less capable of "living up" to the political demands of Third Cinema.[50] Thus a progressive feminist critic aware of this ghetto within a ghetto must traverse a minefield of contradictions, most particularly in that in universalizing man's struggle for social equality Third Cinema and Third Worldism in general localize woman's struggle for gender equality. That there are feminist critics sympathetic to the social and ethical agendas of Third Cinema and who can transcend the limitations of its purview by foregrounding the agency of women in transnational and trans-cultural contexts is amply attested by the ambitious, theoretically rigorous contributions of Ella Shohat and Sumita Chakravarty to this anthology.[51]

Much the same might be argued of Third Cinema's emphasis on class struggle to the near-exclusion of other, "secondary" forms of oppression, forms which have come under more sustained scrutiny with the emergence of such textual approaches as gay/lesbian film criticism.[52] Thus, for instance, the resolutely Third Cinema filmmakers who participated in the New Indian Cinema of the 1970s and 1980s created a considerable body of work which aligned class struggle with male gender oppression of women, but none caused such a stir as Deepa Mehta's fiery first installment in an intended tetralogy based on the classical elements, *Agni* (1997), which in treating the taboo theme of the love of two women won international approbation and awards while provoking Hindu Nationalist riots and government censure in India.

Moreover, when one turns to Third Cinema critics to shed some light on Third Cinema's lacunae it is to discover instead, the resuscitation of hackneyed canons of thought, as for instance Wayne's continued invocation of Fanon in such a way as to suggest a mystic transcendence of place and time, thus granting his words the force of unquestioned authority. Yet no more eloquent an analysis of Fanon's Freudian inheritance (including a mild case of post-Vienna School homophobia in denying that such a "pathology" as homosexuality might exist in Martinique) is to be found than in *Frantz Fanon: Black Skin, White Masks* (1995), Isaac Julien's filmic analysis of the "body" of Fanon's work, presented as poetic reenactment wherein a circuit of gazing suggests that he was regarded with desire by both male and female white patients, and that he wrote from an awareness of this desire. Indeed, not only does a gay, activist filmmaker's "take" on Fanon add significant dimensions to our understanding of Fanon's cultural history, it also attests to the fact that a transnational (and by default First World) *auteur* can indeed fruitfully negotiate what Hamid Naficy terms the "interstitial spaces" between systems of production and cultural margins[53] – in this case, such hotly defended margins as the seemingly barbed-wire-ringed conceptual moat between Second and Third Cinema.

By way of conclusion

There remains to be considered the most fundamental of assumptions made on behalf of Third Cinema; namely, the prescriptive insistence that there is a best theory of film and an optimal form of filmmaking practice to account for Third World issues and that both theory and praxis adhere to a conceptual framework that retains an unchanging, trans-cultural validity in all instances. Challenges to such a notion have taken many forms, as for instance Chakravarty's on Hindi popular cinema in which she succeeded in showing the degree of discursive intersection in the constitution of the "national"; even the pleasure-granting sops of First Cinema, she illustrates, can engage their spectators in democratic, socially productive ways.[54] In fact, the nature of spectatorship in the context of Third Cinema has itself been consistently ignored and under-theorized, with the result that Naficy's contribution to the present work may stand alone in illustrating the degree to which spectatorship partakes of a more phenomenologically complex circuit of perception than the simple model of transmission that the ideals of Third Cinema participation ascribed to its easily-educated and tirelessly receptive audiences.

Yet to be fair none of the filmmaker-theorists who initially conceived of a Third Cinema reified their contentions to the extent of later critics and theorists. Not only did they "fine tune" their theories continually to account for concrete praxis, they also engaged in a fruitful dialogue with each other that led, for example, to the gradual softening of such positions as the absolute necessity of filmmaking collectives based on the Argentine/Cuban model. They certainly did not anathematize those filmmakers who worked outside the frameworks of Third Cinema and in sympathy with their cause, showing considerable tolerance of the imperfection of the latter's strivings for true Imperfection. Moreover, even as they formulated their ideas, more skeptical participants in the dialogue also emerged as Aristophanean satirists of the oft-times clumsy positivism of early Third Cinema. As Robert Stam points out in the seminal essay which sets this anthology in motion, the earliest challenges to the Third Cinema model arose almost at its very inception among similarly-inclined filmmaker-theorists who, aware of the already decomposing boundaries demarcating First, Second and Third, began to suggest that a legitimate countervailing force to monolithic First Cinema was not an equally monolithic alternative but instead a constellation of cinematic forms which embraced hybridity and polyglossia.

The permanent instability of the categories of Cinema and the Worlds which gave rise to them are nowhere better illustrated than in those parts of the world where non-studio-oriented alternatives to First Cinema have emerged. While the majority of such forms have rejected the model of First Cinema proposed by Hollywood's hermetic film language, others have adapted this model in a manner more provocative than Gabriel and his adherents might imagine. As Frank Ukadike illustrates in these pages, for example, valid alternatives to First Cinema, such as the low-budget video films which suddenly sprang up in Anglophone West Africa in the 1990s, may indeed so resemble their model as to confront progressive critics with the painful dilemma of choosing either to celebrate anti-hegemonic Third World initiatives which successfully out-compete imported First Cinema or to condemn their ostentatious capitalism.

Then again, the over-convenient division of cinema into thirds elides the acute problems faced by filmmakers who must contend with Hollywood's far-from-benign linguistic domination of smaller film industries such as those of Britain, Canada, Australia and New Zealand. While one cannot discern any consistent ideological opposition among the latter to the paradigms of First Cinema, the governments of Britain and Canada, especially, once fought unsuccessfully to prevent the swamping of local markets and the stifling of local film industries as the result of becoming dumping grounds for Hollywood's English-language product. Nevertheless, just as Scandinavia and Germany "lost" their most prominent directors to Hollywood in the 1920s, Britain failed to implement quota systems effectively in the 1930s (with the result, in fact, that one of the directors assigned to film the low-budget "quota quickies" that circumvented that very quota system, Alfred Hitchcock, was destined to transplant with singular success the once-despised thriller genre in which he specialized to the receptive, fertile soils of California). Manjunath Pendakur and Tom O'Regan have also catalogued in grim detail the baneful effects of Hollywood's continued, if now subtler predation on the markets and personnel of the Canadian and Australian film industries.[55] Irony seems to be piled on irony in the case of New Zealand, dominated by the industry of its larger, less Middle Earth-like but more "central" neighbor and even more likely, therefore, to lose its leading personnel to the rest of the Anglophone world. History, in this case, provides the convenient example of the freshly rediscovered Len Lye, who immigrated to Australia as a teenager, was deported back there from Samoa a few years later for his Gauginesque rejection of colonial whitewashing, and who eventually settled in Britain to make significant contributions as plastic artist and filmmaker to the British Documentary Movement and to the *avant-gardes* of the 1950s. But consider also the apparently Viconian cycle evidenced by the career of Jane Campion, initially a New Zealand-based feature filmmaker, but trained in Australia and now clearly a Second Cinema *auteur* negotiating the interstitial spaces at the First/ Second margins of the Hollywood/Cannes/Venice festival circuit.

Perhaps the most complex range of issues the three-cinema model fails to account for, let alone to address, are the interactions between varying forms of cinema within national industries diverse enough to sustain coexisting forms of First, Second and Third Cinema. Such conditions may well have obtained in the politically-fraught America of the late 1950s and early 1960s, when Hollywood's studio system had definitively collapsed and directors as disparate as Stan Brakhage, Maya Deren, Jonas Mekas, Orson Welles, Alfred Hitchcock and Ed Wood could each pursue radically different conceptions of cinema. While such a retrospective reading of the categories of Cinema may prove elusive, even unjustifiably anachronistic as it predates the theorization of alternative cinemas by Solanas, Getino, Rocha, Espinosa and Sanjinés, less equivocal examples continue to flourish today in such centers of "Third World" film production as Egypt, where in addition to a thriving regionally popular Arabic-language cinema, an *auteur* cinema such as that of Youssef Chahine and Khaled El Hagar is on occasion paid the compliment of being placed under government interdiction (having one's films banned surely being the supreme accolade for a committed Third Cinema filmmaker).

Presenting an even greater challenge to Third Cinema theorists in this context are the teeming sub-national cinemas of such extended "nations" as Indonesia, where the presence of diverse, culturally- and geographically-distinct nationalities, problematizes the notion of nation even beyond the mess described by O'Regan in the case of Australia. Indeed, as Krishna Sen documents in her contribution to this anthology, the conceptual division of local/regional/national suggested by Benedict Anderson's "imagined communities" has in a sense been overhauled by the process of globalization that has cut across the discursive terrains that once formed the threads of the "national" fabrication. Indeed, so varied are these conceptions of the national that even Homi Bhabha would find the contributions to Dissanayake's *Colonialism and Nationalism in Asian Cinema* bewildering in their disparities.

Perhaps the most interesting example of all, certainly the most maddeningly intricate because of its polymorphous, seemingly-incommensurate diversities, is that of India's various amalgams of First, Second and Third Cinema. The Indian films which pertained most to Third Cinema grew out of the New Indian Cinema of the 1970s and 1980s, and it is this movement to which I devote some attention here for two reasons: it is not treated elsewhere in these pages while remaining one of the important cinemas neglected (for a variety of reasons) by Western criticism – this even though the films produced by these radical filmmakers outnumber those of the *Nouvelle Vague* and the New German Cinema combined; the New Indian Cinema also constitutes a superb illustration all the difficulties and contradictions that filmmakers and film critics encountered and continue to encounter wherever Third Cinema has come into being. India's "Parallel Cinema," as it has come to be known in some quarters, remains unparalleled in its richness as a case study.

It remains an instructive paradox that India's purest forms of Third Cinema were the result of a political miscalculation on the part of then Prime Minister Indira Gandhi who in pursuing the progressive, internationalist policies of her predecessor and father, Jawaharlal Nehru, promoted the formation of the Film Finance Corporation that eventually, in 1980, evolved into the National Film Development Corporation. Ostensibly, it was the task of this body to assess scripts (submitted primarily by students at what was then the national film school and archive in the city of Pune) and to help produce and distribute Indian "art" films at national and international venues; the subterranean agenda was to encourage regional *auteur* cinema on the model of the internationally successful Bengali films of Satyajit Ray, but perhaps also to keep an eye on cinematic expressions of regional discontent for the 1970s proved to be a period of immense political turmoil culminating in the cessation of democratic processes and the imposition of Martial Law in 1975.

If the initial intent of the government had been to facilitate an internationally prominent Second Cinema, its most immediate result was to spawn a Third. The vanguard of the New Indian Cinema that began to emerge in the 1970s either studied under committed leftist filmmaker Ritwik Ghatak at Pune or abroad either at such centers of filmmaking as Moscow (where, notably, Sembène, Sarah Maldoror and a number of Latin American Third Cinema filmmakers also studied) or under the tutelage of such socially-conscious *auteurs* as Robert Bresson. Initially the student cohorts of directors, actors and cinematographers collaborated on projects and, for a brief moment, India produced something akin to the radicalized collective cinema that Solanas and Getino demanded with such optimistic commitment in their manifesto. So immediately distinct was this cinema from that of the mainstream, so unlikely to intersect with it at any point, that it soon acquired the designation of a "Parallel Cinema."[56]

But it was not to last. The NFDC preferred to distribute funds widely, thus ensuring low production values on individual projects, and films very often sat on its shelves for months or even years before being submitted to festivals. Even important award-winning films such as those of Shyam Benegal or, later, Mira Nair very often languished for an equally long time before obtaining proper international distribution.

Thus, India's Third Cinema was denied the vivifying oxygen of international support that sustained it – at least ephemerally, in the *auteurist* manifestation of it that D'Lugo discusses incisively in the case of Latin American cinema – elsewhere, and it was in effect doomed to the same fissures and subject to the same "compromises" as Brazil's Cinema Nôvo. In the 1980s India's equivalent of Cannibalist-tropicalism emerged, although in this case being primarily the result of an autophagy that combined the more palatable morsels of Third Cinema with concessions to fairly conservative popular conventions. This cinema, in turn, came to be known as the Middle Cinema, one whose eye on the box-office and ear for the National Language, Hindi, continues to elicit the disdain of regional *auteurs*. *Auteur* cinema thrives best in states such as

Bengal and Kerala with the highest levels of education and the active support of leftist governments. Curiously, unlike the Cinema Nôvo, India's Third Cinema proper, *auteur* cinema and Middle Cinema have continued to coexist despite Third Cinema remaining in a state of continual, protracted abeyance. India's thriving First Cinema, meanwhile, has shamelessly borrowed plot elements and even the leading actors "discovered" by New Indian Cinema directors such as Benegal and Girish Karnad.

It is as a result of the latter's letter of introduction that in June and July of 1995 I was given access to hundreds of videotapes and a conference room to myself at the NFDC headquarters in Bombay to study the history and development of the New Indian Cinema. And later it was through his intercession that I was invited by Adoor Gopalkrishnan to the set of his *Kathapurushan*, an Indian-Japanese co-production (that most recent manifestation of transnational filmmaking as discussed by D'Lugo) destined to lead a gypsy existence traveling the festival circuit for months. I myself had to travel to various film sets and studios and even as far afield as Madras to meet with Shaji Karun, whose 1988/9 *Piravi*, which lamented the Argentine excesses of the 1975 emergency precipitated by Indira Gandhi's increasingly autocratic policies, repeated the success of Nair's 1988 *Salaam Bombay* in receiving special recognition at Cannes. I asked each of these directors their reaction to the recently released *Bombay* (1995), then undergoing various debacles with the censors despite being the handiwork of India's most popular director, Mani Ratnam.[57] My interrogatory ambitions were two-fold: one strategy consisted of addressing, even if obliquely, the same issues of the "national" and of historical particularity that concern Shohat, Chakravarty and Sen in these pages; another was to attempt to chart the precise relation of the New Indian Cinema to the decidedly First Cinema it paralleled. In the usual course of events Indian popular cinema addresses social issues obliquely, but Ratnam's film succeeded in incorporating the standard quota of singing and dancing into a Hindu-Muslim love story that referred directly to the recent communal riots which had claimed hundreds of lives in the multitudinous city of the title. The only New Indian Cinema filmmaker to have responded as quickly was the ubiquitous documentarist Anand Patwardhan whose views of *Bombay*'s falsification of history were understandably scathing. But his reaction did not differ markedly from that of M.S. Sathyu (whose 1975 *Garam Hava*, treating the same inter-ethnic conflict at the time of India's Partition a quarter of a century previously, was promptly banned for over a year) or from that of Govind Nihalani, whose "loss" to Middle Cinema was tempered by his relentlessly analytical television series, *Tamas* (1993), which also preceded *Bombay* in exposing the political corruption that exacerbated the ethnic catastrophes following Partition.

In most cases, however, I was surprised by the temperate, considered reactions of Third Cinema filmmakers to India's First Cinema, so utterly different were they to the Truffautesque anathemas pronounced on Hollywood's films by Solanas and Getino and repeated by their critical descendents.

Gopalkrishnan, a true *auteur* to the last, expressed disappointment in Ratnam deliberately "courting" censorship and allowing his film to be tampered with. Shaji felt that it was a brave effort for a commercial filmmaker and enjoyed its visual values (he is himself a renowned cinematographer). Shyam Benegal believed it to represent the correct direction for Indian cinema to take, but was less impressed by its anodyne narrative, an elementary reworking of *Romeo and Juliet*. Karnad preferred not to comment but invited me to a party where Mira Nair smiled away my questions about *Bombay* but eyed me, as I then thought, with flattering interest and inquired whether my hair was naturally curly (it was only later that I discovered that she was desperately in search of a eunuch for her new film, *Kama Sutra* [1997]). To my amazement, a few days later I heard again from Karnad, this time to invite me to observe him in Madras, where he was to spend a week acting in a popular Tamil film. "I am quite well known among these audiences, although only as an unredeemable villain, a part I am called upon to play every few months," explained India's most honored playwright, a Rhodes Scholar and the director of subtly sensual films rooted in India's myths, literature and ancient folklore; nor did my inability to attend deter him from dilating on some of his more heinous acts with mordant relish.

Of course, any project undertaken by one of the directors of the New Indian Cinema is a labor of many years spent most often in negotiating labyrinthine governmental bureaucracies, and so the films themselves are seldom topical. What surprised me was not the filmmakers' relative disinterest in tackling the most pressing political issues of the day, but rather their lack of bitterness towards the very cinema whose adamantine hold over a vast audience necessitated their dependence on the caprices of governmental funding and oversight.

Another lesson in tolerance and breadth of vision came in the company of Girish Kasaravalli, whose graduation film at Pune, *Ghatashradda* (1977), together with the films of women filmmakers Prema Karanth and Aparna Sen, remains among the most sensitively observed examples of India's Third Cinema. His response to my obsession with *Bombay* was to invite me to see a rerun of another Mani Ratnam film, *Nayakan* (1987). *Nayakan* simply steals the majority of its plot from the first two parts of Coppola's *Godfather* saga, even quoting some of the shots, but adding a few indigenous scenes and musical numbers. Kasaravalli, whose native language is Kannada and who speaks English better than he speaks Ratnam's Tamil, had to attempt a double translation to allow me to follow the plot. Far from being an embarrassing mélange, however, the film rather brilliantly invokes its models and gave its star, Kamal Hassan, who has to evolve from Robert De Niro into Marlon Brando, the role of a lifetime. Kasaravalli pointed out that Third Cinema filmmakers in India who attempted Middle Cinema could never accomplish what Ratnam did because the forms did not come naturally to them: such a translation was simply impossible. Even in moments of banality (and here he catalogued them in analytical detail), Ratnam is sincere and with sincerity speaks in their language to an audience greater in number than Steven Spielberg's.

I had to wait five years more to meet with one of the founding *auteurs* of the New Indian Cinema, and it was chance that brought me to Mani Kaul on a snowy day at Harvard. Kaul wondered in hindsight if a New Indian Cinema really existed, and upon my rejoinder that it was no more discordant or heterogeneous a movement than Italian Neorealism, suggested that its decline and fragmentation was assured by the way it began. Kaul observed that it was Satyajit Ray himself who inspired a Third Cinema in India and then condemned it by making it known that independent films should win their own audience and be self-sustaining. His point, of course, was that neither the *Nouvelle Vague* nor the New German Cinema would have survived the loss of governmental funding or withstood governmental micro-management of the production and distribution of their films. Middle Cinema is for him no more than a shady compromise. Intellectuals, went on Kaul, the most austere of Indian exponents of Third Cinema, have never appreciated the monumental achievement of the rambunctious popular films. Nowhere else in the world had an indigenous film industry succeeded in "keeping out" Hollywood.

While this sanguine view may soon have to be modified, it remains the most interesting rejoinder of all to the notion that Third Cinema is the only legitimate response to First Cinema. Hollywood's Paleozoic techniques of flooding foreign markets with cheap prints and luring away directors required considerable evolution before even the limited success of Spielberg's *Jurassic Park* (1993) became possible, and this should be viewed against the counterflow of popular Indian cinema to the First World in the form of peripatetic directors such as Shekhar Kapur and films such as *Devdas* (2002), one of the few asymmetries of globalization that has favored the Third World. Nor is Hollywood's foothold the secure beachhead of the colonial past, for despite intense hype *Titanic* (dir. James Cameron, 1997), elsewhere the biggest grossing film of all time, made a comparatively disappointing splash in India before sinking without trace.

Notes

1 See *Film Theory: An Introduction* (Malden: Blackwell Publishers, 2000), p. 281.
2 "The Birth of a New Realism: Painting, Photography and the Advent of Documentary Cinema." Special issue on "Film, Photography and Television." *Film History* Vol. 10.2 (1998), pp. 165–87.
3 Jean-Claude Carrière has made this claim of *Belle de Jour* (see Baxter *Buñuel* pp. 48–9 (New York: Carroll and Graf, 1994)) and Baxter adds that Lacan's showing of *El* in his classes was Buñuel's only "satisfaction" with the film (p. 228).
4 Zizek treats Hitchcock in each of his major works but offers the most concentrated series of analyses in *Everything You Have Always Wanted to Know About Jacques Lacan But Were Afraid to Ask Alfred Hitchcock* (New York: Verso, 1992).
5 See, for instance, John Baxter's discussion in *Buñuel* of the Surrealists in Paris and the fragmentation of the group resulting from André Breton's 1927 decree that all members must join the French Communist Party (pp. 36–9).

6   It should be noted, in fact, that what appeared to turn the critical tide in relation to Ghatak's importance to Third Cinema theory (for he had hitherto been regarded as principally a pedagogue and activist filmmaker working in Satyajit Ray's shadow) were essays by Ashish Rajadhyaksha and Geeta Kapur included in *Questions of Third Cinema* (London: BFI Publishing, 1989, pp. 170–7) edited by Jim Pines and Paul Willemen.

7   I have discussed Pasolini's contribution to the anti-Formalist (and neo-Gramscian) notion of *contenutismo,* i.e. the determination of form and meaning by content, and its relevance to postcolonial discourses and African liberation in a talk entitled "Notes for an African Oresteia: Pier-Paolo Pasolini's Challenge to the Documentary Form," accepted for inclusion among the selected papers of the *Millennium Responses: (Dis) placing Classical Greek Theater* conference hosted by the Aristotle University of Thessaloniki in September, 1997. The value and importance of Pasolini's semiology (which he developed in opposition to that of Metz) is the clarity with which he demonstrates the necessary contiguities of socially relevant filmmaking practice and its theoretical underpinnings.

8   Thompson devotes an entire chapter (pp. 197–217) of *Breaking the Glass Armor* (Princeton: Princeton University Press, 1988) to what remains the model of formal criticism of the film. Note that later, purer examples of Third Cinema (notably Ray's *Pather Panchali* which was embraced by Cesare Zavattini, *The Bicycle Thieves*' scriptwriter, as the only true example of Neorealism up to that point) address some of the very deficiencies – such as star lighting – about which Bazin lacked sufficient rigor, according to Thompson.

9   Translations of these theoretical statements have been collected and reprinted in the first volume of *New Latin American Cinema* (Detroit: Wayne State University Press, 1997) edited by Michael Martin. Perhaps the most perceptive and authoritative discussion of the range of influences that gave rise to a Third Cinema is that of Ella Shohat and Robert Stam (see, especially, pp. 27–8) in *Unthinking Eurocentrism: Multiculturalism and the Media* (London: Routledge, 1994).

10 Note that in "Contemporary Film Studies and the Vicissitudes of Grand Theory," his introduction to *Post-theory* (Madison: The University of Wisconsin Press, 1996), Bordwell confines his attack to the wholesale importation of what he defines as "Grand Theory" (i.e. "subject-position theory and culturalism" p. 26) into film studies. He is evidently more tolerant of what he terms "middle-level research," even mentioning in this context the paradigmatic instance of examining "the relation between African films and indigenous traditions of oral storytelling" (p. 27), an idea acknowledged in a footnote as emanating, in part, from Manthia Diawara's contributions to *Questions of Third Cinema* (see pp. 199–211).

11 *Planet Hong Kong: Popular Cinema and the Art of Entertainment* (Cambridge, MA: Harvard University Press, 2000).

12 See *Political Film: The Dialectics of Third Cinema* (London: Pluto Press, 2001), p. 4.

13 Here I refer to William Over's *Social Justice in World Cinema and Theatre: Civic Discourse for the Third Millennium* (Westport, CT: Ablex Publishing, 2001) and to *Mexico's Cinema: A Century of Film and Filmmakers* (Wilmington, DE: SR Books, 1999) edited by Joanne Hirshfeld and David R. Maciel.

14 I am condensing the introductory arguments (pp. 8–102) to be found in J. Sibber's translation of Hegel's *The Philosophy of History* (New York: Dover Publications, 1956) and those of Lévi-Strauss (pp. 255–63) in *The Savage Mind* (Chicago: University of Chicago Press, 1964). It is indeed a savage irony that at the time Lévi-Strauss wrote, little was known about the ancient Mayan civilization and that it was only with the decipherment of the Mayan system of writing near the close of the last millennium that it emerged that the most time-obsessed and historio-centric culture of all flourished not far from his own chosen site for field research in the Americas.

15 See the first chapter (pp. 30–66) of *Cinematic Uses of the Past* (Minneapolis: University of Minnesota Press, 1996).

16 For a brief overview of the various phases of Cinema Nôvo see the introduction by Stam and Randal Johnson to *Brazilian Cinema* (New York: Columbia UP, 1995), pp. 30–40. The issues surrounding the various manifestations of cinema in Brazil in this period can be

gleaned from Ismail Xavier's *Allegories of Underdevelopment: From the "Aesthetics of Hunger"* *to the "Aesthetics of Garbage"* (Minneapolis: University of Minnesota Press, 1997).

17   See *Unthinking Eurocentrism*, op. cit., p. 25.

18   As Chanan notes in "The changing geography of Third Cinema" (*Screen* Vol. 38.4 [Wint. 1997], pp. 372–88), it was, in fact, the Chinese delegation at Bandung which most readily embraced the terminological distinction (see pp. 373–4).

19   Kissinger's comments in the forward can be found on p. x of *From Third World to First, The Singapore Story: 1965–2000* (New York: HarperCollins, 2000).

20   I have attempted to chart the broad outlines of this "forgotten" history in "Modernism, Modernity and the Rebirth of Singaporean Cinema" in the forthcoming *Theorising the SE Asian City as Text* edited by Brenda Yeoh and Robbie Goh (Singapore: University Press of Singapore).

21   The work in which Chow first articulated this paradoxical problematic was *Primitive Passions: Visuality, Sexuality, Ethnography, and Contemporary Chinese Cinema* (New York: Columbia University Press, 1995), of which the final chapter deals particularly with the issues of cultural transmission via translation (see pp. 175–202).

22   See pp. 34–5 of "Towards a Third Cinema" in Martin, op. cit. (pp. 33–58).

23   Dissanayake has often returned to these issues both within and outside the context of Third Cinema, but an economical treatment of the central issues can be found in the introduction to *Colonialism and Nationalism in Asian Cinema* (Bloomington: Indiana University Press, 1994), pp. ix–xxix.

24   See, especially, the chapters on the consequences of Eurocentrism (pp. 13–54) and the problematic of Third Worldist film (pp. 248–85) in *Unthinking Eurocentrism: Multiculturalism and the Media* (London: Routledge, 1994). The discussion of Orson Welles's aborted film, *It's All True* (pp. 232–5), is also useful in the context of my argument and my later defense of a broadening of the notion of Third Cinema.

25   See *Film Theory*, op. cit., p. 283.

26   See, in particular, pp. 377–80 of "The changing geography of Third Cinema" (*Screen* Vol. 38.4 [Winter 1997], pp. 372–88). Noting the fragmentation that seemed to occur at the 1986 Edinburgh Conference on Third Cinema, Chanan adopts a dynamic model of Third Cinema, one whose terrain (or "geography") shifts with the social situations a particular film addresses, a position that towards the close of his argument veers in the direction of relativism (but see, in this context, my discussion of the even greater danger that inheres to the opposite tendency, the reification of categories of cinema, in my closing remarks to the introduction).

27   See pp. 2–3 of "The Third Cinema Question: Notes and Reflections" in *Questions of Third Cinema*, op. cit., pp. 1–29. Do note that Willemen's argument grows in sophistication and self-reflection, as when he subsequently points out that a dialogical relation exists between modes of authorial address and modes of reception (as on p. 9 when he points out that "In Europe, most Third Cinema products have definitely been consumed in a Second Cinema way"). This, too, raises an important "question" about the uses of *auteur* cinema that Marvin D'Lugo addresses in these pages.

28   Chanan (op. cit.) is so attracted to this position that he quotes him to this effect twice (see, for instance, the conclusion on p. 388).

29   See *Third Cinema in the Third World: An Aesthetics of Revolution* (Ann Arbor: UMI Research Press, 1982).

30   Ibid. pp. 2–4.

31   See *Unthinking Eurocentrism*, op. cit., pp. 29–30.

32   See "Towards a Third Cinema" in Martin, op. cit., p. 41.

33   I refer to "Towards a critical theory of Third World films" in *Questions of Third Cinema* edited by Jim Pines and Paul Willemen (London: British Film Institute, 1989).

34   See, for instance, Nigel Gibson's introduction to his anthology *Rethinking Fanon* (New York: Humanity Books, 1999), wherein he notes (pp. 11–12) various critiques of Fanon's Marxism (and the argument by Lou Turner and John Alan that he was a Marxist-Humanist).

In his contribution to the same volume Henry Louis Gates observes, dispassionately, the "Rashomon-like" series of Fanons that emerge in the analyses of Edward Said, Benita Parry, Gayatri Spivak, Homi Bhabha, and Abdul JanMohammed (pp. 251–68), and Said and Bhabha themselves point to the deep-rooted European intellectual traditions (represented on the one hand by Gyorgy Lukács and the other by Jacques Lacan) which continually informed Fanon's discussion both of class struggle and the psychology of colonialism (pp. 197–214, pp. 179–96).

35 See p. 33 of "Towards a Critical Theory of Third World Films."

36 See, especially, pp. 3–4 of "Marginal Cinemas and Mainstream Critical Theory" in *Screen* Vol. 13.3 (1985), pp. 3–21. Note that the logic of Burton's argument here is, however, limited by her notion that the developed world can more easily consume Third World "raw materials" such as films than peripheral sectors can import and consume such manufactured products of the developed sector such as theoretical and critical writings. Globalization allows us the hindsight of correcting this misperception, for ease of consumption has more to do with ideologies of consumption than with issues of availability and digestibility alone, as "undeveloped" consumers of MacDonalds hamburgers, Coca Cola and such television fare as Bay Watch evidence. Furthermore, the notion that Western Theory was somehow more deeply reflective than those emanating from the Third World would have irked Fanon had he been alive as it might critics as diverse as Aijaz Ahmad or Martin Bernal today.

37 Ibid. p. 5.

38 Ibid. pp. 8–9, pp. 18–19.

39 See pp. 140–1 and pp. 143–4 of "Colonialism and 'Law and Order'," *Screen* Vol. 27.3–4 (1986), pp. 140–7.

40 Ibid. pp. 145–6.

41 I quote from passages scattered throughout "The Third Cinema Question," op. cit.

42 "The Third Cinema Question," op. cit., p. 35.

43 "The changing geography," op. cit., pp. 377, 382.

44 See *Unthinking Eurocentrism*, op. cit., p. 28.

45 See *Film Theory*, op. cit., pp. 283–5.

46 I refer to Patrick Tierney's controversial *Darkness in El Dorado: How Scientists and Journalists Devastated the Amazon* (New York: Norton, 2000). See, also, my earlier critique of the neo-imperialist epistemologies of visual anthropology in "Visual Anthropology, Colonialism and the (Southeast Asian) Voice of Kong," *Southeast Asian Journal of Social Science* Vol. 26.1 (1998), pp. 143–53.

47 Wayne, in fact, argues in *Political Cinema: The Dialectics of Third Cinema* (London: Pluto Press, 2001) that "although theory was always a key component of Third Cinema, as a body of theoretical work, it remains significantly underdeveloped in terms of its grasp of First Cinema and Second Cinema" (p. 6). Wayne's grasp, however, seems rather too firm in that according to him Edward Said blunders in suggesting that *The Battle of Algiers* was "unmatched" in its depiction of an anti-colonial struggle, adding that Stam and Louise Spence only succeed in revealing the film's appeals to a form of "First Cinema" identificatory spectatorship (see, especially, pp. 14–22). Each of these positions (as is the "dialectical" strategy adopted throughout of contrasting one cinematic form to another) stems, as I endeavor to illustrate in the text, from a hermetic and reified division of First, Second and Third Cinema which all the theorists of Third Cinema, including Solanas and Getino, rejected very early on. Note, however, his comparatively measured criticism of Solanas's and Getino's "situationalism" and the spirited defense of *The Hour of the Furnaces* against Steve Neale's unfavorable comparison of it to Godard's more "open" cinematic texts (see pp. 118–36).

48 Ibid. pp. 14 and 19. See also pp. 56–9 for the distinction Wayne draws between Third Cinema and Guerilla Cinema.

49 Ibid. pp. 21–2. Cf. Khanna's "*The Battle of Algiers* and *The Nouba Women of Mont Chenoua*," *Third Text* Vol. 43 (Sum. 1998), pp. 13–32.

50 Note that even in his recent film, *Faat Kine* (2000), Sembène focuses, as he has done periodically throughout his career, on the oppressive structures limiting the role of women in society (whether in France or Senegal); however, with rare exceptions such as Sarah Maldoror, women directors are seldom on the "lists" of the Third Cinema theorists or even on those of writers on the broader terrain of Third World Cinema. Also see Shohat's discussion of *The Battle Of Algiers* in this context.

51 Shohat catalogues some of the remarkable directors who have contested both nationalist agendas and gender oppression. Also noteworthy are women filmmakers – Maria Luisa Bemberg, Marguerite Duras, Laleen Jayamanne, Aparna Sen, Taminei Milani – who have explored the roles of women as multiply marginalized outsiders in Third World contexts.

52 In this context see Stam's discussion in *Film Theory: An Introduction* of the emergence from the critical closet of various theories, especially those which challenged classical "gaze" theory (see pp. 262–7).

53 See *An Accented Cinema: Exilic and Diasporic Filmmaking* (Princeton: Princeton University Press, 2001), pp. 30–1, 46–56. For further reference to Julien's filmmaking and to gay/lesbian interventions in the context of Third Cinema, see Shohat's chapter.

54 See *National Identity In Indian Popular Cinema, 1947–1987* (Austin: University of Texas Press, 1993).

55 I refer to Pendakur's *Canadian Dreams and American Control* (Detroit: Wayne State University Press, 1990) and O'Regan's *Australian National Cinema* (London: Routledge, 1996). The latter, especially, is a central text in any discussion of Third Cinema as it is among the more sophisticated treatments of the nature of a "national cinema," while it scrupulously avoids many of the more elementary and unsatisfactory simplifications of the nature and form of Hollywood's cultural imperialism and industrial predation.

56 And so it is termed, for instance, in Thompson's and Bordwell's *Film History: an Introduction* (New York: McGraw Hill, 1994), where they correctly identify Mrinal Sen's *Bhuvan Shome* (1969) and Basu Chatterji's *Sara Akash* (1969) as the breakthrough films of the movement, but perhaps overstate the case in arguing that the Parallel Cinema was "Bombay-based" and that it soon overshadowed Bengali *auteur* cinema (see pp. 770–4).

57 Ratnam's technical proficiency is readily discernible and he has influenced directors in places as far afield as Australia in the case of Baz Luhrmann.

Part I
Third Cinema theory and beyond

In *Unthinking Eurocentrism* Ella Shohat and Robert Stam have made what is perhaps the most important recent contribution to Third Cinema theory. A comprehensive, yet measured critique of the very forces Third Cinema filmmakers opposed in their practices, it is clearly the result of many years of work in the often embattled terrain of alternative media practices. It is also an eloquent rebuttal, replete with detailed examples, that serves as an historical refutation of the emerging schools of thought that find themselves in denial about the effects of media imperialism and neocolonial exploitation.

Stam's present essay is many things at once. It is a major contribution to a prosaics of cinema inflected by the theories of the Russian classicist and philosopher of language, Mikhail Bakhtin – but this is only to be expected of the author of *Subversive Pleasures: Bakhtin, Cultural Criticism and Film* (Baltimore: Johns Hopkins University Press, 1989). It is also one which shows that filmmakers in the Third World or those operating in the cultural framework of exile/diaspora anticipated the diffusion of Bakhtin's arguments about pluri-spatiality and heterochronicity and used the medium to forge a radical aesthetics that offered direct challenges to the monological aesthetics of First Cinema. At the root of these cinemas, Stam argues, was a genuine heterophony that reflected and celebrated the garbage heaps that, as both metaphor and synecdoche, inspired them.

Perhaps most crucially in the context of this project, Stam's work is also a re-history, a rewriting of the early phase of alternative filmmaking in the Latin American bedrock of Third Cinema; eloquent proof, indeed, that the more sophisticated indigenous critics of Third Cinema never regarded the latter as a universal nostrum or the "ultimate answer" or cure for all Third World ills. Rather than resort to the abjection and what Stam terms "miserabilism" characteristic of early Third Cinema products, these cultural theorists and filmmakers turned their eyes with witty, satiric contempt on the consumerist ethos which underwrote and continues to underwrite First Cinema.

1 Beyond Third Cinema

The aesthetics of hybridity

Robert Stam

In the late 1960s and early 1970s, in the wake of the Vietnamese victory over the French, the Cuban revolution, and Algerian Independence, third world intellectuals called for a "tricontinental revolution" (with Ho Chi Minh, Che Guevara, and Frantz Fanon as talismanic figures). In film, this third-worldist film ideology was crystallized in a wave of militant manifesto essays – Glauber Rocha's "Aesthetic of Hunger" (1965), Fernando Solanas and Otavio Getino's "Towards a Third Cinema" (1969), and Julio García Espinosa's "For an Imperfect Cinema" (1969) – and in declarations and manifestoes from Third World Film Festivals calling for a tricontinental revolution in politics and an aesthetic and narrative revolution in film form. Rocha called for a "hungry" cinema of "sad, ugly films," Solanas and Getino called for militant guerilla documentaries, and Espinosa called for an "imperfect" cinema energized by the "low" forms of popular culture, where the process of communication was more important than the product, where political values were more important than "production values."

The work of Frantz Fanon was a pervasive influence in these theories, and in the films influenced by them. The Solanas and Getino film *La Hora de Los Hornos* (*Hour of the Furnaces*, 1968), not only quotes Fanon's adage that "Every Spectator is a Coward or a Traitor," but also orchestrates a constellation of Fanonian themes – the psychic stigmata of colonialism, the therapeutic value of anti-colonial violence, and the urgent necessity of a new culture and a new human being. The third-worldist film manifestoes also stress anti-colonial militancy and violence, literal/political in the case of Solanas-Getino, and metaphoric/aesthetic in the case of Rocha. "Only through the dialectic of violence," Rocha wrote, "will we reach lyricism."

"Third Cinema" offered a Fanon-inflected version of Brechtian aesthetics, along with a dash of "national culture." At the same time, it offered a practical production strategy which turned scarcity, as Ismail Xavier put it, "into a signifier."[1] While "Third Cinema" represented a valid alternative to the dominant Hollywood model in an early period, it is important to remember that it represents only one model of alternative filmmaking. Rather than measure all alternative models against "Third Cinema" as an ideal type, it is more useful, I think, to envision a wide spectrum of alternative practices.

Indeed, cultural discourse in the Third World, and especially in Latin America and the Caribbean, has been fecund in neologistic aesthetics, both literary and cinematic: *"lo real maravilloso americano"* (Carpentier), the "aesthetics of hunger" (Glauber Rocha), *"megotage"* or "cigarette-butt" cinema (Ousmane Sembène), "Cine imperfecto" (Julio García Espinosa), the "aesthetics of garbage" (Rogerio Sganzerla), the "salamander" (as opposed to the Hollywood dinosaur) aesthetic (Paul Leduc), "termite terrorism" (Gilhermo del Toro), "anthropophagy" (the Brazilian Modernists), "Tropicalia" (Gilberto Gil and Caetano Veloso), "rasquachismo" (Tomas-Ibarra Frausto), "signifying-monkey aesthetics" (Henry Louis Gates), "nomadic aesthetics" (Teshome Gabriel), "diaspora aesthetics" (Kobena Mercer), "neo-hoodoo aesthetics" (Ishmael Reed), and *"santeria"* aesthetics (Arturo Lindsay). Most of these alternative aesthetics revalorize by inversion what had formerly been seen as negative, especially within colonialist discourse. Thus ritual cannibalism, for centuries the very name of the savage, abject other, becomes with the Brazilian *modernistas* an anti-colonialist trope and a term of value. (Recall that even the triumphant literary movement "magic realism" inverts the colonial view of magic as irrational superstition.) At the same time, these aesthetics share the jujitsu trait of turning strategic weakness into tactical strength. By appropriating an existing discourse for their own ends, they deploy the force of the dominant against domination.[2]

Here I would like to focus on three related aspects of these aesthetics, specifically: (1) their constitutive hybridity; (2) their chronotopic multiplicity; and (3) their common motif of the redemption of detritus. After arguing the special qualifications of the cinema for realizing such a hybrid, multitemporal aesthetic, I will conclude with the case of the Brazilian "aesthetics of garbage" as the point of convergence of all our themes, specifically examining three films literally and figuratively "about" garbage.

Hybridity

Although hybridity has been a perennial feature of art and cultural discourse in Latin America – highlighted in such terms as *mestizaje, indianismo, diversalite, creolite, raza cosmica* – it has recently been recoded as a symptom of the postmodern, postcolonial and post-nationalist moment.[3] The valorization of hybridity, it should be noted, is itself a form of jujitsu, since within colonial discourse the question of hybridity was linked to the prejudice against race-mixing, the "degeneration of blood," and the conjectured infertility of mulattoes.[4] But if the nationalist discourse of the 1960s drew sharp lines between First World and Third World, oppressor and oppressed, post-nationalist discourse replaces such binarisms with a more nuanced spectrum of subtle differentiations, in a new global regime where First World and Third World are mutually imbricated.[5] Notions of ontologically referential identity metamorphose into a conjunctural play of identifications. Purity gives way to "contamination." Rigid paradigms collapse into sliding metonymies. Erect, militant postures give way to an orgy of "positionalities." Once secure boundaries become more porous; an iconography of barbed-wire frontiers mutates into images of fluidity and crossing. A rhetoric of unsullied integrity gives way to miscegenated grammars and scrambled metaphors. A discourse of "media imperialism" gives way to reciprocity and "indigenization." Colonial tropes of irreconcilable dualism give way to postcolonial tropes drawing on the diverse modalities of mixedness: religious (syncretism); botanical (hybridity); linguistic (creolization); and genetic (*mestizaje*).

Although hybridity has existed wherever civilizations conflict, combine and synthesize, it reached a kind of violent paroxysm with the European colonization of the Americas. The *conquista* shaped a new world of practices and ideologies of mixing, making the Americas the scene of unprecedented combinations of indigenous peoples, Africans, and Europeans, and later of immigrant diasporas from all over the world. But hybridity has never been a peaceful encounter, a tension-free theme park; it has always been deeply entangled with colonial violence. While for some hybridity is lived as just another metaphor within a Derridean free play, for others it is alive as painful, visceral memory. Indeed, as a descriptive catch-all term, "hybridity" fails to discriminate between the diverse modalities of hybridity, such as colonial imposition (for example, the Catholic Church constructed on top of a destroyed Inca temple), or other interactions such as obligatory assimilation, political cooptation, cultural mimicry, commercial exploitation, top-down appropriation, or bottom-up subversion. Hybridity, in other words, is power-laden and asymmetrical. Hybridity is also cooptable. In Latin America, national identity has often been *officially* articulated as hybrid, through hypocritically integrationist ideologies that have glossed over and concealed subtle racial hegemonies.

Brazilian composer-singer Gilberto Gil calls attention to the power-laden nature of syncretism in his 1989 song "From Bob Dylan to Bob Marley: A Provocation Samba." The lyrics inform us that Bob Dylan, after converting to Christianity, made a reggae album, thus returning to the house of Israel by way of the Caribbean. The lyrics set into play a number of broad cultural parallels, between Jewish symbiology and Jamaican Rastafarianism, between the Inquisition's persecution of Jews (and Muslims) and the European suppression of African religions ("When the Africans arrived on these shores/ there was no freedom of religion"), ultimately contrasting the progressive syncretism of a Bob Marley (who died "because besides being Black he was also Jewish") with the alienation of a Michael Jackson, who "besides turning white … is becoming sad." Gil celebrates hybridity and syncretism, then, but articulates them in relation to the asymmetrical power relations engendered by colonialism. For oppressed people, artistic syncretism is not a game but an arduous negotiation, an exercise, as the song's lyrics put it, both of "resistance" and "surrender."[6]

Chronotopic multiplicity

Current theoretical literature betrays a fascination with the notion of simultaneous, superimposed spatio-temporalities. The widely disseminated trope of the palimpsest, the parchment on which are inscribed the layered traces of diverse moments of past writing, contains within it this idea of multiple temporalities. The postmodern moment, similarly, is seen as chaotically plural and contradictory, while its aesthetic is seen as an aggregate of historically dated styles randomly reassembled in the present. But this oxymoronic space-time is not found only in *recent* theoretical literature. It was anticipated in Benjamin's "revolutionary nostalgia," in Ernst Bloch's conjugation of the now and the "not yet," in Braudel's multiple-speed view of history, in Althusser's "overdetermination" and "uneven development," in Raymond Williams's "residual and emergent" discourses, in Jameson's "nostalgia for the present," and in David Harvey's "time-space compression." Bakhtinian dialogism, in the same vein, alludes to the temporally layered matrix of communicative utterances that "reach" the text not only through recognizable citations but also through a subtle process of dissemination. In a very suggestive formulation, Bakhtin evokes the multiple epochs intertextually "buried" in the work of Shakespeare. The "semantic treasures Shakespeare embedded in his works," Bakhtin writes:

> were created and collected through the centuries and even millennia: they lay hidden in the language, and not only in the literary language, but also in those strata of the popular language that before Shakespeare's time had not entered literature, in the diverse genres and forms of speech communication, in the forms of a mighty national culture (primarily carnival forms) that were shaped through millennia, in theatre-spectacle genres (mystery plays, farces, and so forth), in plots whose roots go back to prehistoric antiquity.[7]
>
> (Bakhtin, 1986: 5)

Bakhtin thus points to the temporally palimpsestic nature of all artistic texts, seen within a millennial, *longue durée*.[8] Nor is this aesthetic the special preserve of canonical writers, since dialogism operates within all cultural production, whether literate or non-literate, highbrow or lowbrow. Rap music's aesthetic of sampling and cut 'n' mix, for example, can be seen as a street-smart, low-budget embodiment of Bakhtin's theories of temporally embedded intertextuality, since rap's multiple strands derive from sources as diverse as African call-and-response patterns, disco, funk, the Last Poets, Gil Scott Heron, Muhammed Ali, doo-wop groups, skip rope rhymes, prison and army songs, signifying and "the dozens," all the way back to the storytelling folk historians, the *griots,* of Nigeria and Gambia.[9] Rap bears the stamp and rhythm of multiple times and meters; as in artistic collage or literary quotation, the sampled texts carry with them the time-connoted memory of their previous existences.

The redemption of detritus

The third shared feature of these hybrid bricolage aesthetics is their common leitmotif of the strategic redemption of the low, the despised, the imperfect, and the "trashy" as part of a social overturning. This strategic redemption of the marginal also has echoes in the realms of high theory and cultural studies. One thinks, for example, of Derrida's recuperation of the marginalia of the classical philosophical text, of Bakhtin's exaltation of "redeeming filth" and of low "carnivalized" genres, of Benjamin's "trash of history" and his view of the work of art as constituting itself out of apparently insignificant fragments, of Deleuze and Guattari's recuperation of stigmatized psychic states such as schizophrenia, of Camp's ironic reappropriation of kitsch, of Cultural Studies' recuperation of sub-literary forms and "subcultural styles," and of James Scott's "weapons of the weak."

In the plastic arts, the "garbage girls" (Mierle Laderman Ukeles, Christy Rupp, Betty Beaumont) deploy waste disposal as a trampoline for art. Ukeles, for example, choreographed a "street ballet" of garbage trucks. (One is reminded of the "dance of the garbage can lids" in the Donen-Kelly musical *It's Always Fair Weather*.) Betty Beaumont makes installation art on toxic waste-dumps using government surplus materials.[10] Joseph Cornell, similarly, turned the flotsam of daily life – broken dolls, paper cutouts, wine glasses, medicine bottles – into luminous, childlike collages. In the cinema, an "aesthetics of garbage" performs a kind of jujitsu by recuperating cinematic waste materials. For filmmakers without great resources, raw-footage minimalism reflects practical necessity as well as artistic strategy. In a film like *Hour of the Furnaces*, unpromising raw footage is transmogrified into art, just as the alchemy of sound-image montage transforms the base metals of titles, blank frames, and wild sound into the gold and silver of rhythmic virtuosity. Compilation filmmakers like Bruce Conner, Mark Rappaport, and Sherry Milner/Ernest Larsen rearrange and reedit preexisting filmic materials, while trying to fly below the radar of bourgeois legalities. Craig Baldwin, a San Francisco film programmer, reshapes outtakes and public domain materials into witty compilation films. In *Sonic Outlaws*, he and his collaborators argue for a media *detournement* that deploys the charismatic power of dominant media against itself, all the time displaying a royal disregard for the niceties of *copyright*. Baldwin's anti-Columbus Quincentennial film *O No Coronado!* (1992), for example, demystifies the conquistador whose desperate search for the mythical Seven Cities of Cibola led him into a fruitless, murderous journey across what is now the American Southwest. To relate this calamitous epic, Baldwin deploys not only his own staged dramatizations but also the detritus of the filmic archive: stock footage, pedagogical films, industrial documentaries, swashbucklers, tacky historical epics.

In an Afro-diasporic context, the redemption of detritus evokes another, historically fraught strategy, specifically the ways that dispossessed New World blacks have managed to transmogrify waste products into art. The Afro diaspora, coming from artistically developed African cultures but now deprived of freedom, education, and material possibilities, managed to tease beauty out of the very guts of deprivation, whether through the musical use of discarded oil barrels (the steel drums of Trinidad), the culinary use of throwaway parts of animals (soul food, *feijoada*), or the use in weaving of throwaway fabrics (quilting).[11] This "negation of the negation" also has to do with a special relationship to official history. As those whose history has been destroyed and misrepresented, as those whose very history has been dispersed and diasporized rather than memorialized and incorporated into the *grand récit* as have dominant histories and as those whose history has often been told, danced and sung rather than written, oppressed people have been obliged to recreate their past out of scraps and remnants and the debris of history. In aesthetic terms, these hand-me-down aesthetics and history-making embody an art of discontinuity – the heterogeneous scraps making up a quilt, for example, incorporate diverse styles, time periods, and materials – whence their alignment with artistic modernism as an art of jazzistic "breaking" and discontinuity, and within an anticipatory postmodernism as an art of recycling and pastiche.[12]

Alternative aesthetics are multi-temporal in still another sense, in that they are often rooted in non-realist, often non-western cultural traditions featuring other historical rhythms, other narrative structures, and other attitudes toward the body and spirituality. By incorporating para-modern traditions into modernizing or postmodernizing aesthetics, they problematize facile dichotomies such as traditional and modern, realist and modernist, modernist and postmodernist. Indeed, the projection of Third World cultural practices as untouched by avant-gardist modernism or mass-mediated postmodernism often subliminally encodes a view of the Third World as "underdeveloped," or "developing," as if it lived in another time zone apart from the global system of the late capitalist world.[13] A less neo-Darwinian stagist conception would see all the "worlds" as living the *same* historical moment, in mixed modes of subordination or domination. Time in all the worlds is scrambled and palimpsestic, with the pre-modern, the modern, and the post-modern coexisting globally, although the "dominant" might vary from region to region.

The world's avant-gardes are also characterized by a paradoxical and oxymoronic temporality. Just as the European avant-garde became "advanced" by drawing on the "primitive," so non-European artists, in an aesthetic version of "revolutionary nostalgia," have drawn on the most traditional elements of their cultures, elements less "pre-modern" (an admittedly dubious term that embeds modernity as telos) than "para-modern." In the arts, the distinction archaic/modernist is often non-pertinent, in that both share a refusal of the conventions of mimetic realism. It is thus less a question of juxtaposing the archaic and the modern than deploying the archaic in order, paradoxically, to modernize, in a dissonant temporality which combines a past imaginary communitas with an equally imaginary future utopia. In their attempts to forge a liberatory language, for example, alternative film traditions draw on para-modern phenomena such as popular religion and ritual magic. In African and Afro-diasporic films such as *Yeelen* (Senegal), *Jitt* (Zimbabwe), *Quartier Mozart* (Cameroon), *The Amulet of Ogum* (Brazil), *Patakin* (Cuba), *The Black Goddess* (Nigeria), and *The Gifted* (the United States), magical spirits become an aesthetic resource, a means for breaking away from the linear, cause-and-effect conventions of Aristotelian narrative poetics, a way of flying beyond the gravitational pull of verism, of defying the "gravity" of chronological time and literal space.

The cinema, I would argue, is ideally equipped to express cultural and temporal hybridity. The cinema is temporally hybrid, first of all, in an intertextual sense, in that it "inherits" all the art forms and millennial traditions associated with its diverse matters of expression. (The music or pictorial art of any historical period can be cited, or mimicked, within the cinema.) But the cinema is also temporally hybrid in another, more technical sense. As a technology of representation, the cinema mingles diverse times and spaces; it is produced in one constellation of times and spaces, it represents still another (diegetic) constellation of times and places, and is received in still another time and space (theatre, home, classroom). Film's conjunction of sound and image means that each track not only presents two kinds of time, but also that they mutually inflect one another in a form of synchresis. Atemporal static shots can be inscribed with temporality through sound.[14] The panoply of available cinematic techniques further multiplies these already multiple times and spaces. Superimposition redoubles the time and space, as do montage and multiple frames within the image. The capacity for palimpsestic overlays of images and sounds facilitated by the new computer and video technologies further amplify possibilities for fracture, rupture and polyphony. An electronic "quilting" can weave together sounds and images in ways that break with linear single-line narrative, opening up utopias (and dystopias) of infinite manipulability. The "normal" sequential flow can be disrupted and sidetracked to take account of simultaneity and parallelism. Rather than an Aristotelian sequence of exposition, identification, suspense, pathos and catharsis, the audio-visual text becomes a tapestry. These media are capable of chameleonic blendings à la *Zelig*, digital insertions à la *Forrest Gump*, and multiple images/ sounds à la *Numéro Deux*. These new media can combine synthesized images with captured ones. They can promote a "threshold encounter" between Elton John and Louis Armstrong, as in the 1991 Diet Coke commercial, or allow Natalie Cole to sing with her long-departed father. Potentially, the audio-visual media are less bound by canonical, institutional and aesthetic traditions; they make possible what Arlindo Machado calls the "hybridization of alternatives."

The cinema in particular, and audio-visual media in general, are in Bakhtinian terms "multichronotopic." Although Bakhtin develops his concept of the "chronotope" (from chronos, time, and topos, place) to suggest the inextricable relation between time and space in the novel, it also seems ideally suited to the cinema as a medium where "spatial and temporal indicators are fused into one carefully thought-out concrete whole."[15] (It also spares us the absurdity of "choosing" between time and space as theoretical focus.) Bakhtin's description of the novel as the place where time "thickens, takes on flesh, becomes artistically visible" and where "space becomes charged and responsive to the movements of time, plot and history" seems in some ways even more appropriate to film than to literature, for whereas literature plays itself out within a virtual, lexical space, the cinematic chronotope is quite literal, splayed out concretely across a screen with specific dimensions and unfolding in literal time (usually 24 frames per second), quite apart from the fictive time-space specific films might construct. Thus cinema embodies the inherent relationality of time (chronos) and space (topos); it is space temporalized and time spatialized, the site where time takes place and place takes time.

The multi-track nature of audio-visual media enables them to orchestrate multiple, even contradictory, histories, temporalities, and perspectives. They offer not a "history channel," but rather multiple channels for multifocal, multiperspectival historical representation. What interests me especially here is a kind of matching between representations of the palimpsestic, multi-nation state and the cinema as a palimpsestic and polyvalent medium which can stage and perform a transgressive hybridity. Constitutively multiple, the cinema is ideally suited for staging what Néstor García Canclini in a very different context, calls "multi-temporal heterogeneity."[16] The fact that dominant cinema has largely opted for a linear and homogenizing aesthetic where track reinforces track within a Wagnerian totality in no way effaces the equally salient truth that the cinema (and the new media) are infinitely rich in polyphonic potentialities.[17] The cinema makes it possible to stage temporalized cultural contradictions not only within the shot, through *mise-en-scène*, decor, costume, and so forth, but also through the interplay and contradictions between the diverse tracks, which can mutually shadow, jostle, undercut, haunt, and relativize one another. Each track can develop its own velocity; the image can be accelerated while the music is slowed, or the soundtrack can be temporally layered by references to diverse historical periods. A culturally polyrhythmic, heterochronic, multiple-velocity and contrapuntal cinema becomes a real possibility.

We catch a glimpse of these possibilities in Glauber Rocha's *Terra em Transe* (*Land in Anguish*, 1967), a baroque allegory about Brazilian politics, specifically the 1964 right-wing *coup d'état* which overthrew Joao Goulart. Set in the imaginary land of Eldorado, the film offers an irreverent, "unofficial" representation of Pedro Alvares Cabral, the Portuguese "discoverer" of Brazil. More important for our purposes, the film exploits temporal anachronism as a fundamental aesthetic resource. The right wing figure of the film (named Porfirio Diaz after the Mexican dictator) arrives from the sea with a flag and a crucifix, suggesting a foundational myth of national origins. Dressed in an anachronistic modern-day suit, Diaz is accompanied by a priest in a Catholic habit, a 16th century conquistador, and a symbolic feathered Indian. Diaz raises a silver chalice, in a ritual evoking Cabral's "first mass," but in an anachronistic manner which stresses the continuities between the conquest and contemporary oppression; the contemporary right-winger is portrayed as the latter-day heir of the conquistadores. But Rocha further destabilizes time and space by making Africa a textual presence. The very aesthetic of the sequence, first of all, draws heavily from the Africanized forms of Rio's yearly samba pageant, with its polyrhythms, its extravagant costumes, and its contradictory forms of historical representation; indeed, the actor who plays the conquistador is Clóvis Bornay, a historian who specialized in carnival "allegories," and himself a well-known figure from Rio's carnival. Secondly, the mass is accompanied not by Christian religious music, but by Yoruba religious chants, evoking the "transe" of the Portuguese title. Rocha's suggestive referencing of African music, as if it had existed in Brazil prior to the arrival of Europeans, reminds us not only of the "continental drift" theory that sees South America and Africa as once having formed part of a single land mass, but also of the theories of van Sertima and others that Africans arrived in the New World "before Columbus."[18] The music suggests that Africans, as those who shaped and were shaped by the Americas over centuries, are in some uncanny sense *also* indigenous to the region.[19] At the same time, the music enacts an ironic reversal since the chants of exaltation are addressed to a reprehensible figure. Although Eurocentric discourse posits African religion as irrational, the film suggests that in fact it is the European elite embodied by Porfirio Diaz which is irrational, hysterical, entranced, almost demonic. The presence of a *mestiço* actor representing the Indian, furthermore, points to a frequent practice in Brazilian cinema during the silent period, when Indians, whose legal status as "wards of the state" prevented them from representing themselves, were often represented by blacks. While in the US white actors performed in blackface, in Brazil blacks performed, as it were, in "redface."

That the entire scene is a product of the narrator-protagonist's delirium as he lays dying, finally, as the past (the "discovery") and the future (the *coup d'état*) flash up before his eyes, adds still another temporalized layer of meaning. Here temporal contradiction becomes a spur to creativity. The scene's fractured and discontinuous aesthetic stages the drama of life in the colonial "contact zone," defined by Mary Louise Pratt as the space in which "subjects previously separated" encounter each other and "establish ongoing relations, usually involving conditions of coercion, radical inequality, and intractable conflict."[20] Rocha's neo-baroque Afro-avant-gardist aesthetic thus figures the discontinuous, dissonant, fractured history of the nation through equally dissonant images and sounds.

Brazilian Cinema proliferates in the signs and tokens of hybridity, drawing on the relational processes of Brazil's diverse communities. Rather than merely reflect a pre-existing hybridity, Brazilian cinema actively hybridizes in that it stages and performs hybridity, counterpointing cultural forces through surprising, even disconcerting juxtapositions. At its best, it orchestrates not a bland pluralism but rather a strong counterpoint between seemingly incommensurable yet nevertheless thoroughly co-implicated cultures. The opening sequence of *Macunaima*, for example, shows a family whose names are indigenous, whose epidermic traits are African and European and mestizo, whose clothes are Portuguese and African, whose hut is indigenous and backwoods, and whose manner of giving birth is indigenous. The plot of *Pagador de Promessas* (*The Given Word*, 1962) revolves around the conflicting values of Catholicism and Candomblé, evoked through the manipulation of cultural symbols. We witness, for instance, a cultural battle between *berimbau* (an African instrument consisting of a long bow, gourd and string) and church bell, which synecdochically encapsulates a larger religious and political struggle. *Tent of Miracles* (1977) counterposes opera and samba to metaphorize the larger conflict between Bahia's white elite and its subjugated mestizos, between ruling-class science and Afro-inflected popular culture.

Latin America, for García Canclini, lives in a postmodern "time of bricolage where diverse epochs and previously separated cultures intersect."[21] In the best Brazilian films hybridity is not just a property of the cultural objects portrayed but rather inheres in the film's very processes of enunciation, its mode of constituting itself as a text. The final shot of *Terra em Transe* exemplifies this process brilliantly. As we see the film's protagonist Paulo wielding a rifle in a Che Guevara-like gesture of quixotic rebellion, we hear a soundtrack composed of Villa-Lobos, Candomblé chants, samba, and machine-gun fire. The mix, in this feverish bricolage, is fundamentally unstable; the Villa-Lobos music never really synchronizes with the Candomblé or the gunfire. We are reminded of Alejo Carpentier's gentle mockery of the innocuous juxtapositions of the European avant-gardists – for example, Lautreamont's "umbrella and a sewing machine" – which he contrasts with the explosive counterpoints of indigenous, African, and European cultures thrown up daily by Latin American life and art, non-homogenizing counterpoints where the tensions are never completely resolved or harmonized, where the cultural dialogue is tense, transgressive, and unassimilated.

Another way that Brazilian culture is figured as a mixed site is through the motif of garbage. Garbage, in this sense, stands at the point of convergence of our three themes of hybridity, chronotopic multiplicity, and the redemption of detritus. Garbage is hybrid, first of all, as the diasporized, heterotopic site of the promiscuous mingling of rich and poor, center and periphery, the industrial and the artisanal, the domestic and the public, the durable and the transient, the organic and the inorganic, the national and the international, the local and the global. The ideal postmodern and postcolonial metaphor, garbage is mixed, syncretic, a radically decentered social text. It can also be seen as what Charles Jencks calls a "heteropolis" and Edward Soja, following Foucault, a "heterotopia," i.e. the juxtaposition in a real place of "several sites that are themselves incompatible."[22] As a place of buried memories and traces, meanwhile, garbage is an example of what David Harvey calls the "time-space compression" typical of the acceleration produced by contemporary technologies of transportation, communication and information. In Foucault's terms, garbage is "heterochronic;" it concentrates time in a circumscribed space. (Archeology, it has been suggested, is simply a sophisticated form of garbology.)[23] The garbage pile can be seen as an archeological treasure trove precisely because of its concentrated, synecdochic, compressed character. As congealed history, garbage reveals a checkered past. As time materialized in space, it becomes coagulated sociality, a gooey distillation of society's contradictions.

As the quintessence of the negative – expressed in such phrases as "talking trash," "rubbish!" and "cesspool of contamination" – garbage can also be an object of artistic jujitsu and ironic reappropriation. An ecologically-aware recycling system in Australia calls itself "reverse garbage." (This is not to say the appreciation of garbage is always marginal: the subversive potential of garbage as metaphor is suggested in Thomas Pynchon's novel *The Crying of Lot 49*, where the heroine collects hints and traces that reveal the alternative network of W.A.S.T.E. as a kind of counterculture outside of the dominant channels of communication.) In aesthetic terms, garbage can be seen as an aleatory collage or surrealist enumeration, a case of the definitive by chance, a random pile of *objets trouvés* and *papiers collés*, a place of violent, surprising juxtapositions.[24]

Garbage, like death and excrement, is a great social leveler, the trysting point of the funky and the shi shi. It is the terminus for what Mary Douglas calls "matter out of place." In social terms, it is a truth-teller. As the lower stratum of the *socius*, the symbolic "bottom" or *cloaca maxima* of the body politic, garbage signals the return of the repressed; it is the place where used condoms, bloody tampons, infected needles and unwanted babies are left, the ultimate resting place of all that society both produces and represses, secretes and makes secret. The final shot of Buñuel's *Los Olvidados*, we may recall, shows the corpse of the film's lumpen protagonist being unceremoniously dumped on a Mexico City garbage pile; the scene is echoed in Babenco's *Kiss of the Spider Woman*, where Molina's dead body is tossed on a garbage heap while the voice-over presents the official lies about his death. Grossly material, garbage is society's id; it steams and smells below the threshold of ideological rationalization and sublimation. At the same time, garbage is reflective of social prestige; wealth and status are correlated with the capacity of a person (or a society) to discard commodities, i.e. to generate garbage. (The average American discards five pounds of garbage per day.)[25] Like hybridity, garbage too is power-laden. The power elite can gentrify a slum, make landfill a ground for luxury apartments, or dump toxic wastes in a poor neighborhood.[26]

It is one of the utopian, recombinant functions of art to work over dystopian, disagreeable and malodorous materials. Brazil's *udigrudi* (underground) filmmakers of the 1960s were the first, to my knowledge, to speak of the "aesthetics of garbage" (estetica do lixo). The movement's film-manifesto, Sganzerla's *Red Light Bandit* (1968), began with a shot of young *favelados* dancing on burning garbage piles, pointedly underlined by the same Candomblé music that begins Rocha's *Terra em Transe*. The films were made in the Sao Paulo neighborhood called "boca de lixo" (mouth of garbage), a red-light district named in diacritical contrast with the high-class red light district called "boca de luxo" (mouth of luxury). Brazilian plastic artist Regina Vater played on these references in her mid-1970s work "Luxo/Lixo" (Luxury/Garbage) where she photographically documented the quite different trash discarded in neighborhoods representing different social classes.

For the underground filmmakers, the garbage metaphor captured the sense of marginality, of being condemned to survive within scarcity, of being the dumping ground for transnational capitalism, of being obliged to recycle the materials of the dominant culture.[27] And if the early 1960s trope of hunger – as in Rocha's "aesthetics of hunger" – evokes the desperate will to dignity of the famished subject, token of the self-writ large of the third world nation itself, then the trope of garbage is more decentered, post-modern, post-colonial.

Three recent Brazilian documentaries directly address the theme of garbage. Eduardo Coutinho's *O Fio da Memoria* (*The Thread of Memory*, 1991), a film made as part of the centenary of abolition commemoration, reflects on the sequels of slavery in the present. Instead of history as a coherent, linear narrative, the film offers a history based on disjunctive scraps and fragments. Here the interwoven strands or fragments taken together become emblematic of the fragmentary interwovenness of black life in Brazil. One strand consists of the diary of Gabriel Joaquim dos Santos, an elderly black man who had constructed his own dream house as a work of art made completely out of garbage and detritus: cracked tiles, broken plates, empty cans. For Gabriel, the city of Rio represents the "power of wealth," while his house, constructed from the "city's leftovers," represents the "power of poverty." Garbage thus becomes an ideal medium for those who themselves have been cast off, broken down, who have been "down in the dumps," who feel, as the blues line had it, "like a tin can on that old dumping ground."[28] A transformative impulse takes an object considered worthless and turns it into something of value. Here the restoration of the buried worth of a cast-off object analogizes the process of revealing the hidden worth of the despised, devalued artist himself. At the same time, we witness an example of a strategy of resourcefulness in a situation of scarcity. The trash of the haves becomes the treasure of the have-nots; the dank and unsanitary is transmogrified into the sublime and the beautiful; what had been an eyesore is transformed into a sight for sore eyes. The burned-out light bulb, wasted icon of modern inventiveness, becomes an emblem of beauty. With great improvisational flair, the poor, tentatively literate Gabriel appropriates the discarded products of industrial society for his own recreational purposes, in procedures which inadvertently evoke those of modernism and the avant-garde: the Formalists' "defamiliarization," the Cubists' "found objects," Brecht's "refunctioning," the Situationists' "detournement." This recuperation of fragments also has a spiritual dimension in terms of African culture. Throughout West and Central Africa, "the rubbish heap is a metaphor for the grave, a point of contact with the world of the dead."[29] The broken vessels displayed on Congo graves, Robert Farris Thompson informs us, serve as reminders that broken objects become whole again in the other world.[30]

The title of another "garbage" video, Coutinho's documentary *Boca de Lixo* (translated as *The Scavengers*, 1992) directly links it to the "aesthetics of garbage," since its Portuguese title refers to the Sao Paulo red light district where the "garbage" films were first produced. The film centers on impoverished Brazilians who survive thanks to a garbage dump outside of Rio, where they toil against the backdrop of the outstretched, ever-merciful arms of the Christ of Corcovado. Here the camera is witness to social misery. Ferreting through the garbage, the participants perform a triage of whatever is thrown up by the daily lottery of ordure, sorting out plastic from metal from edible matter. Since many of the faces are female and dark-skinned, the film also reveals the feminization and the racialization of social misery. Here we see the endpoint of an all-permeating logic of commodification, logical telos of the consumer society and its ethos of planned obsolescence. Garbage becomes the morning after of the romance of the new. (Italo Calvino's novel *Invisible Cities* speaks of a city so enamored of the new that it discards all of its objects daily.) In the dump's squalid phantasmagoria, the same commodities that had been fetishized by advertising, dynamized by montage and haloed through backlighting, are now stripped of their aura of charismatic power. We are confronted with the seamy underside of globalization and its facile discourse of one world under a consumerist groove. The world of transnational capitalism and the "post-"s, we see, is more than ever a world of constant, daily immiseration. At last we witness the hidden face of the global system, all the sublimated agonies masked by the euphoric nostrums of "neo-liberalism."

If *Thread of Memory* sees garbage as an artistic resource, *Boca de Lixo* reveals its human-existential dimension. Here the garbage dwellers have names (Jurema, Enoch), nicknames ("Whiskers"), families, memories, and hopes. Rather than take a miserabilist approach, Coutinho shows us people who are inventive, ironic, and critical, who tell the director what to look at and how to interpret what he sees. While for Coutinho the stealing of others' images for sensationalist purposes is the "original sin" of TV-reportage,[31] the garbage dwellers repeatedly insist that "Here nobody steals," as if responding to the accusations of imaginary middle-class interlocutors. Instead of the suspect pleasures of a condescending "sympathy," the middle-class spectator is obliged to confront vibrant people who dare to dream and to talk back and even criticize the filmmakers. The "natives," in this ethnography of garbage, are not the object but rather the agents of knowledge. At the end of the film, the participants watch themselves on a VCR, in a reflexive gesture which goes back to the African films of Jean Rouch and which is now familiar from "indigenous media." Rather than pathetic outcasts, the film's subjects exist on a continuum with Brazilian workers in general; they encapsulate the country as a whole; they have held other jobs, they have worked in other cities, they have labored in the homes of the elite. And critically they have absorbed and processed the same media representations as everyone else and so have "lines out" to the center; they disprove what Janice Perlman calls the "myth of marginality." A vernacular philosopher in the film tells the filmmakers that garbage is a beginning and an end in a cyclical principle of birth and rebirth –

what goes around comes around. Garbage is shown as stored energy, containing in itself the seeds of its own transformation. Garbage becomes a form of social karma, the deferred rendezvous between those who can afford to waste and those who cannot afford not to save what has been wasted. Those who live off garbage also decorate their homes with it. While the elite wastes food almost as a matter of principle, the poor are obliged to lick their own plates, and those of others, clean.[32]

Jorge Furtado's *Isle of Flowers* (1989) brings the "garbage aesthetic" into the postmodern era, while also demonstrating the cinema's capacity as a vehicle for political/aesthetic reflexion. Rather than an aestheticization of garbage, here garbage is both theme and formal strategy. Described by its author as a "letter to a Martian who knows nothing of the earth and its social systems," Furtado's short uses Monty Python-style animation, archival footage, and parodic/reflexive documentary techniques to indict the distribution of wealth and food around the world. The "Isle of Flowers" of the title is a Brazilian garbage dump where famished women and children, in groups of ten, are given five minutes to scrounge for food. But before we get to the garbage dump, we are given the itinerary of a tomato from farm to supermarket to bourgeois kitchen to garbage can to the "Isle of Flowers." Furtado's edited collage is structured as a social lexicon or glossary, or better surrealist enumeration of key words such as "pigs," "money," and "human beings." The definitions are interconnected and multi-chronotopic; they lead out into multiple historical frames and historical situations. In order to follow the trajectory of the tomato, we need to know the origin of money: "Money was created in the seventh century before Christ. Christ was a Jew, and Jews are human beings." As the audience is still laughing from this abrupt transition, the film cuts directly to the photographic residue of the Holocaust, where Jews, garbage-like, are thrown into Death Camp piles. (The Nazis, we are reminded, had their own morbid forms of recycling.) Throughout, the film moves back and forth between minimalist definitions of the human to the lofty ideal of freedom evoked by the film's final citation: "Freedom is a word the human dream feeds on, that no one can explain or fail to understand."

But this summary gives little sense of the experience of the film, of its play with documentary form and expectations. First, the film's visuals – old TV commercials, newspaper advertisements, health care manuals – themselves constitute a kind of throwaway, visual garbage. (In the silent period of cinema, we are reminded, films were seen as transient entertainments rather than artistic durables and therefore as not worth saving; during the First World War they were even recycled for their silver and lead content.) Many of the more banal shots – of pigs, of tomatoes, and so forth – are repeated, in defiance of the decorous language of classical cinema which suggests that shots should be both beautiful and unrepeated. Second, the film, whose preamble states that "this is not a fiction film," mocks the positivist mania for factual detail by offering useless, gratuitous precision: "We are in Belem Novo, city of Porto Alegre, state of Rio Grande do Sul. More precisely, at thirty degrees, twelve minutes and thirty seconds latitude south, and fifty one degrees eleven minutes and twenty three seconds longitude west." Third, the film mocks the apparatus and protocols of rationalist science, through absurd classificatory schemas, "Dona Anete is a Roman Catholic female biped mammal," and tautological syllogisms, "Mr. Suzuki is Japanese, and therefore a human being." Fourth, the film parodies the conventions of the educational film, with its authoritative voice-over and quiz-like questions such as "What is a history quiz?" The overture music is a synthesized version of the theme song of *Voice of Brazil*, the widely-detested official radio program that has been annoying Brazilians since the days of Vargas. Humor becomes a kind of trap; the spectator who begins by laughing ends up, if not crying, at least reflecting very seriously. Opposable thumbs and a highly developed telencephalon, we are told, have given "human beings the possibility of making many improvements in their planet;" a shot of a nuclear explosion serves as illustration. Thanks to the universality of money, we are told, we are now "Free!;" a snippet of the "Hallelujah Chorus" punctuates the thought. Furtado invokes the old carnival motif of pigs and sausage, but with a political twist; here the pigs, given inequitable distribution down the food chain, eat better than people.[33] In this culinary recycling, we are given a social examination of garbage; the truth of a society is in its detritus. The socially peripheral points to the symbolically central. Rather than having the margins invade the center as in carnival, here the center creates the margins, or better, there are no margins; the tomato links the urban bourgeois family to the rural poor via the sausage and the tomato within a web of global relationality.[34]

In these films, the garbage dump becomes a critical vantage point from which to view society as a whole. It reveals the social formation as seen "from below." As the overdetermined depot of social meanings, as a concentration of piled up signifiers, garbage is the place where hybrid, multi-chronotopic relations are re-invoiced and re-inscribed. Garbage defines and illuminates the world; the trashcan, to recycle Trotsky's aphorism, *is* history. Garbage offers a database of material culture from which one can read social customs or values. Polysemic and multivocal, garbage can be seen literally – garbage as a source of food for poor people, garbage as the site of ecological disaster – but it can also be read symptomatically, as a metaphorical figure for social indictment – poor people treated like garbage, garbage as the "dumping" of pharmaceutical products or of "canned" TV programs, slums (and jails) as human garbage dumps. These films reveal the "hidden transcripts" of garbage, reading it as an allegorical text to be deciphered, a form of social colonics where the truth of a society can be "read" in its waste products.

Notes

1 See Ismail Xavier, *Allegories of Underdevelopment: Aesthetics and Politics in Modern Brazilian Cinema* (Minneapolis: University of Minnesota Press, 1997).

2   This work evolves out of an address first presented at the second installment of the "Hybrid Cultures and Transnational Identities" Conference held at UCLA March 7–8, 1997. The session was organized by Randal Johnson.

3   For those of us working in the area of Latin American culture, where "hybridity" and "mestizaje" have been critical commonplaces for decades, it is always a surprise to learn that Homi Bhabha, through no fault of his own, has been repeatedly "credited" with the concept of "hybridity".

4   The genealogy of these racist clichés extends even beyond Gobineau's extremely influential and pseudo-scientific *Essay on the Inequality of the Races* issued by the author in four volumes between 1853 and 1855, the first of which has been reprinted by Howard Fertig (New York, 1999).

5   For more on "post-Third Worldism," see Ella Shohat/Robert Stam, *Unthinking Eurocentrism: Multiculturalism and the Media* (London: Routledge, 1994) and Ella Shohat, "Post-Third-Worldist culture," in the present volume.

6   The mutually enriching collaborations between the diverse currents of Afro-diasporic music, yielding such hybrids as "samba reggae," "samba-rap," "jazz tango," "rap reggae" and "roforenge" (a blend of rock, forro, and merengue), in the Americas offer examples of "lateral syncretism," i.e. syncretism on a "sideways" basis of rough equality. Diasporic musical cultures mingle with one another, while simultaneously also playing off the dominant media-disseminated tradition of First World, especially American, popular music, itself energized by Afro-diasporic traditions. An endlessly creative multidirectional flow of musical ideas thus moves back and forth around the "Black Atlantic" (Gilroy), for example, between cool jazz and samba in bossa nova, between soul music and ska in reggae. Afro-diasporic music displays an anthropophagic capacity to absorb influences, including western influences, while still being driven by a culturally African bass-note.

7   M.M. Bakhtin, "Response to a Question from the *Novy Mir* editorial staff," in Vern McGee (ed.) *Speech Genres and Other Late Essays* (Austin: University of Texas Press, 1986), p. 5.

8   Ibid., p. 3.

9   See David Toop, *The Rap Attack: African Jive to New York Hip Hop* (New York: Pluto Press, 1984).

10   See "The Garbage Girls," in Lucy Lippard's *The Pink Glass Swan: Selected Essays on Feminist Art* (New York: The New Press, 1995).

11   In his fascinating intervention at the "Hybrid Cultures and Transnational Identities" Conference, Teshome Gabriel showed slides of the salvage art of African-American artist Lefon Andrews, who uses paper bags as his canvas, and dry leaves for paint. Teshome demonstrated the method by showing the audience a paper bag and some leaves, revealing them to be the basic materials that went into the beautiful artifacts pictured in the slides.

12   The African-American environmental artist known as Mr Imagination has, according to Suzanne Seriff, "created bottle-cap thrones, paintbrush people, cast-off totems, and other pieces salvaged from his life as a performing street artist." See page 23 of "Folk Art from the Global Scrap Heap: The Place of Irony in the Politics of Poverty," in Charlene Cerny and Suzanne Seriff (eds) *Recycled, Re-seen: Folk Art from the Global Scrap Heap* (New York: Harry N. Abrams, 1996), pp. 8–29.

13   Commenting on the Afro-Brazilian musical group Olodum, which contributed to Paul Simon's compact disk *The Spirit of the Saints*, Caetano Veloso remarked in a recent interview that: "It is not Paul Simon who brings modernity to Olodum; no, Olodum is itself modern, innovative." See Christopher Dunn's interview with Caetano: "The Tropicalista Rebellion." Introduction and Interview with Caetano Veloso, *Transition* 70 (October, 1996), pp. 116–38.

14   See Michel Chion, *Audio-Vision: Sound on Screen* (New York: Columbia University Press, 1994), especially the first chapter "Projections of Sound on Image."

15   See Bakhtin, *The Dialogic Imagination,* edited by Michael Holquist and Caryl Emerson (Austin: University Of Texas Press, 1981), p. 84. the terms in the discussion that follows can be found on pages 84–5 of the "Chronotope Essay" (pp. 84–258).

16 See Néstor García Canclini, *Culturas Hibridas: Estrategias para entrar y salir de la modernidad* (Mexico City: Grijalbo, 1989, translated by Lucy Lopez as *Hybrid Cultures: Strategies For Entering and Leaving Modernity* (Minneapolis: University of Minnesota Press, 1995).

17 Ella Shohat and I try to call attention to the vast corpus of films that explore these potentialities in our *Unthinking Eurocentrism: Multiculturalism and the Media* (London: Routledge, 1994).

18 See Ivan van Sertima, *They Came Before Columbus* (New York: Random House, 1975).

19 A 1992 samba pageant presentation, *Kizombo*, also called attention to the putative pre-Columbian arrival of Africans in the New World, both in the lyrics and through gigantic representations of the Mexican Olmec statues with their often-remarked Negroid features.

20 Mary Louise Pratt, *Imperial Eyes: Travel Writing and Transculturation* (London: Routledge, 1992), p. 7.

21 See Néstor García Canclini, "Los Estudios Culturales de los 80 a los 90: Perspectivas Antropologicas y Sociologicas em America Latina," *Iztapalapa: Revista de Ciencias Sociales y Humanidades*, Vol. 11.24, p. 24.

22 See Charles Jencks, *Heteropolis: Los Angeles, the Riots and the Strange Beauty of Hetero-Architecture* (London: Academy Editions, 1993) and Edward W. Soja, *Thirdspace: Journeys to Los Angeles and Other Real-and-Imagined Places* (Oxford: Blackwells, 1996).

23 Note also that another form of garbology is the study of celebrity garbage, for example that of Bob Dylan or O.J. Simpson, for purposes of meta-psychological investigation.

24 For a survey of recycled art from around the world, see Charlene Cerny and Suzanne Seriff, eds *Recycled, Reseen: Folk Art from the Global Scrap Heap* (New York: Harry N. Abrams in conjunction with the Museum of International Folk Art, Santa Fe, 1996).

25 Artist Milenko Matanoviè has developed a project called "Trash Hold" in which high-profile participants drag especially designed bags of their garbage around with them for a week, at the end of which the participants gather to recycle. See Lucy Lippard *op. cit.* p. 265.

26 For more on the discourse of garbage, see Michael Thompson, *Rubbish Theory: The Creation and Destruction of Value* (Oxford: Oxford University Press, 1979); Judd H. Alexander, *In Defense of Garbage* (Westport, CT: Praeger, 1993); William Rathje and Cullen Murphy, *Rubbish! The Archeology of Garbage* (New York: HarperCollins, 1992); and Katie Kelly, *Garbage: The History and Future of Garbage in America* (New York: Saturday Review Press, 1973).

27 For an analysis of Brazil's "udigrudi" films, see Ismail Xavier, *Allegories of Underdevelopment: From the "Aesthetics of Hunger" to the "Aesthetics of Garbage"* (Minneapolis: University of Minnesota Press, 1997).

28 My formulation obviously both echoes and Africanizes the language of Frederic Jameson's well-known essay "Third World Literature in the Era of Multinational Capitalism," *Social Text*, No. 15 (Fall, 1986).

29 See Wyatt MacGaffey, "The Black Loincloth and the Son of Nzambi Mpungu," in Bernth Lindfors (ed.) *Forms of Folklore in Africa: Narrative, Poetic, Gnomic, Dramatic* (Austin: University of Texas Press, 1977), p. 78.

30 See Robert Farris Thompson and Joseph Cornet, *The Four Moments of the Sun: Congo Art in Two Worlds* (Washington: National Gallery, 1981), p. 179.

31 Quoted in *Revista USP*, No. 19 (September/October/November, 1993), p. 148.

32 Juan Duran-Luzio has kindly given me a copy of a Costa Rica "garbage novel," Fernando Contreras Castor's *Unica Mirando al Mar* (*Unica looking toward the sea*; San José: Farben, 1994). In the novel, the protagonist's husband writes to the President of the Republic concerning the fate of those who live off the garbage dumps.

33 The pig, as Peter Stallybrass and Allon White point out, was despised for its specific habits, "its ability to digest its own and human faeces as well as other garbage; its resistance to full domestication; its need to protect its tender skin from sunburn by wallowing in the mud." See *The Politics and Poetics of Transgression* (Ithaca: Cornell University Press, 1986).[AU: please provide the page ref.]

34 Jorge Furtado's *Esta nao e a sua Vida* (*This is Not Your Life*, 1992) prolongs the director's reflexions on the nature of documentary, posing such questions: how does the documentarist find a topic? What does it mean to "know" about someone's life? How much has the spectator learned about someone's life by seeing a documentary? How do you film your subject?

Part II
Challenging Third World legacies
Issues of gender, culture, and representation

The theorist-filmmakers who promulgated a Third Cinema made demands that few women directors (with notable exceptions) could meet, for challenges to authority within patriarchal cultures are less likely to emerge from the most dispossessed members of societies than from those better equipped to resist authoritarian discursive structures. Nevertheless, as Ella Shohat shows, the neglect of women's contributions to post-Third-Worldist feminism by metropolitan criticism is a byproduct both of an essentializing Eurocentric feminism and the foregrounding of nationalist agendas by the early proponents of Third Cinema.

Her contribution also addresses the larger issue of what may be termed "gaze history" ("gaze theory" already being a well-worn terrain of critical inquiry), for as she shows the contributions of such radical post-Third-World feminist filmmakers as Sarah Maldoror, Moufida Tlatli, Mona Hatoum, Farida Benlyazid and Tracey Moffat can only be appreciated properly in the light of their abjuration of the historically-precipitated Europeanization of what John Berger called "ways of seeing," ways of which we are all to varying degrees victims as dwellers in a post-Imperial (globalistic) regime of image diffusion. They, and their sisters, who have launched a critique from within the centers of hegemony, challenge not only Eurocentrism but also the ways in which such early exponents of Third Cinema as Glauber Rocha saw.

In contrast Sumita Chakravarty's principal concern is the very act of troping, the symbolic use of women's bodies as signifiers of nation and of national integrity and fecundity. Noting that the discourse of the woman-centered film now deployed by post-Third-World directors belongs to a larger repertoire of images, one drawn upon by (mostly male) directors since the inception of cinema, Chakravarty engages critical approaches as varied as those of Georges Bataille, Marsha Kinder and Rey Chow to theorize this "erotics of history" in an attempt to elucidate its social, cultural and ethical valences.

What is most striking about her analysis is her refusal to compartmentalize this erotics of history, to limit herself to the products of a single director or a unitary film movement or national industry. This, after all, was one of the major drawbacks of works like Roy Armes's *Third World Filmmaking and the West*, which isolated (and thus disaggregated) common threads by recapitulating a Eurocentric tendency to categorize by geographic, regional, topographic, national and conceptual boundaries. Chakravarty will see bodies whole and undivided, wherever they originate and whatever they represent, thus herself embodying a new, inter-cultural critical trend among writers on non-Western cinemas of treating fluid fields of representation.

2 Post-Third-Worldist culture

Gender, nation, and the cinema[a]

Ella Shohat

At a time when the *grands récits* of the West have been told and retold ad infinitum, when a certain postmodernism (Lyotard) speaks of an "end" to metanarratives, and when Fukuyama speaks of an "end of history," we must ask: precisely whose narrative and whose history is being declared at an "end"?[1] Hegemonic Europe may clearly have begun to deplete its strategic repertoire of stories, but Third-World peoples, First-World minoritarian communities, women, and gays and lesbians have only begun to tell, and deconstruct, theirs. For the "Third World," this cinematic counter-telling basically began with the postwar collapse of the European empires and the emergence of independent nation-states. In the face of Eurocentric historicizing, the Third World and its diasporas in the First World have rewritten their own histories, taken control over their own images, spoken in their own voices, reclaiming and re-accentuating colonialism and its ramifications in the present in a vast project of remapping and renaming. Third-World feminists, for their part, have participated in these counternarratives, while insisting that colonialism and national resistance have impinged differently on men and women, and that remapping and renaming is not without its fissures and contradictions.

Although relatively small in number, women directors and producers in the "Third World" already played a role in film production in the first half of this century: Aziza Amir, Assia Daghir, and Fatima Rushdi in Egypt; Carmen Santos and Gilda de Abreu in Brazil; Emilia Saleny in Argentina; and Adela Sequeyro, Matilda Landeta, Candida Beltran Rondon, and Eva Liminano in Mexico. However, their films, even when focusing on female protagonists, were not explicitly feminist in the sense of a declared political project to empower women in the context of both patriarchy and (neo)colonialism. In the post-independence or post-revolution era, women, despite their growing contribution to the diverse aspects of film production, remained less visible than men in the role of film direction. Furthermore, Third-Worldist revolutionary cinemas in places such as China, Cuba, Senegal, and Algeria were not generally shaped by an anti-colonial feminist imaginary. As is the case with First-World cinema, women's participation within Third-World

a ©1996 from *Feminist Genealogies, Colonial Legacies, Democratic Futures*, Alexander and Mohanty, eds. Reproduced by permission of Routledge, Inc., part of The Taylor & Francis Group.

cinema has hardly been central, although their growing production over the last decade corresponds to a worldwide burgeoning movement of independent work by women, made possible by new, low-cost technologies of video communication. But quite apart from this relative democratization through technology, post-independence history, with the gradual eclipse of Third-Worldist nationalism and the growth of women's grass roots local organizing, also helps us to understand the emergence of what I call "post-Third-Worldist"[2] feminist film and video.

Here, I am interested in examining recent feminist film and video work within the context of post-Third-Worldist film culture as a simultaneous critique both of Third-Worldist anti-colonial nationalism and of First-World Eurocentric feminism. Challenging white feminist film theory and practice that emerged in a major way in the 1970s in First-World metropolises, post-Third-Worldist feminist works have refused a Eurocentric universalizing of "womanhood," and even of "feminism." Eschewing a discourse of universality, such feminisms claim a "location,"[3] arguing for specific forms of resistance in relation to diverse forms of oppression. Aware of white women's advantageous positioning within (neo)colonialist and racist systems, feminist struggles in the Third World (including the "third world" in the First World) have not been premised on a facile discourse of global sisterhood, and have often been made within the context of anti-colonial and anti-racist struggles. But the growing feminist critique of Third-World nationalisms translates those many disappointed hopes for women's empowerment invested in a Third-Worldist national transformation. Navigating between the excommunication as "traitors to the nation" and "betraying the race" by patriarchal nationalism, and the imperial rescue fantasies of clitoridectomized and veiled women proffered by Eurocentric feminism, post-Third-Worldist feminists have not suddenly metamorphosized into "Western" feminists. Feminists of color have, from the outset, been engaged in analysis and activism around the intersection of nation/race/gender. Therefore, while still resisting the ongoing (neo)colonized situation of their "nation" and/or "race," post-Third-Worldist feminist cultural practices also break away from the narrative of the "nation" as a unified entity so as to articulate a contextualized history for women in specific geographies of identity. Such feminist projects, in other words, are often posited in relation to ethnic, racial, regional, and national locations.

Feminist work within national movements and ethnic communities has not formed part of the generally monocultural agenda of Euro-"feminism." In cinema studies, what has been called "feminist film theory" since the 1970s has often suppressed the historical, economic, and cultural contradictions among women. Prestigious feminist film journals have too often ignored the scholarly and cultural feminist work performed in relation to particular Third-Worldist national and racial media contexts; feminist work to empower women within the boundaries of their Third-World communities was dismissed as merely nationalist, not "quite yet" feminist. Universalizing the parameters for feminism and using such ahistorical psychoanalytical categories as "desire," "fetishism," and "castration" led to a discussion of "the female body" and "the female spectator" that was ungrounded in the many different – even opposing – women's experiences, agendas, and political visions. Any dialogue with feminist scholars or filmmakers who insisted on working from and within particular locations was thus inhibited. Is it a coincidence that throughout the 1970s and most of the 1980s, it was Third-World cinema conferences and film programs that first gave prominence to Third-Worldist women filmmakers (for example, the Guadeloupian Sarah Maldoror, the Colombian Marta Rodriguez, the Lebanese Heiny Srour, the Cuban Sara Gomez, the Senegalese Safi Faye, the Indian Prema Karanth, the Sri Lankan Sumitra Peries, the Brazilian Helena Solberg Ladd, the Egyptian Atteyat El-Abnoudi, the Tunisian Selma Baccar, the Puerto Rican Ana Maria Garcia) rather than feminist film programs and conferences? A discussion of Ana Maria Garcia's documentary *La Operación*, a film which focuses on US-imposed sterilization policies in Puerto Rico, for example, reveals the historical and theoretical aporias of such concepts as "the female body" when not addressed in terms of race, class, and (neo)colonialism. Whereas a white "female body" might undergo surveillance by the reproductive machine, the dark "female body" is subjected to a dis-reproductive apparatus within a hidden, racially coded demographic agenda.

In fact, in the 1970s and most of the 1980s, prestigious feminist film journals paid little attention to the intersection of heterosexism with racism and imperialism; that task was performed by some "Third-World cinema" academics who published in those leftist film and cultural journals that allotted space to Third-World alternative cinema (for example, Jumpcut, Cineaste, The Independent, Framework, and Critical Arts). Coming in the wake of visible public debates about race and multiculturalism, the task-force on "race" (established in 1988) at the Society for Cinema Studies, along with the increasingly substantial representation of the work of women of color in Women Make Movies (a major New York-based distribution outlet for independent work by women film- and video-makers), began to have an impact on white feminist film scholars, some of whom gradually came to acknowledge and even address issues of gender in the context of race. Discourses about gender and race still tend not to be understood within an anti-colonial history, however, while the diverse recent post-Third-Worldist feminist film and video practices tend to be comfortably subsumed as a mere "extension" of a "universal" feminist theory and practice. Applying old paradigms onto new (dark) objects implies, to some extent, "business as usual." Post-Third-Worldist feminist practices now tend to be absorbed into the preoccupations of Eurocentric feminist theories within the homogenizing framework of the shared critique of patriarchal discourse. Examining recent Third-World feminist cultural practices only in relation to theories developed by what has been known as "feminist film theory" reproduces a Eurocentric logic whose narrative beginnings for feminism will inevitably always reside with "Western" cultural practices and theories seen as straightforwardly pure "feminism," unlike Third-World feminisms, seen as "burdened" by national and ethnic hyphenated identities. Notions of nation and race, along with community-based work, are implicitly dismissed as both too "specific" to qualify for the theoretical realm of "feminist film theory" and as too "inclusive" in their concern for nation and race that they presumably "lose sight" of feminism.

Rather than merely "extending" a preexisting First-World feminism, as a certain Euro-"diffusionism"[4] would have it, post-Third-Worldist cultural theories and practices create a more complex space for feminisms open to the specificity of community culture and history. To counter some of the patronizing attitudes toward (post-) Third-World feminist filmmakers – the dark women who now also do the "feminist thing" – it is necessary to contextualize feminist work in national/racial discourses locally and globally inscribed within multiple oppressions and resistances. Third-World feminist histories can be understood as feminist if seen in conjunction with the resistance work these women have performed within their communities and nations. Any serious discussion of feminist cinema must therefore engage the complex question of the "national." Third-Worldist films are often produced within the legal codes of the nation-state, often in (hegemonic) national languages, recycling national intertexts (literatures, oral narratives, music), projecting national imaginaries. But if First-World filmmakers have seemed to float "above" petty nationalist concerns, it is because they take for granted the projection of a national power that facilitates the making and the dissemination of their films. The geopolitical positioning of Third-World nation-states continues to imply that their filmmakers cannot assume a substratum of national power.

Here, I am interested in examining the contemporary work of post-Third-Worldist feminist film- and video-makers in light of the ongoing critique of the racialized inequality of the geopolitical distribution of resources and power as a way of looking into the dynamics of rupture and continuity with regard to the antecedent Third-Worldist film culture. These texts, I argue, challenge the masculinist contours of the "nation" in order to continue a feminist decolonization of Third-Worldist historiography, as much as they continue a multicultural decolonization of feminist historiography. My attempt to forge a "beginning" of a post-Third-Worldist narrative for recent film and video work by diverse Third-World, multicultural, diasporic feminists is not intended as an exhaustive survey of the entire spectrum of generic practices. Rather, by highlighting works embedded in the intersection between gender/sexuality and nation/race, this essay attempts to situate such cultural practices. It looks at a moment of historical rupture and continuity, when the macronarrative of women's liberation has long since subsided yet sexism and heterosexism prevail, and in an age when the metanarratives of anti-colonial revolution have long since been eclipsed yet (neo)colonialism and racism persist. What, then, are some of the new modes of a multicultural feminist aesthetics of resistance? And in what ways do they simultaneously continue and rupture previous Third-Worldist film culture?

The eclipse of the revolutionary paradigm

Third-Worldist films by women assumed that revolution was crucial for the empowering of women, that the revolution was integral to feminist aspirations.

Sarah Maldoror's short film *Monangambe* (Mozambique, 1970) narrates the visit of an Angolan woman to see her husband who has been imprisoned by the Portuguese, while her feature film *Sambizanga* (Mozambique, 1972), based on the struggle of the ruling party, the MPLA in Angola, depicts a woman coming to revolutionary consciousness. Heiny Srour's documentary *Saat al Tahrir* (*The Hour of Liberation*, Oman, 1973) privileges the role of women fighters as it looks at the revolutionary struggle in Oman, and her *Leila wal dhiab* (*Leila and the Wolves*, Lebanon, 1984) focuses on the role of women in the Palestine Liberation Movement. Helena Solberg Ladd's *Nicaragua Up From the Ashes* (US, 1982) foregrounds the role of women in the Sandinista revolution. Sara Gomez's well-known film *De cierta manera* (*One Way or Another*, Cuba, 1975), often cited as part of the late 1970s and early 1980s Third-Worldist debates around women's position in revolutionary movements, interweaves documentary and fiction as part of a feminist critique of the Cuban revolution. From a decidedly pro-revolutionary perspective, the film deploys images of building and construction to metaphorize the need for further revolutionary changes. Macho culture is dissected and analyzed within the overlaid cultural histories (African, European, and Cuban), in terms of the need to revolutionize gender relations in the post-revolution era.

These developments must be seen in the context of the initial Third Cinema manifestoes that amplified declarations from Third-World film festivals calling for a tricontinental revolution in politics and an aesthetic and narrative revolution in film form.[5] But the resistant practices of the films advocated by Glauber Rocha, Julio García Espinosa, Fernando Solanas and Octavio Getino are neither homogeneous nor static; they vary over time, from region to region, and, in genre, from epic costume drama to personal small-budget documentary. Their aesthetic strategies range from "progressive realist" to Brechtian deconstructivist to avant-gardist, tropicalist, and resistant postmodern.[6] In their search for an alternative to the dominating style of Hollywood, such films shared a certain preoccupation with First-World feminist independent films which sought alternative images of women. The project of digging into "herstories" involved a search for new cinematic and narrative forms that challenged both the canonical documentaries and mainstream fiction films, subverting the notion of "narrative pleasure" based on the "male gaze." As with Third-Worldist cinema and with First-World independent production, post-Third-Worldist feminist films and videos conduct a struggle on two fronts, at once aesthetic and political, synthesizing revisionist historiography with formal innovation.

The early period of Third-Worldist euphoria has given way to the collapse of Communism, the indefinite postponement of the devoutly wished for "tricontinental revolution," the realization that the "wretched of the earth" are not unanimously revolutionary (nor necessarily allies to one another), the appearance of an array of Third-World despots, and the recognition that international geopolitics and the global economic system have forced even the "Second World" to be incorporated into transnational capitalism.

Recent years have even witnessed a crisis around the term "Third World" itself; it is now seen as an inconvenient relic of a more militant period. Some have argued that Third-World theory is an open-ended ideological interpellation that papers over class oppression in all three worlds, while limiting socialism to the now nonexistent Second World.[7] Third-World theory not only flattens heterogeneities, masks contradictions, and elides differences, but also obscures similarities (for example, the common presence of the "Fourth-World," or indigenous, peoples in both "Third-World" and "First-World" countries). Third-World feminist critics such as Nawal El-Saadawi (Egypt), Vina Mazumdar (India), Kumari Jayawardena (Sri Lanka), Fatima Mernissi (Morocco), and Leila Gonzales (Brazil) have explored these differences and similarities in a feminist light, pointing to the gendered limitations of Third-World nationalism.

But even within the current situation of "dispersed hegemonies" (Arjun Appadurai),[8] the historical thread or inertia of First-World domination remains a powerful presence. Despite the imbrication of "First" and "Third" worlds, the global distribution of power still tends to make the First-World countries cultural "transmitters" and the Third-World countries "receivers." (One byproduct of this situation is that First-World "minorities" have the power to project their cultural productions around the globe.) While the Third World is inundated with North American films, TV series, popular music, and news programs, the First World receives precious little of the vast cultural production of the Third World, and what it does receive is usually mediated by multi-national corporations.[9] These processes are not entirely negative, of course. The same multinational corporations that disseminate inane blockbusters and canned sitcoms also spread Afro-diasporic music, such as reggae and rap, around the globe. The problem lies not in the exchange but in the unequal terms on which the exchange takes place.[10]

At the same time, the media-imperialism thesis, which was dominant in the 1970s, needs drastic retooling. First, it is simplistic to imagine an active First World simply forcing its products on a passive Third World. Second, global mass culture does not so much replace local culture as coexist with it, providing a cultural lingua franca remarked by a "local" accent.[11] Third, there are powerful reverse currents as a number of Third-World countries (Mexico, Brazil, India, Egypt) dominate their own markets and even become cultural exporters.[12] We must distinguish, furthermore, between the ownership and control of the media – an issue of political economy – and the specifically cultural issue of the implications of this domination for the people on the receiving end. The "hypodermic needle" theory is as inadequate for the Third World as it is for the First: everywhere spectators actively engage with texts, and specific communities both incorporate and transform foreign influences.[13] In a world of transnational communications, the central problem becomes one of tension between cultural homogenization and cultural heterogenization, in which hegemonic tendencies, well-documented by Marxist analysts like Mattelart and Schiller, are simultaneously "indigenized" within a complex, disjunctive global cultural economy. At the same time, discernible patterns of domination channel the "fluidities" even of a "multipolar" world; the same hegemony that unifies the world through global networks of circulating goods and information also distributes them according to hierarchical structures of power, even if those hegemonies are now more subtle and dispersed.

Although all cultural practices are on one level products of specific national contexts, Third-World filmmakers (men and women) have been forced to engage in the question of the national precisely because they lack the taken-for-granted power available to First-World nation-states. At the same time, the topos of a unitary nation often camouflages the possible contradictions among different sectors of Third-World society. The nation-states of the Americas, of Mrica and Asia often "cover" the existence, not only of women, but also of indigenous nations (Fourth World) within them. Furthermore, the exaltation of "the national" provides no criteria for distinguishing exactly what is worth retaining in the "national tradition." A sentimental defense of patriarchal social institutions simply because they are "ours" can hardly be seen as emancipatory. Indeed, some Third-World films criticize exactly such institutions: *Xala* (1990) criticizes polygamy; *Finzan* (1989) and *Fire Eyes* (1993) critique female genital mutilation; films like *Allah Tanto* (1992) focus on the political repression exercised even by a pan-Africanist hero like Sekou Touré; and Sembène's *Guelwaar* (1992) satirizes religious divisions within the Third-World nation. Morever, all countries, including Third-World countries, are heterogeneous, at once urban and rural, male and female, religious and secular, native and immigrant. The view of the nation as unitary muffles the "polyphony" of social and ethnic voices within heteroglot cultures. Third-World feminists, especially, have highlighted the ways in which the subject of the Third-World nationalist revolution has been covertly posited as masculine and heterosexual. Fourth, the precise nature of the national "essence" to be recuperated is elusive and chimerical. Some locate it in the pre-colonial past, or in the country's rural interior (e.g. the African village), or in a prior stage of development (e.g. the pre-industrial), or in a non-European ethnicity (e.g. the indigenous or African strata in the nation-states of the Americas); and each narrative of origins has had its gender implications. Recent debates have emphasized the ways in which national identity is mediated, textualized, constructed, "imagined," just as the traditions valorized by nationalism are "invented."[14] Any definition of nationality, then, must see nationality as partly discursive in nature, must take class, gender, and sexuality into account, must allow for racial difference and cultural heterogeneity, and must be dynamic, seeing "the nation" as an evolving, imaginary construct rather than an originary essence.

The decline of the Third-Worldist euphoria, which marked feminist films like *One Way or Another*, *The Hour of Liberation*, and *Nicaragua Up From the Ashes*, brought with it a rethinking of political, cultural, and aesthetic possibilities, as the rhetoric of revolution began to be greeted with a certain skepticism. Meanwhile, the socialist-inflected national-liberation struggles of the 1960s and 1970s were harassed economically and militarily, violently discouraged from becoming revolutionary models for post-independence societies. A combination of IMF pressure, cooptation, and "low-intensity warfare" obliged even socialist regimes to make a sort of peace with trans-national capitalism. Some regimes repressed those who wanted to go beyond a purely nationalist bourgeois revolution to restructure class, gender, religion, and ethnic relations. As a result of external pressures and internal self-questioning, the cinema also gave expression to these mutations, with the anti-colonial thrust of earlier films gradually giving way to more diversified themes and perspectives. This is not to say that artists and intellectuals became less politicized but that cultural and political critique took new and different forms. Contemporary cultural practices of post-Third-World and multicultural feminists intervene at a precise juncture in the history of the Third World.

Third Worldism under feminist eyes

Largely produced by men, Third-Worldist films were not generally concerned with a feminist critique of nationalist discourse. It would be a mistake to idealize the sexual politics of anti-colonial Third-Worldist films like the classic *The Battle of Algiers*, for example. On one level, it is true that Algerian women are granted revolutionary agency. In one sequence, three Algerian women fighters are able to pass for Frenchwomen and, consequently, slip through the French checkpoints with bombs in their baskets. The French soldiers treat the Algerians with discriminatory scorn and suspicion but greet the Europeans with amiable "bonjours." The soldiers' sexism leads them to misperceive the three women as French and flirtatious when, in fact, they are Algerian and revolutionary. *The Battle of Algiers* thus underlines the racial and sexual taboos of desire within colonial segregation. As Algerians, the women are the objects of the military as well as the sexual gaze; they are publicly desirable for the soldiers, however, only when they masquerade as French. They use their knowledge of European codes to trick the Europeans, putting their own "looks" and the soldiers' "looking" (and failure to see) to revolutionary purpose. (Masquerade also serves the Algerian male fighters, who veil as Algerian women to better hide their weapons.) Within the psychodynamics of oppression, the colonized knows the mind of the oppressor, while the converse is not true. In *The Battle of Algiers*, the women deploy this cognitive asymmetry to their own advantage, consciously manipulating ethnic, national, and gender stereotypes in the service of their struggle.

On another level, however, the women in the film largely carry out the orders of the male revolutionaries. They certainly appear heroic, but only insofar as they perform their sacrificial service for the "nation." The film does not ultimately address the two-fronted nature of their struggle within a nationalist but still patriarchal revolution.[15] In privileging the nationalist struggle, *The Battle of Algiers* elides the gender, class, and religious tensions that fissured the revolutionary process, failing to realize that, as Anne McClintock puts it, "nationalisms are from the outset constituted in gender power" and that "women who are not empowered to organize during the struggle will not be empowered to organize after the struggle."[16] The final shots of a dancing Algerian woman waving the Algerian flag and taunting the French troops, accompanied by a voice-over announcing, "July 2, 1962: Independence. The Algerian Nation is born," has the woman "carry" the allegory of the "birth" of the Algerian nation. But the film does not raise the contradictions that plagued the revolution both before and after victory. The nationalist representation of courage and unity relies on the image of the revolutionary woman precisely because her figure might otherwise evoke a weak link, the fact of a fissured revolution in which unity vis-à-vis the colonizer does not preclude contradictions among the colonized.

Third-Worldist films often favored the generic and gendered space of heroic confrontations, whether set in the streets, the casbah, the mountains, or the jungle. The minimal presence of women corresponded to the place assigned to women both in the anti-colonialist revolutions and within Third-Worldist discourse, leaving women's homebound struggles unacknowledged. Women occasionally carried the bombs, as in *The Battle of Algiers*, but only in the name of a "Nation." More often, women were made to carry the "burden" of national allegory: the woman dancing with the flag in *The Battle of Algiers*, the Argentinian prostitute whose image is underscored by the national anthem in *La Hora de Los Hornos* (*The Hour of the Furnaces*), the mestiza journalist in *Cubagua*, embodying the Venezuelan nation; or else the symbolic women are scapegoated as personifications of imperialism, for example, the allegorical "whore of Babylon" figure in Rocha's films. Gender contradictions have been subordinated to anti-colonial struggle: women were expected to "wait their turn."

A more recent Tunisian film, *Samt al Qusur* (*The Silence of the Palace*, 1994) by Moufida Tlatli, a film editor who had worked on major Tunisian films of the post-independence, "Cinema Jedid" (New Cinema) generation, and who has now directed her first film, exemplifies some of the feminist critiques of the representation of the "nation" in the anti-colonial revolutionary films. Rather than privileging direct, violent encounters with the French, which would necessarily have to be set in male-dominated spaces of battle, the film presents 1950s Tunisian women at the height of the national struggle as restricted to the domestic sphere. Yet, it also challenges middle-class assumptions about the domestic sphere as belonging to the isolated wife-mother of a (heterosexual) couple. *The Silence of the Palace* focuses on working-class women, the servants of the rich, pro-French Bey elite, subjugated to hopeless servitude, including at times sexual servitude, but for whom life outside the palace, without the guarantee of shelter and food, would mean the even worse misery of, for example, prostitution. Although they are bound to silence about what they see and know within the palace, the film highlights their survival as a community. As an alternative family, their emotional closeness in crisis and happiness and their supportive involvement in decision-making show their ways of coping with a no exit situation. They become a non-patriarchal family within a patriarchal context. Whether through singing as they cook for an exhibitionist banquet, through praying as one of them heals a child who has fallen sick, or through dancing and eating in a joyous moment, the film represents women who did not plant bombs but whose social positioning turns into a critique of failed revolutionary hopes as seen in the postcolonial era. The information about the battles against the besieging French is mediated through the radio and by vendors, who report to the always "besieged" women on what might lead to an all-encompassing national transformation.

Yet, this period of anti-colonial struggle is framed as a recollection narrative of a woman singer, a daughter of one of the female servants, illuminating the continuous pressures exerted on women of her class. (With some exceptions, female singers/dancers are still associated in the Middle East with being just a little above the shameful occupation of prostitution.) The gendered and classed oppression that she witnessed as an adolescent in colonized Tunisia led her to believe that things would be different in an independent Tunisia. Such hopes were encouraged by the promises made by the middle-class male intellectual, a tutor for the Bey's family, who suggests that in the new Tunisia not knowing her father's name will not be a barrier for establishing a new life. Their passionate relationship in the heat of revolution, where the "new" is on the verge of being born, is undercut by the framing narrative. Her fatherless servant-history and her low status as a singer haunt her life in the post-independence era; the tutor lives with her but does not marry her, yet gives her the protection she needs as a singer. The film opens on her sad, melancholy face singing a famous Um Kulthum song from the 1960s, "Amal Hayati" (The Hope of My Life). Um Kulthum, an Egyptian, was the leading Arab singer of the twentieth century. Through her unusual musical talents – including her deep knowledge of "fusha" (literary) Arabic – she rose from her small village to become "kawkab al sharq" (the star of the East). Her singing accompanied the Arab world in all its national aspirations and catalyzed a sense of Arab unity that managed to transcend, at least on the cultural level, social tensions and political conflicts. She was closely associated with the charismatic leadership of Gamal Abdul Nasser and his anti-imperial pan-Arab agenda, but the admiration, respect, and love she elicited continued well after her death in 1975. Um Kulthum's transcendental position, however, has not been shared by many female singers or stars in the Arab world.

The protagonist of *The Silence of the Palace* begins her public performance at the invitation of the masters of the palace. This invitation comes partly because of her singing talent but no less because of the sexual advances she begins to experience as soon as one of the masters notices that the child has turned into a young woman. The mother who manages to protect her daughter from sexual harassment is herself raped by one of the masters. On the day of the daughter's first major performance at a party in the palace, the mother dies of excessive bleeding from medical complications caused by aborting the product of the rape. In parallel scenes, the mother shouts from her excruciating pain and the daughter courageously cries out the forbidden Tunisian anthem.

The sequence ends with the mother's death and with her daughter leaving the palace for the promising outside world of young Tunisia. In post-independent Tunisia, the film implies, the daughter's situation has somewhat improved. She is no longer a servant but a singer who earns her living, yet needs the protection of her boyfriend against gender-based humiliations. Next to her mother's grave, the daughter articulates, in a voice-over, her awareness of some improvements in the conditions of her life in comparison with that of her mother. The daughter has gone through many abortions, despite her wish to become a mother, in order to keep her relationship with her boyfriend – the revolutionary man who does not transcend class for purposes of marriage. At the end of the film, she confesses at her mother's grave that this time she cannot let this piece of herself go. If, in the opening, the words of Um Kulthum's song relay a desire for the dream not to end – "Khalini, gambak, khalini/ fi hudhni albak, khalini/ oosibni ahlam bik/ Yaret Zamani ma yesahinish (Leave me by your side/ in your heart/ and let me dream/ wish time will not wake me up) – the film ends with an awakening to hopes unfulfilled with the birth of the nation. Birth, here, is no longer allegorical as in *The Battle of Algiers*, but concrete, entangled in taboos and obstacles, leaving an open-ended narrative, far from the euphoric closure offered by nationhood.

The cinema of displacement

Third-World nationalist discourse has often assumed an unquestioned national identity, but most contemporary nation-states are "mixed" formations. A country like Brazil, arguably Third World in both racial terms (a *mestizo* majority) and economic ones (given its economically dependent status), is still dominated by a Europeanized elite. The US, a "First-World" country, which always had its Native American and African American minorities, is now becoming even more "Third-Worldized" by waves of post-independence migrations. Contemporary United States' life intertwines First- and Third-World destinies. The song "Are My Hands Clean," by Sweet Honey in the Rock, traces the origins of a blouse on sale at Sears to cotton in El Salvador, oil in Venezuela, refineries in Trinidad, factories in Haiti and South Carolina. Thus, there is no Third World, in Trinh T. Minh-ha's pithy formulation, without its First World, and no First World without its Third. The First-World/Third-World struggle takes place not only between nations but also *within* them.

A number of recent diasporic film and video works link issues of post-colonial identity to issues of post-Third-Worldist aesthetics and ideology. The Sankofa production *The Passion of Remembrance* (1986) by Maureen Blackwood and Isaac Julien thematizes post-Third-Worldist discourses and fractured diasporic identity – in this case, Black British identity – by staging a "polylogue" between the 1960s black radical as the (somewhat puritanical) voice of nationalist militancy and the "new," more playful voices of gays and lesbians, all within a derealized reflexive aesthetic. Film and video works such as Assia Djebar's *Nouba Nisa al Djebel Chenoua* (*The Nouba Women of Mount Chenoua*)

(1977), Lourdes Portillo's *After the Earthquake* (1979), Lucia Salinas's *Canto a la Vida* (Song to Life) (1990), Mona Hatoum's *Measures of Distance* (1988), Pratibha Parmar's *Khush* (1991), Trinh T. Minh-ha's *Surname Viet Given Name Nam* (1989) and *Shoot for the Content* (1991), Prajna Paramita Parasher and Den Ellis's *Unbidden Voices* (1989), Lucinda Broadbent's *Sex and the Sandinistas* (1991), Mona Smith's *Honored by the Moon* (1990), Indu Krishnan's *Knowing Her Place* (1990), Christine Chang's *Be Good My Children* (1992), Teresa Osa and Hidalgo de la Rivera's *Mujeria* (1992), and Marta N. Bautis's *Home is the Struggle* (1991) break away from earlier macronarratives of national liberation, re-envisioning the nation as a heteroglossic multiplicity of trajectories. While remaining anti-colonialist, these experimental films call attention to the diversity of experiences within and across nations. Since colonialism had simultaneously aggregated communities fissured by glaring cultural differences and separated communities marked by equally glaring commonalities, these films suggest, many Third-World nation-states were highly artificial and contradictory entities. The films produced in the First World, in particular, raise questions about dislocated identities in a world increasingly marked by the mobility of goods, ideas, and peoples attendant with the "multinationalization" of the global economy.

Third Worldists often fashioned their idea of the nation-state according to the European model, in this sense remaining complicit with a Eurocentric Enlightenment narrative. And the nation-states they built often failed to deliver on their promises. In terms of race, class, gender, and sexuality, in particular, many of them remained, on the whole, ethnocentric, patriarchal, bourgeois, and homophobic. At the same time, a view of Third-World nationalism as the mere echo of European nationalism ignores the international realpolitik that made the end of colonialism coincide with the beginning of the nation-state. The formation of Third-World nation-states often involved a double process of, on the one hand, joining diverse ethnicities and regions that had been separate under colonialism, and, on the other, partitioning regions in a way that forced regional redefinition (Iraq/Kuwait) and a cross-shuffling of populations (Pakistan/India, Israel/Palestine). Furthermore, political geographies and state borders do not always coincide with what Edward Said calls "imaginary geographies," whence the existence of internal émigrés, nostalgics, rebels (i.e. groups of people who share the same passport but whose relations to the nation-state are conflicted and ambivalent). In the postcolonial context of a constant flux of peoples, affiliation with the nation-state becomes highly partial and contingent.

While most Third-Worldist films assumed the fundamental coherence of national identity, with the expulsion of the colonial intruder fully completing the process of national becoming, the post-nationalist films call attention to the fault lines of gender, class, ethnicity, region, partition, migration, and exile. Many of the films explore the complex identities generated by exile – from one's own geography, from one's own history, from one's own body – within innovative narrative strategies. Fragmented cinematic forms homologize cultural disembodiment. Caren Kaplan's observations about a reconceived "minor" literature as deromanticizing solitude and rewriting "the connections between different parts of the self in order to make a world of possibilities out of the experience of displacement,"[17] are exquisitely appropriate to two autobiographical films by Palestinians in exile, Elia Suleiman's *Homage by Assassination* (1992) and Mona Hatoum's *Measures of Distance*. *Homage by Assassination* chronicles Suleiman's life in New York during the Persian Gulf War, foregrounding multiple failures of communication: a radio announcer's aborted efforts to reach the filmmaker by phone; the filmmaker's failed attempts to talk to his family in Nazareth (Israel/Palestine); his impotent look at old family photographs; and despairing answering-machine jokes about the Palestinian situation. The glorious dream of nationhood and return is here reframed as a Palestinian flag on a TV monitor, the land as a map on a wall, and the return (*awda*) as the "return" key on the computer keyboard. At one point, the filmmaker receives a fax from a friend, who narrates her family history as an Arab-Jew, her feelings during the bombing of Iraq and Scud attacks on Israel, and the story of her displacements from Iraq, through Israel/ Palestine, and then on to the US.[18] The mediums of communication become the imperfect means by which dislocated people struggle to retain their national imaginary, while also fighting for a place in a new national context (the US, Britain), in countries whose foreign policies have concretely impacted on their lives. *Homage by Assassination* invokes the diverse spatialities and temporalities that mark the exile experience. A shot of two clocks, in New York and in Nazareth, points to the double time-frame lived by the diasporic subject, a temporal doubleness underlined by an intertitle saying that, due to the Scud attacks, the filmmaker's mother is adjusting her gas mask at that very moment. The friend's letter similarly stresses the fractured space-time of being in the US while identifying with relatives in both Iraq and Israel.

In *Measures of Distance*, the Palestinian video and performance artist Mona Hatoum explores the renewal of friendship between her mother and herself during a brief family reunion in Lebanon in the early 1980s. The film relates the fragmented memories of diverse generations: the mother's tales of the "used-to-be" Palestine, Hatoum's own childhood in Lebanon, the civil war in Lebanon, and the current dispersal of the daughters in the West. (It should be noted that the cinema, from *The Sheik* through *The King and I* to *Out of Africa*, has generally preferred showing Western women travelers in the East rather than Eastern women in the West.) As images of the mother's handwritten Arabic letters to the daughter are superimposed over dissolves of the daughter's color slides of her mother in the shower, we hear an audiotape of their conversations in Arabic, along with excerpts of their letters as translated and read by the filmmaker in English.

The voice-over and script of *Measures of Distance* narrate a paradoxical state of geographical distance and emotional closeness. The textual, visual, and linguistic play between Arabic and English underlines the family's serial dislocations, from Palestine to Lebanon to Britain, where Mona Hatoum has been living since 1975, gradually unfolding the dispersion of Palestinians over very diverse geographies. The foregrounded letters, photographs, and audio-tapes call attention to the means by which people in exile negotiate cultural identity. In the mother's voice-over, the repeated phrase "My dear Mona" evokes the diverse "measures of distance" implicit in the film's title. Meanwhile, background dialogue in Arabic, recalling their conversations about sexuality and Palestine during their reunion, recorded in the past but played in the present, parallels shower photos of the mother, also taken in the past but looked at in the present. The multiplication of temporalities continues in Hatoum's reading of a letter in English: to the moments of the letter's sending and its arrival is added the moment of Hatoum's voice-over translation of it for the English-speaking viewer. Each layer of time evokes a distance at once temporal and spatial, historical and geographical; each dialogue is situated, produced, and received in precise historical circumstances.

The linguistic play also marks the distance between mother and daughter, while their separation instantiates the fragmented existence of a nation. When relentless bombing prevents the mother from mailing her letter, the screen fades to black, suggesting an abrupt end to communication. Yet the letter eventually arrives via messenger, while the voice-over narrates the exile's diffi-culties of maintaining contact with one's culture(s). The negotiation of time and place is here absolutely crucial. The videomaker's voice-over reading her mother's letters in the present interferes with the dialogue recorded in the past in Lebanon. The background conversations in Arabic give a sense of present-tense immediacy, while the more predominant English voice-over speaks of the same conversation in the past tense. The Arabic speaker labors to focus on the Arabic conversation and read the Arabic scripts, while also listening to the English. If the non-Arabic speaking spectator misses some of the film's textual registers, the Arabic-speaking spectator is overwhelmed by competing images and sounds. This strategic refusal to translate Arabic is echoed in Suleiman's *Homage by Assassination* where the director (in person) types out Arab proverbs on a computer screen, without providing any trans-lation. These exiled filmmakers thus cunningly provoke in the spectator the same alienation experienced by a displaced person, reminding us, through inversion, of the asymmetry in social power between exiles and their "host communities." At the same time, they catalyze a sense of community for the minoritarian speech community, a strategy especially suggestive in the case of diasporic filmmakers, who often wind up in the First World precisely because colonial/imperial power has turned them into displaced persons.

Measures of Distance also probes issues of sexuality and the female body in a kind of self-ethnography, its nostalgic rhetoric concerned less with the "public sphere" of national struggle than with the "private sphere" of sexuality, pregnancy, and children. The women's conversations about sexuality leave the father feeling displaced by what he dismisses as "women's nonsense." The daughter's photographs of her nude mother make him profoundly uncomfort-able, as if the daughter, as the mother writes, "had trespassed on his possession."

To videotape such intimate conversations is not a common practice in Middle Eastern cinema or, for that matter, in any cinema. (Western audiences often ask how Hatoum won her mother's consent to use the nude photographs and how she broached the subject of sexuality.) Paradoxically, the exilic distance from the Middle East authorizes the exposure of intimacy. Displacement and separation make possible a transformative return to the inner sanctum of the home; mother and daughter are together again in the space of the text.

In Western popular culture, the Arab female body, whether in the form of the veiled, bare-breasted women who posed for French colonial photographers or the Orientalist harems and belly dancers of Hollywood film, has functioned as a sign of the exotic. But rather than adopt a patriarchal strategy of simply censuring female nudity, Hatoum deploys the diffusely sensuous, almost pointillist images of her mother naked to tell a more complex story with nationalist overtones. She uses diverse strategies to veil the images from voyeuristic scrutiny: already hazy images are concealed by text (fragments of the mother's correspondence, in Arabic script) and are difficult to decipher. The superimposed words in Arabic script serve to "envelop" her nudity. "Barring" the body, the script metaphorizes her inaccessibility, visually undercutting the intimacy verbally expressed in other registers. The fragmented nature of existence in exile is thus underlined by superimposed fragmentations: fragments of letters, dialogue, and the mother's *corps morcelle* (rendered as hands, breasts, and belly). The blurred and fragmented images evoke the dispersed collectivity of the national family itself.[19] Rather than evoke the longing for an ancestral home, *Measures of Distance*, like *Homage by Assassination*, affirms the process of recreating identity in the liminal zone of exile.[20] Video layering makes it possible for Mona Hatoum to capture the fluid, multiple identities of the diasporic subject.

Interrogating the aesthetic regime

Exile can also take the form of exile from one's own body. Dominant media have long disseminated the hegemonic white-is-beautiful aesthetic inherited from colonialist discourse, an aesthetic which exiled women of color from their own bodies. Until the late 1960s, the overwhelming majority of Anglo-American fashion journals, films, TV shows, and commercials promoted a canonical notion of beauty within which white women (and, secondarily, white men) were the only legitimate objects of desire. In so doing, the media extended a longstanding philosophical valorization of whiteness. European writing is replete with homages to the ideal of white beauty, implicitly de-valorizing the appearance of people of color. For Gobineau, the "white race originally possessed the monopoly of beauty, intelligence and strength."[21] For Buffon, "[Nature] in her most perfect exertions made men white."[22] Fredrich Bluembach called white Europeans "Caucasians" because he believed that the Caucasus mountains were the original home of the most beautiful human species.[23]

Gendered racism left its mark on Enlightenment aesthetics. The measurements and rankings characteristic of the new sciences were wedded to aesthetic value judgments derived from an Apollonian reading of a de-Dionysianized Greece. Thus, Aryanists like Carl Gustav Carus measured the divine in humanity through resemblance to Greek statues. The auratic religion of art, meanwhile, also worshipped at the shrine of whiteness. Clyde Taylor, Cornel West, and bell hooks, among others, have denounced the normative gaze that has systematically de-valorized non-European appearance and aesthetics.[24] Where but among Caucasians, the British surgeon Charles White asked rhetorically, does one find "that nobly arched head, containing such a quantity of brain....In what other quarter of the globe shall we find the blush that overspreads the soft features of the beautiful women of Europe?"[25] Although White's tumescent descriptions clearly hierarchize male brains over female beauty, they ultimately embrace white women for their genetic membership in the family of (white) Man. In this spirit, countless colonial adventure novels, not to mention films like *Trader Horn* (1930) and *King Kong* (1933), show "natives" in naked adoration of the fetish of white beauty. It is only against the backdrop of this long history of glorification of whiteness and the de-valorization of blackness that one can appreciate the emotional force of the counter-expression "Black is Beautiful."

If cinema itself traced its parentage to popular sideshows and fairs, ethnographic cinema and Hollywoodean ethnography were the heirs of a tradition of exhibitions of "real" human objects, a tradition going back to Columbus's importation of "New World" natives to Europe for purposes of scientific study and courtly entertainment. Exhibitions organized the world as a spectacle within an obsessively mimetic aesthetic.[26] Africans and Asians were exhibited as human figures bearing kinship to specific animal species, thus literalizing the colonialist zeugma yoking "native" and "animal," the very fact of exhibition in cages implying that the cages' occupants were less than human. Lapps, Nubians, and Ethiopians were exhibited in Germany in anthropological-zoological exhibits.[27] The conjunction of "Darwinism, Barnumism, [and] pure and simple racism" resulted in the exhibition of Ota Benga, a pygmy from the Kasai region, alongside the animals in the Bronx Zoo.[28] The 1894 Antwerp World's Fair featured a reconstructed Congolese village with sixteen "authentic" villagers. In many cases, the people exhibited died or fell seriously ill. "Freak shows," too, paraded before the bemused eyes of the West a variety of "exotic" pathologies. A recent video, *The Couple in the Cage: A Gautinaui Odyssey* (1993) by Coco Fusco and Paula Heredia, "writes back" by readdressing the notion of pathology to its scientist "senders." The video is based on a satirical performance by Guillermo Gomez-Peña and Coco Fusco in which they placed themselves in a cage in public squares and museums performing as two newly discovered Gautinaui from an island in the Gulf of Mexico. The video juxtaposes responses of spectators, many of whom took the caged humans to be "real," with archival footage from ethnographic films in a kind of media jujitsu that returns the colonial gaze.

One of the best-known cases of the exhibition of an African woman is that of Saartje Baartman, the "Hottentot Venus," who was exhibited on the entertainment circuit in England and France.[29] Although her protrusive buttocks constituted the main attraction, the rumored peculiarities of her genitalia also drew crowds, with her racial/sexual "anomaly" constantly being associated with animality.[30] The zoologist and anatomist George Cuvier studied her intimately and presumably dispassionately, and compared her buttocks to those of "female mandrills, baboons … which assume at certain epochs of their life a truly monstrous development."[31] After her death at the age of twenty-five, Cuvier received official permission for an even closer look at her private parts, and dissected her to produce a detailed description of her body, inside out.[32] Until their return to the Khoisan nation, now in South Africa, in May 2002, her genitalia rested on a shelf in the Musée de l'Homme in Paris alongside the genitalia of "*une negresse*" and "*une peruvienne*,"[33] monuments to a kind of imperial necrophilia. The final placement of the female parts in the patriarchally designated "Museum of Man" provides a crowning irony.

A collage by the artist Renée Green on the subject of the "Hottentot Venus" looks ironically at this specific form of colonizing the black female body. The supposedly oxymoronic naming of the "Hottentot Venus" was aggressive and Eurocentric. The collage turns this same "oxymoron" against its originators. The piece juxtaposes a photograph of a white man looking through a camera; a fragment of a nineteenth-century drawing of the torso of a white woman in a hoop skirt; a fragment of another torso, this time of the nude Hottentot; and finally, an image of the *Grand Tetons* (the Big Breasts). A text accompanying the collage calls attention to the undercurrents of desire within the scientific enterprise:

> The subinterpreter was married to a charming person, not only a Hottentot in figure, but in that respect a Venus among Hottentots. I was perfectly aghast at her development. I profess to be a scientific man, and was exceeding anxious to obtain accurate measurements of her shape.

The collage evokes a hierarchy of power. The man looking evokes Cuvier, the scientist who measured the historical Hottentot Venus. By fragmenting the African woman's buttocks, Green exaggerates what for the white scientists was already exaggerated. Juxtaposing this image with a fragmented depiction of a white woman whose fashionably hooped skirt also shapes artificially outsized buttocks, she implies that both the African and the European woman have been constructed for masculinist pleasures: one as the acme of coy virginal beauty, adorned with flowers and a delicately held fan; the other, naked, imagined as an exemplum of gross corporality supposedly to be looked at without pleasure, only for the sake of the austere discipline of science. Both drawings easily slide into the image of Nature, the *Grand Tetons*. The letter "A" appears next to the white woman, "B" next to the Black, and "AB" next to the *Grand Tetons*, and a punning "C" ("see") next to the white man with a camera. The strategic use of European representations of an African woman to underline social ironies about sexuality, gender, and race exploits a boomerang technique; a descendant of Africans literally re-frames the prejudicial images of an earlier African woman as a kind of posthumous accusation.

The hegemony of the Eurocentric gaze, spread not only by First-World media but even at times by Third-World media, explains why *morena* women in Puerto Rico, like Arab-Jewish (Sephardi) women in Israel, paint their hair blond, and why Brazilian TV commercials are more suggestive of Scandinavia than of a black-majority country, and why "Miss Universe" contests can elect blond "queens" even in North African countries, and why Asian women perform cosmetic surgery in order to appear more Western. (I am not questioning the partial "agency" involved in such transformations but highlighting the patterns informing the agency exercised.) Multicultural feminists have criticized the internalized exile of Euro-"wannabes" (who transform themselves through cosmetic surgery or by dying their hair) while at the same time seeking an open, non-essentialist approach to personal aesthetics. The mythical norms of Eurocentric aesthetics come to inhabit the intimacy of self-consciousness, leaving severe psychic wounds. A patriarchal system contrived to generate neurotic self-dissatisfaction in *all* women (whence anorexia, bulimia, and other pathologies of appearance) becomes especially oppressive for women of color by excluding them from the realms of legitimate images of desire.

Set in a Hollywood studio in the 1940s, Julie Dash's *Illusions* (1982) underscores these exclusionary practices by foregrounding a black singer who lends her singing voice to a white Hollywood star. Like Hollywood's classic *Singin' in the Rain*, *Illusions* reflexively focuses on the cinematic technique of post-synchronization, or dubbing. But while the former film exposes the intra-ethnic appropriation whereby silent movie queen Lina Lamont (Jean Hagen) appropriates the silky dubbed voice of Kathy Selden (Debbie Reynolds), *Illusions* reveals the racial dimension of constructing eroticized images of female stars. The film features two "submerged" black women: Mignon Duprée (Lonette McKee), invisible as an African American studio executive "passing for white," and Esther Jeeter (Rosanne Katon), the invisible singer hired to dub the singing parts for a white film star (Lila Grant). Jeeter performs the vocals for a screen role denied her by Hollywood's institutional racism. Black talent and energy are sublimated into a haloed white image. But by reconnecting the black voice with the black image, the film makes the black presence "visible" and therefore "audible," while depicting the operation of the erasure and revealing the film's indebtedness to black performance. But if Gene Kelly can expose the injustice and bring harmony in the world of *Singin' in the Rain*, Lonette McKee – who is far from being a "tragic mulatta" and is portrayed as a woman with agency, struggling to rewrite her community's history – has no such power in *Illusions*, in a studio significantly named the "national studio." *Illusions* references the historical fading in of the African American image into Euro-American entertainment, suggesting that while black sounds were often welcome (for example, on the radio) black images remained taboo, as if their iconic presence would be incendiary after such a long disappearing act.

The existential life of the racialized body has been harsh, subject not only to the indignities of the auction block, to rape, branding, lynching, whipping, stun gunning, and other kinds of physical abuse but also to the kind of cultural erasure entailed in aesthetic stigmatization. Many Third-World and minoritarian feminist film and video projects offer strategies for coping with the psychic violence inflicted by Eurocentric aesthetics, calling attention to the sexualized/racialized body as the site of both brutal oppression and creative resistance. Black creativity turned the body, as a singular form of "cultural capital," into what Stuart Hall calls a "canvas of representation."[34] A number of recent independent films and videos – notably Ayoka Chenzira's *Hairpiece: A Film for Nappy-Headed People* (1985), Ngozi A. Onwurah's *Coffee Coloured Children* (1988), Deborah Gee's *Slaying the Dragon* (1988), Shu Lea Cheang's *Color Schemes* (1989), Pam Tom's *Two Lies* (1989), Maureen Blackwood's *Perfect Image?* (1990), Helen Lee's *Sally's Beauty Spot* (1990), Camille Billop's *Older Women and Love* (1987), and Kathe Sandler's *A Question of Color* (1993) – meditate on the racialized/sexualized body in order to narrate issues of identity. These semiautobiographical texts link fragmented diasporic identities to larger issues of representation, recovering complex experiences in the face of the hostile condescension of Eurocentric mass culture. *Perfect Image?*, for example, satirizes the mass-mediated ideal of a "perfect image" by focusing on the representation and self-representation of two black British women, one light-skinned and the other dark, lampooning the system that generates self-dissatisfaction in very diverse women, all of whom see themselves as "too" something – too dark, too light, too fat, too tall. Their constant shifting of personae evokes a diversity of women, and thus prevents any essentialist stereotyping along color lines in the Afro-diasporic community.

Pathological syndromes of self-rejection – black skins/white masks – form the psychic fall-out of racial hegemony. Given the construction of dark bodies as ugly and bestial, resistance takes the form of affirming black beauty. The Black Power movement of the 1960s, for example, transformed kinky hair into proud Afro hair. Sandler's *A Question of Color* traces tensions around color-consciousness and internalized racism in the African American community, a process summed up in the popular dictum: "If you're white, you're all right/ if you're yellow, you're mellow/ if you're brown, stick around/ but if you're black, stay back." (Such tensions formed the subject of Duke Ellington's musical composition "Black, Brown and Beige.") Hegemonic norms of skin color, hair texture, and facial features are expressed even within the community through such euphemisms as "good hair" (i.e. straight hair) and "nice features" (i.e. European-style features), and in inferentially prejudicial locutions like "dark *but* beautiful," or in admonitions not to "look like a Ubangi." The film registers the impact of the "Black is Beautiful" movement, while regarding the present moment as the contradictory site both of the resurgent Afrocentrism of some rap music along with lingering traces of old norms. One interview features a Nigerian cosmetic surgeon who de-Africanizes the appearance of black women, while the film reflects on the valorization of light-skinned black women in rap videos and MTV. Sandler also probes intimate relations in order to expose the social pathologies rooted in color hierarchies; the darker-skinned feel de-valorized and desexualized, the lighter-skinned – to the extent that their own community assumes they feel superior to it – are obliged to "prove" their blackness. Filtering down from positions of dominance, chromatic hierarchies sow tensions among siblings and friends, all caught by Sandler's exceptionally sensitive direction.

In all these films, internalized models of white beauty become the object of a corrosive critique. Not coincidentally, many of the films pay extraordinary attention to hair as the scene both of humiliation ("bad hair") and of creative self-fashioning, a "popular art form" articulating "aesthetic solutions," in Kobena Mercer's words, to the "problems created by ideologies of race and racism."[35] Already, since the Afro hair style of the late 1960s and 1970s and especially recently, there have been reverse currents linked to the central role of African Americans in mass-mediated culture: whites who thicken their lips and sport dreadlocks, fades, or cornrows. From a multicultural feminist perspective, these cross-cultural transformations (cosmetic surgery, dyeing the hair) on one level are exempla of "internal exile" or "appropriation." But on another level they evoke the possibility of an open, non-essentialist approach to looks and identity. Ayoka Chenzira's ten-minute animated short *Hairpiece: A Film for Nappy-Headed People* addresses hair and its vicissitudes in order to narrate African Americans' history of exile from the body as the utopia of empowerment through Afro-consciousness. In a dominant society where beautiful hair is that which "blows in the wind," *Hairpiece* suggests an isomorphism between vital, rebellious hair that refuses to conform to Eurocentric norms and the vital, rebellious people who "wear" the hair. Music by Aretha Franklin, James Brown, and Michael Jackson accompanies a collage of black faces (from Sammy Davis to Angela Davis). Motown tunes underscore a quick-paced visual inventory of relaxers, gels, and curlers, devices painfully familiar to black people, and particularly to black women. The film's voice-over and "happy ending" might seem to imply an essentialist affirmation of "natural African beauty," but as Kobena Mercer points out in another context, "natural hair" is not itself African; it is a syncretic construct.[36] Afro-diasporic hair styles, from the Afro to dreadlocks, are not emulations of "real" African styles but rather neologistic projections of diasporic identity. The styles displayed at the film's finale, far from being examples of "politically correct" hair, rather assert a cornucopia of diasporic looks, an empowering expression of a variegated collective body. Satirizing the black internalization of white aesthetic models, this provokes a comic catharsis for spectators who have experienced the terror and pity of self-colonization.[37]

Ngozi A. Onwurah's lyrical semiautobiographical film *Coffee Coloured Children*, meanwhile, speaks of the black body as hemmed in by racism. The daughter of a white mother and an absent Nigerian father, the film's narrator recalls the pain of growing up in an all-white English neighborhood. The opening sequence immediately demonstrates the kind of racist harassment the family suffered: a neo-Nazi youth defiles their front door with excrement, while the mother, in voice-over, worries about protecting her children from feeling somehow responsible for the violence directed at them. The narrative conveys the traumatic self-hatred provoked by imposed paradigms. In one scene, the daughter doffs a blonde wig and white makeup in front of a mirror, trying to emulate a desired whiteness. If *The Battle of Algiers* made the mirror a revolutionary tool, here, it becomes the speculum for a traumatized identity, literally that of a black skin masked with whiteness. The simple act of looking in a mirror is revealed to be multiply specular, as one looks even at oneself through the eyes of many others – one's family, one's peers, one's racial others, as well as the panoptic eyes of the mass media and consumerist culture. The scar inflicted on the victims of this aesthetic hegemony are poignantly suggested in a bath sequence in which the children, using cleaning solutions, frantically try to scrub off a blackness lived as dirt.[38] The narrator's voice-over relating the cleansing ritual is superimposed on a close shot of rapid scrubbing, blurred so as to suggest bleeding, an apt image for colonialism's legacy inscribed on the body of children, a testament to the internalized stigmata of a devastating aesthetic regime.

Rewriting the exotic body

While Third-World and First-World minoritarian women have experienced diverse histories and sexual regimes, they have also shared a common status as colonial exotics. They have been portrayed as wiggling bodies graced with Tutti Frutti hats, as lascivious dark eyes peering from behind veils, as feathered dark bodies slipping into trance to accelerating rhythms. In contrast to the Orientalist harem imaginary, all-female spaces have been represented very differently in feminist independent cinema, largely directed by Arab women. Documentaries such as Atteyat El-Abnoudi's *Ahlam Mumkina (Permissible Dreams)* (Egypt, 1989) and Claire Hunt's and Kim Longinotto's *Hidden Faces* (Britain, 1990) examine female agency within a patriarchal context. Both films feature sequences in which Egyptian women, speaking together about their lives in the village, recount in ironic terms their dreams and struggles with patriarchy. Through its critical look at the Egyptian feminist Nawal El-Saadawi, *Hidden Faces* explores the problems of women working together to create alternative institutions. Elizabeth Fernea's *The Veiled Revolution* (1982) shows Egyptian women redefining not only the meaning of the veil but also the nature of their own sexuality. And Moroccan filmmaker Farida Benlyazid's feature film *Bab Ila Sma Maftouh (A Door to the Sky,* 1988) offers a positive gloss on the notion of an all-female space, counterposing Islamic feminism to Orientalist phantasies.

A Door to the Sky tells the story of a Moroccan woman, Nadia, who returns from Paris to her family home in Fez. That she arrives in Morocco dressed in punk clothing and hair style makes us expect an ironic tale about a Westernized Arab feeling out of place in her homeland. But instead, Nadia rediscovers Morocco and Islam and comes to appreciate the communitarian world of her female relatives, as well as her closeness with her father. She is instructed in the faith by an older woman, Kirana, who has a flexible approach to Islam: "Everyone understands through his own mind and his own era." As Nadia awakens spiritually, she comes to see the oppressive aspects of Western society. At the same time, she sees Arab/Muslim society as a possible space for fulfillment. Within the Islamic tradition of women using their wealth for social charity, she turns part of the family home into a shelter for battered women. The film is not uncritical of the patriarchal abuses of Islam – for example, the laws which count women as "half-persons" and which systematically favor the male in terms of marriage and divorce. The film's aesthetic, however, favors the rhythms of contemplation and spirituality, in slow camera movements that caress the contoured Arabic architecture of courtyards and fountains and soothing inner spaces. Dedicated to a historical Muslim woman, Fatima Fihra, the tenth-century founder of one of the world's first universities, *A Door to the Sky* envisions an aesthetic that affirms Islamic culture, while inscribing it with a feminist consciousness, offering an alternative both to the Western imaginary and to an Islamic fundamentalist representation of Muslim women. Whereas contemporary documentaries show all-female gatherings as a space for resistance to patriarchy and fundamentalism, *A Door to the Sky* uses all-female spaces to point to a liberatory project based on unearthing women's history within Islam, a history that includes female spirituality, prophecy, poetry, and intellectual creativity, as well as revolt, material power, and social and political leadership.[39]

Negotiating between past and present is also seen in Tracey Moffat's *Nice Coloured Girls*, which interweaves tales about contemporary urban Australian Aboriginal women and their "captains" (sugar daddies) with tales of Aboriginal women and white men from over 200 years before. Moffat interrogates the hackneyed conventions of the "Aboriginal Film," proposing instead the formal experimentalism of *Nice Coloured Girls* itself.[40] And in sharp contrast to the colonial construction of the Aboriginal "female body" seen as a metaphorical extension of an exoticized land, *Nice Coloured Girls* places dynamic, irreverent, resourceful Aboriginal women at the center of the narrative, offering a multitemporal perspective on their "nasty" actions – mild forms of prostitution and conning white Australian men into spending money. By shuttling between present-day Australia and past texts, voices, and images, the film contextualizes their behavior in relation to the asymmetrical exchanges typical of colonial encounters. Two temporally and spatially distinct but conceptually inter-connected frames – one associated with images of the sea (or its painterly representation) and set in the past, the other set in a pub in contemporary Australia – contextualize the encounter. In one early pub sequence, an Aboriginal man and woman step behind a frosted glass door to smoke a joint. As their film-noirish silhouettes undulate to the diegetic pub music, a British-accented male voice-over reads excerpts from a historical journal describing an Aboriginal woman's breasts, teeth, and face. The evocation of an earlier historical meeting conditions the viewer's comprehension of latter-day encounters.

Rather than search for an "authentic" Aboriginal culture, *Nice Coloured Girls* constructs a "genealogy" of criminality. While from the vantage point of Eurocentric decorum the Aboriginal women are amoral schemers, the historical context of settler colonialism and its sexualized relations to both land and women switches the ethical and emotional valence. In the pub, the women demonstrate their resilient capacity to survive and to outwit marginalization. Whereas images of the past are set inside a ship or in daylight on shore, images from the present are set in the night-time city, pointing to the historical "neonization," as it were, of Aboriginal space. The film can thus be seen as a "revenge" narrative in which Aboriginal women trick Euro-Australian men into fantasizing a "fair" exchange of sex and goods, then take their money and run.

Racial and sexual relations from past (the initial encounter between Europeans and Aborigines in 1788) and present (1987) are interwoven through overlapping images, music, texts, and voice-over. The opening sequence superimposes a text by an early English "explorer" over a dark urban skyscraper, accompanied by the sounds of rowing and of labored rhythmic breathing. While the male voice-over narrates excerpts from journals of the "discovery" of Australia in 1788, subtitles convey the thoughts of present-day Aboriginal women. While the voice-over is in the first-person, the subtitles relay a collective voice. The images reinforce the subtitled version, offering the women's perspective on their trapped "captains," deconstructing the journals not by correcting the historical record but rather through a discursive critique of their racist and masculinist thrust.

The title of *Nice Coloured Girls* is itself ironic, foreshadowing the film's subversion of the "positive" image of "nice" colored girls as the objects of colonial exoticization, and the valorization of the "negative" image of "nastiness." The historical encounters are reconstructed in a minimalist anti-realist style, a symbolic evocation rather than a "realistic" depiction. By reflexively foregrounding the artifice of its production through stylized sets, excessive performance style, and ironic subtitles, the film undermines any expectation of sociologically "authentic" or ethnically "positive" representations. Image, sound, and text amplify and contextualize one another, militating against any authoritative history. The constant changes of discursive register – vérité-style hand-held camera, voice-over ethnographic texts, subtitled oral narratives, American soul music of obscure diegetic status – undermine any univocal mode of historical narration. *Nice Coloured Girls* challenges a whole series of discursive, generic, and disciplinary traditions.

Looking at official Anglo-Australian discourse through the deconstructive eyes of the Aboriginal women, this densely layered text mocks the prurient "ethnographic" fascination with Aboriginal sexuality. Rather than reverse the dichotomy of sexualized Third-World women and virginal European women by proposing an equally virginal image of Aboriginal women, the film rejects the binaristic mode altogether. Finding the kernel of contemporary power relations in the colonial past, *Nice Coloured Girls* shows "nastiness" as a creative response to a specific economic and historical conjuncture.

A discourse which is "purely" feminist or "purely" nationalist, I have tried to argue, cannot apprehend the layered, dissonant identities of diasporic or post-independent feminist subjects. The diasporic and post-Third-Worldist films of the 1980s and 1990s, in this sense, do not so much reject the "nation" as interrogate its repressions and limits, passing nationalist discourse through the grids of class, gender, sexuality, and diasporic identities. While often embedded in the autobiographical, they are not always narrated in the first person, nor are they "merely" personal; rather, the boundaries between the personal and communal, like the generic boundaries between documentary and fiction, the biographic and the ethnographic, are constantly blurred. The diary form, the voice-over, the personal written text, now bear witness to a collective memory of colonial violence and postcolonial displacement. While early Third-Worldist films documented alternative histories through archival footage, interviews, testimonials, and historical reconstructions, generally limiting their attention to the public sphere, the films of the 1980s and 1990s use the camera less as a revolutionary weapon than as a monitor of the gendered and sexualized realms of the personal and the domestic, seen as integral but repressed aspects of national history. They display a certain skepticism toward metanarratives of liberation but do not necessarily abandon the notion that emancipation is worth fighting for. Rather than fleeing from contradiction, they install doubt and crisis at their very core. Rather than a grand anti-colonial metanarrative, they favor heteroglossic proliferations of difference within polygeneric narratives, seen not as embodiments of a single truth but rather as energizing political and aesthetic forms of communitarian self-construction.

Since all political struggle in the postmodern era necessarily passes through the simulacral realm of mass culture, the media are absolutely central to any discussion of post-Third-Worldist multicultural and transnational feminist practices. I have tried to link the often ghettoized debates concerning race and identity politics, on the one hand, and nationalism and postcolonial discourse, on the other, as part of an attempt to put in dialogue, as it were, diverse post-Third-Worldist feminist critiques. The global nature of the colonizing process and the global reach of the contemporary media virtually oblige the cultural critic to move beyond the restrictive framework of the nation-state. Within postmodern culture, the media not only set agendas and frame debates but also inflect desire, memory, and fantasy. The contemporary media shape identity; indeed, many argue that they now exist close to the very core of identity production. In a transnational world typified by the global circulation of images and sounds, goods, and peoples, media spectatorship impacts complexly on national identity, communal belonging, and political affiliations. By facilitating a mediated engagement with distant peoples, the media "deterritorialize" the process of imagining communities. And while the media can destroy community and fashion solitude by turning spectators into atomized consumers or self-entertaining monads, they can also fashion community and alternative affiliations. Just as the media can exoticize and disfigure cultures, they have the potential power not only to offer countervailing representations but also to open up parallel spaces for anti-racist feminist transformation. In this historical moment of intense globalization and immense fragmentation, the alternative spectatorship established by the kind of film and video works I have discussed can mobilize desire, memory, and fantasy, where identities are not only the given of where one comes from but also the political identification with where one is trying to go.

Notes

1 Lyotard, despite his skepticism about "metanarratives," supported the Persian Gulf War in a collective manifesto published in *Liberation*, thus endorsing George Bush's metanarrative of a "New World Order."

2 I am proposing here the term "post-Third-Worldist" to point to a move beyond the ideology of Third Worldism. Whereas the term "postcolonial" implies a movement beyond anti-colonial nationalist ideology and a movement beyond a specific point of colonial history, post-Third-Worldism conveys a movement "beyond" a specific ideology – Third-Worldist nationalism. A post-Third-Worldist perspective assumes the fundamental validity of the anti-colonial movement, but also interrogates the fissures that rend the Third-World nation. See Ella Shohat, "Notes on the Post-Colonial," *Social Text* Nos. 31–2 (Spring, 1992).

3 For more on the concept of "location," see, for example, Chandra Talpade Mohanty, "Feminist Encounters: Locating the Politics of Experience," *Copyright* No. 1 (Fall, 1987); Michele Wallace, "The Politics of Location: Cinema/Theory/Literature/Ethnicity/Sexuality/Me," *Framework* No. 36 (1989); Lata Mani, "Multiple Mediations: Feminist Scholarship in the Age of Multinational Reception," *Inscriptions* No. 5 (1989); and Inderpal Grewal, "Autobiographic Subjects and Diasporic Locations: Meatless Days and Borderlands," and Caren Kaplan, "The Politics of Location as Transnational Feminist Practice," in Inderpal Grewal and Caren Kaplan, eds, *Scattered Hegemonies: Postmodernity and Transnational Feminist Practice* (Minneapolis: University of Minnesota Press, 1994).

4 See J.M. Blaut, *The Colonizer's Model of the World: Geographical Diffusionism and Eurocentric History* (New York and London: Guilford Press, 1993).

5 The various film festivals – in Havana, Cuba (dedicated to New Latin American cinema), in Carthage, Tunisia (for Arab and African Cinemas), in Ougadoogoo, Burkina Faso (for African and Afro-diasporic cinemas) – gave further expression to these movements.

6 In relation to cinema, the term "Third World" has been empowering in that it calls attention to the collectively vast cinematic productions of Asia, Africa, and Latin America, as well as the minoritarian cinema in the First World. While some, such as Roy Armes (1987), define "Third-World cinema" broadly as the ensemble of films produced by Third-World countries (including films produced before the very idea of the "Third World" was current), others, such as Paul Willemen (1989), prefer to speak of "Third Cinema" as an ideological project (i.e. as a body of films adhering to a certain political and aesthetic program, whether or not they are produced by Third-World peoples themselves). As long as they are not taken as "essential" entities but as collective projects to be forged, both "Third-World cinema" and "Third Cinema" retain important tactical and polemical uses for a politically inflected cultural practice. In purely classificatory terms, we might envision overlapping circles of denotation: (1) a core circle of "Third-Worldist" films produced by and for Third-World people (no matter where those people happen to be) and adhering to the principles of "Third Cinema"; (2) a wider circle of the cinematic productions of Third-World peoples (retroactively defined as such), whether or not the films adhere to the principles of

"Third Cinema" and irrespective of the period of their making; (3) another circle consisting of films made by First- or Second-World people in support of Third-World peoples and adhering to the principles of "Third Cinema"; and (4) a final circle, somewhat anomalous in status, at once "inside" and "outside," comprising recent diasporic hybrid films (for example, those of Mona Hatoum or Hanif Kureishi), which both build on and interrogate the conventions of "Third Cinema." See Shohat/Stam, *Unthinking Eurocentrism*.

7 See Aijaz Ahmad, "Jameson's Rhetoric of Otherness and the National Allegory," *Social Text* No. 17 (Fall, 1987), pp. 3–25; Julianne Burton, "Marginal Cinemas," *Screen* Vol. 26, Nos. 3–4 (May–August, 1985).

8 See Arjun Appadurai, "Disjuncture and Difference in the Global Cultural Economy," *Public Culture* Vol. 2, No. 2 (1990). A similar concept, "scattered hegemonies," is advanced by Inderpal Grewal and Caren Kaplan, who offer a feminist critique of global-local relations in their introduction to *Scattered Hegemonies*.

9 In the cinema, this hegemonizing process intensified shortly after World War I, when US film distribution companies (and, secondarily, European companies) began to dominate Third-World markets, and was further accelerated after World War II, with the growth of transnational media corporations. The continuing economic dependency of Third-World cinemas makes them vulnerable to neocolonial pressures. When dependent countries try to strengthen their own film industries by setting up trade barriers to foreign films, for example, First-World countries can threaten retaliation in some other economic area such as the pricing or purchase of raw materials. Hollywood films, furthermore, often cover their costs in the domestic market and can, therefore, be profitably "dumped" on Third-World markets at very low prices.

10 Although direct colonial rule has largely come to an end, much of the world remains entangled in neocolonial globalization. Partially as a result of colonialism, the contemporary global scene is now dominated by a coterie of powerful nation-states, consisting basically of Western Europe, the US, and Japan. This domination is economic ("the Group of Seven," the IMF, the World Bank, GATT), political (the five veto-holding members of the UN Security Council), military (the new "unipolar" NATO), and techno-informational-cultural (Hollywood, UPI, Reuters, France Presse, CNN). Neocolonial domination is enforced through deteriorating terms of trade and the "austerity programs" by which the World Bank and the IMF, often with the self-serving complicity of Third-World elites, impose rules that First-World countries would themselves never tolerate.

11 For a similar argument, see Grewal and Kaplan's introduction to *Scattered Hegemonies*.

12 The Indian TV version of the *Mahabharata* won a 90 percent domestic viewer share during a three-year run, and Brazil's *Rede Globo* now exports its telenovelas to more than eighty countries around the world.

13 For Appadurai, the global cultural situation is now more interactive; the US is no longer the puppeteer of a world system of images, but only one mode of a complex transnational construction of "imaginary landscapes." In this new conjuncture, he argues, the invention of tradition, ethnicity, and other identity markers becomes "slippery, as the search for certainties is regularly frustrated by the fluidities of transnational communication." See Appadurai, "Disjuncture and Difference in the Global Cultural Economy", in Mike Featherstone, ed. *Global Culture: Globalisation and Modernity* (London: Sage Publications, 1990), pp. 259–310.

14 See Benedict Anderson, *Imagined Communities: Reflexions on the Origins and Spread of Nationalism* (London: Verso, 1983); and E.J. Hobsbawm and Terence Ranger (eds) *The Invention of Tradition* (Cambridge: Cambridge University Press, 1983).

15 Pontecorvo returned to Algiers in 1991 to make *Gillo Pontecorvo Returns to Algiers*, a film about the evolution of Algeria during the twenty-five years that have elapsed since *The Battle of Algiers* was filmed, and focusing on such topics as Islamic fundamentalism, the subordinate status of women, the veil, and so forth.

16 Anne McClintock, "No Longer in a Future Heaven: Women and Nationalism in South Africa," *Transition* No. 51 (1991), p. 120.
17 Caren Kaplan, "Deterritorializations: The Rewriting of Home and Exile in Western Feminist Discourse," *Cultural Critique* No. 6 (Spring, 1987), p. 198.
18 The friend in question is Ella Habiba Shohat.
19 Or as the letters put it: "This bloody war takes my daughters to the four corners of the world." This reference to the dispersion of the family, as metonym and metaphor for the displacement of a people, is particularly ironic given that Zionist discourse itself has often imaged its own national character through the notion of the ingathering of exiles from the four corners of the globe.
20 In this sense, *Measures of Distance* goes against the tendency criticized by Hamid Naficy which turns nostalgia into a ritualized denial of history. See "The Poetics and Practice of Iranian Nostalgia in Exile," *Diaspora* No. 3 (1992).
21 Quoted in Brian V. Street, *The Savage in Literature* (London: Routledge and Kegan Paul, 1975), p. 99.
22 Georges-Louis Leclerc de Buffon, *The History of Man and Quadrupeds*, trans. William Smellie (London: T. Cadell and W. Davies, 1812), p. 422.
23 George Mosse, *Toward the Final Solution: A History of European Racism* (London: Dent, 1978), p. 44.
24 See Cornel West, *Prophesy Deliverance: An Afro-American Revolutionary Christianity* (Philadelphia: Westminster, 1982); Clyde Taylor, "Black Cinema in the Post-Aesthetic Era," in Jim Pines and Paul Willemen, eds, *Questions of Third Cinema* (London: BFI, 1989); and bell hooks, *Black Looks: Race and Representation* (Boston: South End Press, 1992).
25 Charles White, *Account of the Regular Gradation in Man*, quoted in Stephen Jay Gould, *The Mismeasure of Man* (New York: W. W. Norton, 1981), p. 42.
26 Egyptians at an Orientalist exposition were amazed to discover that the Egyptian pastries on sale were authentic. See Tim Mitchell, *Colonizing Egypt* (Berkeley: University of California Press, 1991), p. 10.
27 See Jon Pietersie, *White on Black: Images of Africa and Blacks in Western Popular Culture* (New Haven: Yale University Press, 1992). On the colonial safari as a kind of traveling mini-society, see Donna Haraway, "Teddy Bear Patriarchy: Taxidermy in the Garden Of Eden, New York City, 1908–1936," *Social Text* No. 11 (Winter, 1984–5).
28 See Phillips Verner Bradford and Harvey Blume, *Ota Benga: The Pygmy in the Zoo* (New York: St Martins, 1992).
29 The real name of the "Hottentot Venus" remains unknown since it was never referred to by those who "studied" her.
30 For further discussion on science and the racial/sexual body, see Sander Gilman, "Black Bodies, White Bodies: Toward an Iconography of Female Sexuality in Late Nineteenth-Century Art, Medicine, and Literature," *Critical Inquiry* Vol. 12, No. 1 (Autumn, 1985); and, in conjunction with early cinema, see Fatimah Tobing Rony, "Those Who Squat and Those Who Sit: The Iconography of Race in the 1895 Films of Felix-Louis Regnault," *Camera Obscura* No. 28 (1992), a special issue on "Imaging Technologies, Inscribing Science," edited by Paula A. Treichler and Lisa Cartwright.
31 "Flower and Murie on the Dissection of a Bushwoman," *Anthropological Review* No. 5 (July, 1867), p. 268.
32 Richard Altick, *The Shows of London* (Cambridge and London: Harvard University Press, 1978), p. 272.
33 Stephen Jay Gould, *The Flamingo's Smile* (New York: W. W. Norton & Co., 1985), p. 292. On a recent visit to the Musée de l'Homme, I found no traces of the Hottentot Venus; neither the official catalogue, nor officials themselves, acknowledged her existence.
34 Stuart Hall, "What Is This 'Black' in Black Popular Culture?" in Gina Dent, ed. *Black Popular Culture* (Seattle: Bay Press, 1992), p. 27.
35 Kobena Mercer, "Black Hair/Style Politics," *New Formations* No. 3 (Winter, 1987), pp. 33–54.

36 Ibid., p. 34.

37 Not surprisingly, the film has been screened in museums and churches, and even for social workers and hair stylists, as a provocative contemplation of the intersection of fashion, politics, and identity.

38 This association is especially ironic given the colonial legacy of slavery and servitude in which black men (janitors) and women (maids) were obliged to clean up the "mess" created by white Europeans.

39 See Fatima Mernissi, *The Forgotten Queens of Islam*, trans. Mary Jo Lakeland (Minneapolis: University of Minnesota Press, 1993).

40 The juxtaposition of ethnographic diaries/writings and Aboriginal images in *Nice Coloured Girls* is hardly coincidental, since the first photographic and cinematographic representations of Aborigines reflected the culture-bound ethnography of white settlers. (Walter Baldwin Spencer's 1901 footage of the Arrente tribe performing a kangaroo dance and rain ceremony marks the historical beginning of ethnographic filmmaking about the Aborigines.) See Karl C. Heider, *Ethnographic Film* (Austin: University of Texas Press, 1976), p. 19.

3 The erotics of history

Gender and transgression in the new Asian cinemas

Sumita S. Chakravarty

In his perceptive study *The Colonial Harem*, Malek Alloula dissects the sexual fantasies of French colonists as embodied in postcards of veiled and unveiled Algerian women, presenting his own critique as a form of exorcism of the evil eye or gaze of the oppressors. He states that the reading he undertakes is necessary, for "in the absence of a confrontation of opposed gazes, I attempt here, lagging far behind History, to return this immense postcard to its sender" (Alloula, 1986: 5). Alloula's response encapsulates what are by now the classic tropes of colonial and post-colonial discourse: the territorial, economic and symbolic rape of a civilization; fixity in a deformed Otherness; the pained and self-conscious process of reclaiming one's own history and traditions. What I wish to highlight in the present context, however, is Alloula's strategy of reading and mapping, whereby erotic imagery becomes meaningful (for the violated group) as the bearer of an entire historical and ideological complex. In other words, offensive as the pictures are to Alloula as a form of sexual traffic, it is what they signify (the traumatic colonial encounter between France and Algeria) that he needs to address.[1]

In this essay, I am concerned with a similar tendency in some non-Western films of the 1980s and 1990s to revisit the national past using the bodies and psyches of women as at once sites for the play of historical forces as well as instruments of critique available to the filmmakers in the present. Unlike Alloula, however, it is not the colonizing Western power that is being excoriated, but the split body of the nation, at once patriarchal and feminized, and hence erupting in tension and conflict. The question I want to pose is: what are the implications of treating history as if it were a woman?[2]

My concern is with the woman-centered film that has been a prominent feature of many non-Western new cinemas. In these films, male directors tend to present the oppression of women and the tensions arising out of transgressive sexual desires as allegories of social or national history. I analyze this tendency through a theorization of the concept of the "erotic" in which eroticism connects sexuality to a political and/or ethical vision, a vision that records and interrogates the failed narratives of the national past. What are the challenges that this revisionary project poses to the filmmakers? What sense can we make of the figuring of history as a woman? Does the trope of the transgressive female body serve as an adequate instrument of social critique? How are gender relations played out in these films? In trying to answer these questions, my larger goal is to rethink the notion of eroticism as used in cultural/media criticism, a notion that is ubiquitous but rarely theorized in a systematic way.

Eroticism, as I use the concept here, is a meaning system that seeks to capture the force of that which is unspeakable and suppressed in history, but needs to be articulated to make some kind of redemption possible for the collectivity. As such, it is the beast in the social belly. By constructing this framework of analysis, I wish to engage in cross-cultural or comparative analysis that cuts across the rubric of "national cinemas," one which has traditionally isolated discussion of them within a matrix of nation-specific "Third World" socio-economic conditions. (Interestingly, the notion of "Third Cinema" which first emerged as a resolutely transnational or supranational rubric, focused on individual filmmakers and their political goals and aesthetic strategies, so that the comparative framework was assumed rather than explored or foregrounded.) While some excellent studies of Asian cinemas have appeared in recent years, they tend not to go beyond existing paradigms. Even those analyses that claim to advance the cause of "post-colonial" criticism end up revisiting yet again a West-non-West relational schema. Few studies exist that look for patterns across national cinemas.

The issue of gender and sexuality seems particularly suited to a rethinking of the bifurcated paths of a "universalist," psychoanalysis-based feminist critique of women's representation on the one hand and a particularist, "national-cultural" focus on the other. For what initiated my own inquiry into eroticism was a dissatisfaction with the available models, neither of which adequately explained the "treatment" of women characters across a range of cinematic texts of diverse origins. A focus on gender *difference* seemed to exclude the way men and women seek to *relate* to each other – on emotional, social, ideological, creative and symbolic planes. It is to get at "the total social fact" that it is necessary to go beyond "male domination" theories, not because male domination does not exist in a wide range of contexts but because monolithic systems, in explanation as in other spheres of activity, repress other truths, negate other possibilities.

The films that I have chosen as examplars of an alternative "erotic" approach reflect diverse national traditions and varied narrative and visual strategies. My intent is not to homogenize them or to erase their marks of cultural difference. Chen Kaige's *Yellow Earth* (mainland China) has little that is obviously in common with Satyajit Ray's *The Home and the World* (India), Zhang Yimou's concerns and style as a filmmaker are distinct from those of Lino Brocka or Ishmael Bernal of the Philippines, and India's Middle Cinema (as exemplified, say, by the films of Ketan Mehta or Shyam Benegal) is a category unknown in the Philippines. And all of these visual texts may seem to have nothing to do with a literary text such as Salman Rushdie's *Shame*. Yet all these diverse texts clearly espouse a critical attitude towards developments within their countries and use women's sufferings to denote the failures of national ideals or movements. These nationalist dramas portray women as powerful, though ultimately vulnerable and defeated, while the men are uniformly ineffectual, manipulative, callous and evil. To suggest a past that has failed its citizens, these films show women who have not borne, or cannot bear, children.[3] Thus the films deny their audiences refuge in myths of maternity and fertility. Violence, either physical or psychological, inflicted on the women and resulting in the victimization or death of the female protagonist, points to the culture of violence that props up the dominant social order. The women serve to mediate the historical span that links the diegetic past to the filmmaking present, the past being the displaced site of the tensions, failures and anxieties of the present.

These films are part of various New Cinemas that are characterized by a critical attitude to the past, whether it be the failures of nationalism and modernization (the Indian "new wave" and recent Korean and Taiwanese New Cinemas), the trauma of the Cultural Revolution (Chinese New Cinema), or the painful memory of Nazism (New German Cinema).[4] Coupled with a political critique is the rebellion of many "new" film directors against the established practices and products of the mainstream industry, whether native or foreign (Hollywood). In recent years, moreover, the viability of an international film forum through a proliferation of film festivals and the success of many New Cinema products in the US market may be said to have contributed to a shared filmic sensibility (in which exoticism plays a role) whereby film directors can serve both local and international audiences simultaneously. In a provocative analysis, Rey Chow explains how, in the case of the Chinese Fifth Generation films, a desire for new beginnings in the post-Mao period is expressed through "primitivism" or the projection of China as primary and unique. She writes,

> like their counterparts from many areas of the non-Western world, contemporary Chinese films, even though they are always made with the assumption that they represent the ongoing problems within China, become the space where "China" is exhibited in front of audiences overseas.
> (Chow, 1995: 37)

A question that circles this inquiry, therefore, is how "the erotics of history" are inflected by the erotics of a successfully exported "way of seeing" (to borrow John Berger's famous expression) that we can think of as an increasingly "global visual culture." Self-projections of a so-called Third World as feminized may then be seen to feed the narcissistic assumptions of power and potency in the "advanced" Western countries.[5]

Defining the erotic

On the face of it, a discussion of eroticism in the cinema and the vocabulary that traditionally goes with it, such as "desire," "sexuality," "romance" and the like, seems somewhat redundant. As Geoffrey Nowell-Smith notes, the "cinema is an erotic art" in which the norms of (hetero)sexual coupling are played out: "The content of narrative has also been traditionally seen as the channelling and shaping of desire in the interests of social cohesion, with couple formation, marriage, and reproduction as the explicit or implicit goal of stories the world over" (Nowell-Smith, 1995: 756). This is an instrumental view of the role of sexuality in cinema narrative. While this view applies no doubt to mainstream cinemas everywhere, it also suggests that sexual meanings are self-evident, universally conformative to one culturally-specific ideal of monogamy and patriarchal nuclear bonding and that they need not be elaborated upon beyond these externalities of narrative or plot mechanism. The other major approach, stemming from Laura Mulvey's classic formulation, in which the patriarchal relations governing society are reflected/instituted in mainstream cinema, may have elided or even hypostatized the issue of eroticism altogether. Despite the enormous critical productivity of this model, its tendency to dichotomize male and female desire does not lend itself to a more philosophical understanding of the erotic. In its Lacanian adherence to a notion of eroticism as sexual objectification, it leaves no room for contradictions, for the erotic as life-in-death and death-in-life, at once a creative and a destructive force. In its latter sense, the erotic signifies a structural arrangement of forces in which the scenario of love and longing takes on meaning only as part of a larger political project of self-understanding, simultaneously social and subjective. The erotic can function as a composite metaphor for the invocation of value-systems, beliefs and practices through which a society calls itself into being at specific historical and cultural moments. The erotic, in what follows, is the clash of the old and the new on the semantic body of woman. "Woman!" says a character in Salman Rushdie's *Shame*, "what a term! Is there no end to the burdens this word is capable of bearing? Was there ever such a broad-backed and also such a dirty word?" (Rushdie, 1983: 62).

Far more complex in his view of human sexuality than Nowell-Smith (or Lacan), Georges Bataille takes a dialectical view of the erotic, seeing tension and contradiction at its very heart. Drawing heavily on Nietzsche and Schopenhauer, Bataille's founding premise is that human beings are discontinuous or separate and isolated, and it is the aim of erotism to escape this state and create continuity through the merging implied in sexual union. Thus, for him "eroticism is assenting to life up to the point of death." Bataille juxtaposes sensuality and death because each gives meaning to the other: the individual person must "die" metaphorically *as a separate being* in order to feel erotic oneness with a sexual partner, while death as the end of life is feared and yet desired as a means of liberation from the prospect of an endless life. Thus, paradoxically, "the domain of eroticism is the domain of violence, of violation" (Bataille, 1986: 16). Thus Bataille associates the erotic with transgressive sexual desires and acts, since they appear to violate the social order while affirming its norms and procedures.[6]

In extending Bataille's insights to the films discussed below, I focus on the interplay of taboo and transgression that implicates the central female character in erotic experience, with violence unleashed against herself and others. The woman thus feels in her own body the conflicts over the prohibitions that the society of men has instituted and seeks to enforce. History unfolds as a succession of these prohibitions and the female characters' struggle against them. But the texts undercut their own potential for a truly erotic sense of the revaluation of the past. For if the aim of the filmmakers is to reject or rethink particular configurations of history, insofar as the women are sexually inscribed in these scenarios, and symbolically annihilated for their sexual disobedience, the films reinstitute the same social order that is condemned in the first place. This is the double bind of these reflexive texts: to exorcise the past and yet to hold on to it; to represent sexual desire and yet to know it as entrapment; to celebrate the female figure and yet to exploit it within the terms of the classical grammar of film narrative.

Women's bodies/historical bodies

Before we turn to the films in question, I would like to invoke briefly a literary text as a paradigmatic, though particularly harsh and poignant, instance of what I am calling the erotics of history and historical recollection. Salman Rushdie's *Shame* presents to the reader a grim portrayal of the birth of Pakistan and its later history through the warped sensibilities of two women characters, a mother and daughter, both of whom are psychically and sexually burdened with feelings of shame. Rushdie transforms stereotypically "female" emotion into a metaphor for the linking of the individual and the national body, and makes it possible for the fictive author to revisit his erstwhile "homeland." Weaving fact with fiction in the way that Robert Rosenstone designates as one of the hallmarks of what he terms the "historical film," Rushdie cites a real-life event as the nucleus for his macabre tale, an incident in London's East End in which a Pakistani father murdered his only child, a daughter, "for making love to a white boy." Here is the classic scenario that Bataille has drawn for us of taboo, transgression, and violence that culminates in death, so closing the circle and reactivating the taboo. But rather than accept this cycle as the motor of social life, Rushdie explores its sexual and cultural politics. The erotic union of a white boy and "Pakistani" girl brings not symbolic but real death to one of the partners. The separation between human beings that eroticism might have transcended leads to further estrangement and rupture. What is erotic love to the young couple is animal sexuality and shameful behavior to the enraged parent. Thus notions of communal pride and norms governing sexuality mediate erotic behavior. Rushdie notes,

> We who have grown up on a diet of honour or shame can still grasp what must seem unthinkable to peoples living in the aftermath of the death of God and of tragedy: that men will sacrifice their dearest love on the implacable altars of their pride.
>
> (Rushdie, 1983: 115)

Shame is an allegory of the defeat of eroticism under degrading conditions of political and moral imbalance. Where power relations govern all human intercourse, sexuality can find expression only in acts that are furtive, aberrant, destructive. Not only does a transgressive sexual act provide the motivation for the novel (the author decides to present a reincarnated version of the murdered girl), but Pakistan's history and politics are continually linked to symbols of the enraged and thwarted sexual psyches of women. In a telling passage, Rushdie in his persona as the outer narrator, contemplates the role accorded to women in his novel:

> I had thought, before I began, that what I had on my hands was an almost excessively masculine tale, a saga of sexual rivalry, ambition, power, patronage, betrayal, death, revenge. But the women seem to have taken over; they marched in from the peripheries of the story to demand an inclusion of their own tragedies, histories and comedies, obliging me to couch my narrative in all manner of sinuous complexities, to see my "male" plot refracted, so to speak, through the prisms of its reverse and "female" side. It occurs to me that the women knew precisely what they were up to – that their stories explain, and even subsume, the men's. Repression is a seamless garment; a society which is authoritarian in its social and sexual codes, which crushes its women beneath the intolerable burdens of honour and propriety, breeds repressions of other kinds as well. Contrariwise: dictators are always – or at least in public, on other people's behalf – puritanical. So it turns out that my "male" and "female" plots are the same story, after all.
>
> (Rushdie, 1983: 173)

These words provide a powerful rationale not only to rethink history from below, but also for newly-conceptualized deployments of eroticism. There could hardly be a more damning indictment of the patriarchal and authoritarian values that have governed Pakistani politics and the toll they have exacted from women. If eroticism here appears in the guise of misogyny, as a befuddled Aijaz Ahmad (1992: 123–58) claimed, Rushdie's point is that at a certain point a falsely engendered sense of shame spills over into revenge, fuelling erotic energies that can bring down dictatorial or corrupt male figures.[7]

The seductions of nationalism

The embodiment of the nation in oppressed female figures, so powerfully evoked in *Shame*, is a hallmark of many films in which the ideology of nationalism itself is questioned and critiqued. Satyajit Ray's *The Home and the World* (1984) and Chen Kaige's *Yellow Earth* (1984) show female protagonists attached to charismatic male figures whose self-identification as national symbols of liberation is problematized by the filmmakers. As in Rushdie's *Shame*, the vanity and emptiness of male-dominated histories are reconfigured through women's physical and emotional states. While the men remain unchanged through the course of the films, women both reflect change and are victims (often willingly so) of change happening around them. Thus Bimala in *Home* bears the harsh consequences of an adulterous love affair and Ciacao in *Yellow Earth* gets drowned in the course of trying to escape her narrowly confined village existence.

As stated earlier, different stagings of female transgression convey historical crises as meeting points of the personal and the social.[8] *Ghare Baire* (*The Home and the World*), based on a 1915 novella of the same name written by Bengal's literary giant Rabindranath Tagore, foregrounds a brief moment in Indian colonial history, specifically the convulsive effects that followed Bengal's partition by Lord Curzon in 1902. The film is set in 1905 and the political content is mediated through the story of a love triangle between a rich land-owner, Nikhil, his wife, Bimala, and his boyhood friend-turned-politician, Sandip. But if Tagore's novella was written at the height of the nationalist movement and is an autobiographical exploration of his own stance towards different political strategies,[9] Ray's film has the effect of telescoping several decades of Indian history.

For viewers in 1984, exploitative political leaders, communal conflicts, the fading away of nationalist ideals were the sum and substance of public life, and could be projected onto the filmic experience of the past. One way in which Ray communicates this dark and somber post-nationalist mood is in the use of subdued lighting throughout most of the film, and the somewhat overdetermined nobility and vileness respectively of the two male characters. As Nicholas Dirks has pointed out, the film's ending (the death of Nikhil) is contained in the opening shots, so that the filmmaker positions himself in the present and aligns his perspective with that of the female character whose narration enables us to enter the story. Dirks writes,

> The voice, and the story of the film, belong to the mourning woman, Bimala; the tragedy is simultaneously that of her marriage and that of her motherland, the nation.
>
> (Dirks, 1995: 45)

Eroticism is central to Bimala's dual signification (she is herself at once woman and mother-goddess),[10] since her story communicates the inextricability of love, transgression and death. Bimala is intensely desired by two men, her husband Nikhil and their house-guest and nationalist idol, Sandip. She in turn has to fall in love with Sandip in order to realize her love for her husband, a realization that comes too late, that is followed almost immediately by his death, and remains to haunt her widowhood. Through Bimala is literalized the film's title, for it is she who traverses both home and world, the women's quarters and the drawing-room, the world of domesticity, fashion and leisure and that of political speeches, riots, protests, intrigues and machinations. Ray's Bimala is first a rich and indulgent landlord's wife who preens herself in front of her mirror in lavishly-tailored European clothing, under the gaze of her adoring husband. But when she meets Sandip who is passing by to rouse sentiments against the British among the rural folk, she also enters the realm of political consciousness. The scene that captures, in slow motion and to Tagorean music on the soundtrack, her frontal movement down a corridor is clearly orchestrated as highly symbolic.

Thereafter, as Bimala slowly, almost unconsciously, responds to Sandip's seductions, she becomes simultaneously a participant in political debate, an ardent nationalist, and less attentive to herself as spectacle. She will go to great lengths to help Sandip's cause, including selling her gold jewelry and parting with her fortune. Thus her marital transgression goes hand in hand with her political awakening.

It is of course the tragedy of this film that Bimala's commitment is to a lost or unworthy cause. "Swadeshi" politics as purveyed by Sandip is shown to be divisive and morally despicable in comparison to the more conciliatory and pragmatic stance of Nikhil. In first loving and then turning away from Sandip, Bimala loses face, and soon thereafter, loses her husband. It is thus the woman who pays the price for historical knowledge, her erotic awakening now associated with witchcraft by a member of her own sex, her angry and always-envious sister-in-law. Bimala's brief experiment in autonomy signals the risks inherent in transgressing age-old social taboos. At this point we can return briefly to the scene mentioned earlier. Bimala, accompanied by Nikhil, crosses the fateful space that separates home and world. Sandip is waiting on the other side. The scene is at once triumphal and subdued, Bimala wearing a slight smile of hope and daring, Nikhil of pride and serene authority. The two walk side by side towards the camera, in slow motion, down a corridor, then the shot is repeated to prolong the scene. From a feminist perspective, this is a utopian moment in the film, when the three characters enjoy a rare instance of sexual equality, when the past and the future merge in the possibilities of the present. Both the adventure and the danger of Bimala's passage are signified by the scene in a way that makes it the central point of the narrative.

If the eroticized figure of Bimala in *The Home and the World* is meant to convey the libidinal force and danger in nationalism, its unstable character, Cuiqiao in Chen Kaige's *Yellow Earth* (1984), is also an ambivalent figure of identification with a history at once immemorial and particularized. The two characters are very different, yet they are both transitional (even liminal) figures, aware of the risks involved in their social transgressions. In both films, these characters symbolize larger historical forces: *Yellow Earth*'s director stated, "Cuiqiao is Cuiqiao; Cuiqiao is not-Cuiqiao. She is both concrete and transcendent. From her we can see the hope for our people" (quoted in Chow, 1995: 100). Both Bimala and Cuiqiao, in other words, come from traditions in which female figures are perennially subject to invocation: as cultural repositories of the distilled essence of the past; as mirroring surfaces which capture and render meaningful a culture's struggles with itself; as sacrificial body for cultural purification and renewal. New Cinema pioneers seem particularly conscious of their own need to break with the past, but tend to do so by "reinvesting" in the past through such symbolic invocations.

As the film that heralded the advent of China's Fifth Generation and a New Cinema emerging from decades of state-controlled film production, *Yellow Earth* has understandably drawn substantial critical attention. My own attempt here can do no better than to engage with some dominant strands of this response, particularly with regard to its erotic potential. Before doing so, however, it is tempting to cite, albeit briefly and suggestively, the parallels between the founding moments of the Chinese and the Indian New Cinemas, as personified by Chen Kaige and Satyajit Ray. Rey Chow has located her analysis of Chen's film in the broader context of the representational politics of East-West, the nation, ethnicity, exoticism, and the like; others have pointed out the difficult conditions in which such endeavors are undertaken, all reminiscent of Ray's early struggles in India and showing how, where the cinema is concerned, Communist and bourgeois nationalist politics can converge. Like Ray's *Pather Panchali*, *Yellow Earth* was given the stamp of official approval at home after its favorable critical reception in the West; like the former, Chen's film was accused of purveying rural poverty abroad, thus showing the country in a "bad light" to foreigners; and like *Pather Panchali*, *Yellow Earth* is a complex negotiation between "nativist" conceptions of space and time and the (narrative and visual) demands of the cinematic medium. Both films were vulnerable to easy ascriptions of "Chineseness" and "Indianness," a tendency that, as Chow shows us, is fraught with problematic assumptions.

Unfortunately, the critical consequence of such a "Third Worldist" frame of reference has to date not been adequately considered, perhaps even by Chow herself. One suspects that a substantially different account of international film dynamics might emerge if one were, for instance, to compare *Pather Panchali* and *Yellow Earth*'s "exhibitionary complex" as common responses to their own internal social situations rather than to hegemonic Western demands for "otherness." My own discomfort with Chow's excellent and nuanced examination of the textual, critical, and cultural dimensions of *Yellow Earth*, then, is that she restricts herself, as she finds others doing, to the same Western frame of reference she critiques. Hence her question: "... what is it that enables Chinese intellectuals on the mainland to produce works that are so relevant to the contemporary West...?" But given that non-Western societies such as China and India share a "borrowed" relationship to the Western technology of cinema, their stylistic and ideological negotiations with this technology can at least be as fruitful an avenue of inquiry as the way they "inevitably conjure the historical relations between 'East' and 'West' " (Chow, 1995: 104).

Perhaps it is this "inevitability" that leads Chow to dismiss the erotic potential of the figure of Cuiqiao and to limit the concept itself to Western feminism's coinage, "*woman-as-sexed-subject* (heterosexual erotics)" (Chow, 1995: 87). Given that neither the Red Army soldier, Gu Qing, nor the rural child-woman, Cuiqiao, are Hollywoodean figures or protagonists in any traditional sense, "heterosexual erotics" is absent in the film. Sexuality as a *separate* domain has no place in *Yellow Earth*; however, events of a sexual nature – marriage, bondage to a man, emotional loneliness and grief – center on Cuiqiao and link her to her community, her environment, and her fate. Cuiqiao's fascination with Gu Qing, her longing for what he represents, misguided though it is, links them together in a way that any overt suggestions of romantic involvement can hardly do. In this sense, eroticism is at the heart of the film, linking its varied strands – its ominous death-in-life and life-in-death – conceived in accordance with Bataille's notion of eroticism as acceding to life unto the point of death. In an interview (Semsel: 137–8), Chen and his cinematographer relate how the land shown in the film is emblematic of Chinese history and civilization, an emblem that, that I would contend is in turn symbolized by the archetype of the silent, suffering woman tormented by her budding sexuality.

Sexuality is the means whereby many of the social and psychic structures of the film are articulated. This relates not only to plot elements, but to the film's thematic and stylistic features as well. Thus sexuality here is what Bataille, following Lévi-Strauss, called "a total social fact" (Bataille, 1993: 40), that which lays bare the human community's inner workings. The film shows two weddings taking place, one early on and portrayed with documentary thoroughness, the other (Cuiqiao's) presented briefly, as a gesture of repetition. Cuiqiao is also defined in relation to female and household labor: she takes care of her father and her brother Han han, and will be "exchanged" in marriage with another family's daughter who will in turn take her place as Han han's wife. Cuiqiao's transgression is that she despises this arrangement emotionally and tries to escape. The rain-god prayer sequence at the end of the film may be taken as a collective punishment visited on the community for the transgression of one of its members.

The film is, on one level, about the relationship of outsiders (including the filmmakers themselves) to China's far west, where "land" and "people" merge and become indistinguishable. Gu Qing is already an outsider at the beginning of the film and the first shots show him only as a dot, as it were, against a forbidding landscape as he walks towards the mountain village which is the setting of the narrative. Here are the much-talked about empty spaces on screen, suggestive of Chinese painting and Daoist aesthetics (Yau, Farquhar), to which Gu Qing remains only marginally (and ambivalently) related throughout the film. Against the stillness of the landscape he is usually shown in movement, crossing its expanses but often seemingly getting nowhere. His task is to record folk songs, and he is often shown doing just that, while also singing the praises of the Red Army and its progressive agenda. He is obviously set up as the voice of reason and the agent of deliverance for a backward people, and audiences are invited to view village practices through his questioning eyes. And yet, Gu Qing remains the sympathetic but detached outsider. As Cuiqiao finds her tremulous emotions fastening on him, she wants him to stay or to take her away, but he will do neither. This is how the film sets up the dialectic of production and expenditure that Bataille tells us characterizes human societies. Both the world that Gu Qing represents and the feudalist village world of Cuiqiao's entrapment are characterized by the values of production. Gu Qing can sew, he helps in farming and household chores; above all, he not only records songs but teaches them as well. Cuiqiao's father is highly conscious of conserving resources, admonishing Cuiqiao's waste of firewood, licking his bowl clean when he eats, and maintaining the circuit of labor by marrying Cuiqiao off at fourteen.

Against these highly ordered worlds, Cuiqiao represents or renders, paradoxically, what is "unspeakable" in the film. Chen Kaige stated, "A single word sums up the essence of the film's style: 'concealment'." The film derives its force from the internal tension between its ethic of "concealment" and its goal-directedness, what on one level may be called its documentary thrust, and on the other, its sensory awareness rendered through spectacular landscape shots and an ear-filling soundtrack. The redundancy of raw erotic power is dispersed onto many levels but is located most obviously in Cuiqiao herself. From the start, Cuiqiao is invested with a knowledge and passions strangely in excess of her diminutive body and youth. Her singing, which, as Rey Chow points out, often seems to be disconnected with any lip movement on her part, fills the landscape and gives voice to the hills and valleys; in shots with obvious mythic overtones, she appears against the wide expanse of the Yellow River or near the deep troughs of water she draws from; and her final fatal journey shows a desperation that exceeds the bounds of "normal" peasant girl behavior (after all, the practice of marrying young girls to older men in this village setting is routine, as the first wedding sequence shows). But it is perhaps in the realm of sexuality that the film's "unspeakability" is most palpable. The film sternly refuses any recourse to the structures of dominant cinema whereby Gu Qing and Cuiqiao could be romantically linked and her life "saved." Quite the contrary: Gu Qing early on asks Cuiqiao to call him "Brother Gu," thus setting up a taboo (of incest) which defines the parameters of their relationship. Cuiqiao's passions are displaced onto "the cause," the "impossibility" of which in terms of the film's own conditions and context of production is symbolically rendered by Cuiqiao's death by drowning. Thus a film set in 1934 "spills over" into 1984; a film revisiting the founding of the Communist Party in China subtly suggests its failures and ideological ambiguities; a film that eschews narrative seduction orchestrates a romance of landscape and local color; and a film that focuses on the victimization of rural women also subscribes to the regenerative powers of primordial myths.

The erotics of *Yellow Earth*, therefore, go far beyond any easy identifications of "woman-as-sexed-subject." Such paradigms do not even begin to address the weight of historicity, national self-reflection, and the confusions of contemporary consciousness as embodied in the figure of Cuiqiao. Like Bimala, Cuiqiao is central to an understanding of the contradictory forces that assail the body politic, as they are both seduced and destroyed by utopian projections of "the nation." Cuiqiao may also be taken as a meditation on the politics of transgression embodied by the Chinese New Cinema (and New Cinemas in general): the charges of self-indulgence often leveled against them, their uncertain mandate as the critical conscience of a generation, their privileging of stylistic experimentation rather than storytelling, and, above all, their ambivalent political relationship to their (usually governmental) sponsors. Cuiqiao's uncertainties and vulnerabilities point to the transgressive self-definition of China's Fifth Generation.

Transgressive pasts and inadmissible futures

Zhang Yimou's lush films, controversial in their depiction of China, have, more than the works of any other fifth generation filmmaker, used central female figures to represent past and present injustices in mainland Chinese society. In an interview given some years ago Zhang noted, "what I want to express is the Chinese people's oppression and confinement, which has been going on for thousands of years. *Women express this more clearly on their bodies because they bear a heavier burden than men*" (Yang, 1993: 300; italics added).[11] Two such films which view history in terms of women's bodies and were initially banned in China are *Judou* (1990) and *Raise the Red Lantern* (1991), films in which sexual desire and transgression are the narrative means of interrogating the past and its grip on the present. Interestingly, this feminized portrayal of history has been the source of intense controversy in the critical reception of Zhang's films (see, for instance, Dai Qing's "Raised Eyebrows for *Raise the Red Lantern*" *Public Culture* 10/1993: 333–7), drawing charges of a putative "Orientalism" and aestheticization. Rey Chow notes that

> the seduction of Zhang's films – the appeal of his visual ethnography – is that they keep crossing boundaries and shifting into new spheres of circulation. The wish to "liberate" Chinese women, which seems to be the "content," shifts into the liberation of "China," which shifts into the liberation of the "image" of China on film, which shifts into the liberation of "China" on film in the international culture market, and so on.
>
> (Chow, 1995: 149)

Chow does acknowledge that in Zhang Yimou's films "Femininity ... is the place where the contradictory nature of culture-writing – as a retrospective capturing of the past's violence and chaos, and as a progressive, forward-looking investment in the possibilities of rewriting and enlightenment – becomes clearest" (Chow, 1995: 146). However, she goes on to fault him for the trite nature of his narratives, the deliberate attempt at popularization, and the exoticization of feudal China. Zhang's films, she argues, in blurring the specificities of time period and class markers, are primarily ethnographic in intent, with women enabling the construction of "ethnic primitivism." Moreover, she cites a number of critical responses (both within and outside mainland China) to these two films, all of which seem to be in agreement over the films' "misrepresentation" of China and the seductions of Zhang's visual style as it pertains to women's bodies. What we are dealing with here seems to be Zhang's own "transgressions" against his society/people, effected by means of that transgressive Western technological mode of surveillance and objectification, the camera, all compounded by the textual-sexual transgressions of his female characters. Chow's painstaking recounting of all the criticisms leveled against Zhang's "exploitation" of Chinese history and culture provides a valuable perspective on the vexed issue of cultural representation and the degree to which fictional films may be implicated in ethnographic modalities. My problem with this conflation is that it can easily slide into the tired binaries of West/East, male/female, popular art/high art, nature/culture: in short, binaries that can only valorize one pole in terms of its (negative) other.[12] However, accepting them for the moment, the questions I want to raise are: what constitutes the "sexual content" of Zhang's films? What role does eroticism play in *Judou* and *Red Lantern*? How is sexuality articulated with history? What are the components of a "pornographic" as opposed to an "erotic" style?

No matter whether Zhang's Chinese critics are moved or repelled by his films, they seem to be drawn to sexual metaphors to describe aspects of his narrative or style. Jane Ying Zha is impatient with the "Orientalizing" charge and writes:

> In a way, seeing these movies is like using a Western man's hand – the arm of a Western movie camera – to slowly caress the Chinese landscape and Chinese people; it provides a pleasure and stimulation at once familiar and strange.
>
> (Zha, 1993: 22)

Rey Chow, on the other hand, compares Zhang's gendered preoccupations to Butterfly fiction, adding that "his films do not change the mundane nature of the stories but enlarge the possibilities of our enjoyment of precisely those unspeakable, at times pornographic fantasies, that are, shall we say, a culture's 'shame'" (Chow, 1995: 147). Dai Qing, while criticizing *Red Lantern*'s exoticism and lack of attention to authentic historical detail, writes:

> Why is the film so circumspect, even prudish, in its depiction of sex, when sex in fact figures so importantly in the entire plot of the movie, from the heroine's winning favor with the master initially to her eventual fall into disgrace and final dementia? It seems to me that, in keeping with the mood and meaning of the film, it would have been entirely appropriate, even necessary, for the director to have included a few well-placed scenes of explicit love-making, for the purposes of advancing both plot development and character portrayal. Instead it appears that while the director and scriptwriters did not hesitate to take outrageous liberties with such details as decor, dialogue, and diction, they were unwilling to claim the more daring artistic licence of filming erotic scenes.
>
> (Qing, 1993: 336)

Given that perceived sexuality is such a prominent register of response to Zhang's films, it is worthwhile to consider what role it plays within the overall schema which these films represent. I would argue that, as in the case of Bimala and Cuiqiao, the sexuality of Judou and Songlian denotes the expenditure of material and psychic gift-giving that Bataille has designated as senseless and extravagant when seen from the normalized perspective of the historical order of production. Bimala/Cuiqiao and Judou/Songlian represent two ways of dealing with the ethical dilemma of representation that calls on the filmmaker to denote as well as allegorize. Bimala and Cuiqiao are etherealized, their identities invested with the "spirit" of India/China, but Judou and Songlian are not extricated from the "excremental" world of useless expenditure. It is his refusal to ultimately valorize this womanly domain, to align himself with it, that may be more responsible for Zhang's "dark" vision.[13]

Judou and *Red Lantern* are set in China's pre-Communist past: in the 1920s and the 1940s respectively, although they have been criticized for their lack of historical authenticity. But Zhang's decision to locate these films in a non-specified past may also be seen as arising from the need to highlight its structures all the more clearly and starkly, as well as to deny a sense of historical rupture between the past and the present. Just as Bataille's move to focus on the problem of abundance in human societies rather than of scarcity arose out of Mauss's notion of the potlatch, a practice found among native Americans in the northwest, so the heightened "primitivism" of China in these films helps to render structural patterns in sharper relief. And it is through structures – real, solid, physical structures – that the films most graphically *work* their visual meanings. These structures, the home-cum-dye factory in *Judou* and the sprawling old mansion in *Red Lantern*, signify not only order and hierarchy but also work, production, and labor which includes the work that has gone into the production of beauty and formal harmony to which both houses bear visual testimony.[14] In *Red Lantern*, the very layout of the mansion, its courtyard within courtyard and symmetrically placed units in which the wives of the landowner live their separate lives, denotes the essence of an age-old civilization dominated by Confucian values of the maintenance of custom and tradition (see Joann Lee, 1996: 120). What happens when the values of "waste" and "expenditure" in terms of sexual energy are introduced into these worlds?

Both films focus on female characters (both played by Gong Li) whose youth and beauty make them vulnerable to the instrumental designs of older men. Yang Jinshan in *Judou* and Chen in *Red Lantern* need young women for similar purposes: to bear a male heir for the one and to stimulate an aging virility for the other. If, as scholars have noted, and Zhang Yimou has himself confirmed, *Red Sorghum*, *Judou* and *Raise the Red Lantern* form a trilogy, it might be said that the films progressively portray a diminution of the pleasurable potential of sexual passion. While Jiuer and her lover can freely abandon themselves to their initial passion (prudishly outside the camera's range), the love affair between Judou and Tianqing is guilt-ridden from the start, while Songlian may be said to have suppressed passion altogether as an option. Nevertheless, both *Judou* and *Red Lantern*, in posing sexuality as the site of crisis and tension, allow the viewer to explore the relationships between the sexual and the larger social world which defines, constrains and punishes it. In blatantly inviting our sympathies to rest with the thwarted desires of the protagonists, Zhang may be taking the easy way out in terms of condemning an outmoded old order which is vicious and impotent (Yang Jinshan) or facelessly destructive (Chen). It is the cinema's phantasmatic mission, after all, to castigate the world of order and authority and to celebrate pleasure and rebellion. Yet the fact that Judou is undone by her own love-child and Songlian by her sexual scheming may give pause to any unproblematical assumption of pleasure as moral rectitude. Rather, in bringing the forces of non-productive expenditure center-stage, the films highlight the entangling of the erotic with social dynamics.

Two scenes in *Judou* are pivotal not only to the conflictual dynamics of the narrative, its speakable and unspeakable strands, but to the display of celebratory modes within the normative social world of the film. One marks the birthday party that Yang Jinshan throws for his "son," actually the offspring resulting from Judou and Tianqing's clandestine relationship. Here all the rituals are followed, but when Tianqing is asked to make a speech congratulating the boy, he can only burst into tears and blabber incoherently. The hopelessness of his situation is forcefully brought home to him and to the viewers who know his predicament but not to the assembled guests. The other scene shows the funeral procession of Yang Jinshan and the bizarre practice of ritual mourning in which his widow and nephew must try to stop the cortege from reaching its destination forty-nine times. This scene is one of those that critics have cited as a distortion of historical authenticity and evidence of Zhang's Orientalizing of Chinese cultural practices. Its impact is certainly visceral, a literalization of the dead weight of the past and its continued power over the filmic present. But what is uncanny is that the very occasion that sets Judou and Tianqing free, namely the death of her husband, encircles them in social obligations more firmly than ever so that their moment of triumph is simultaneously their most bitter. In *Red Lantern*, structures have closed in even more firmly on human society, here symbolized by the mansion which also functions as "brothel," prison and slaughter-house, in short an efficient machinery of control. The film presents an interplay of (male) prohibition and (female) transgression, those twin processes out of which human history emerges. Bataille has noted that desire accompanies prohibition, as it does horror. The film evokes these contradictory emotions through its use of the mansion both as a source of visual pleasure and fearful alienation. As Songlian slowly succumbs to the norms and behavior patterns of this household, she hovers perilously between victimhood and victimization, her rebelliousness crushed and transformed by the weight of normative practices.

Bataille's critique of history and its relentless utilitarianism, then, may well be Zhang's own. Scattered throughout his writings, they appear succinctly in this passage:

The intellect ... constructs, under the name of science, a world of abstract things, copied from the things of the profane world, a partial world dominated by utility. Nothing is stranger, once we have surpassed it, than this world of the intellect where each thing must answer the question "What is the use of that?" We then realize that the mental process of abstraction never gets out of a cycle in which one thing is related to another, for which the first is useful; the other thing in turn must be useful ... for something else. The scythe is there for the harvest, the harvest for food, the food for labor, the labor for the factory where scythes are made ... Nowhere do we find a totality that is an end in itself, that is meaningful as such, that doesn't need to justify itself by pleading its usefulness for some other thing ...

To make this radical difference between two worlds perceptible, there is no finer example than the domain of erotic life, where the object is rarely situated on another plane than the subject.

(Bataille, 1993: 112)

The world of Zhang's films is clearly closed to the non-conformity that comes with a celebration of erotic excess and is signified only as that other realm of possibility in whose absence is contained the film's indictment of the existing order.

Eroticism and the mystical experience: Ishmael Bernal's *Himala*

So far, we have been examining the role of eroticism in certain New Cinemas as a way of articulating history's unspeakable paradoxes. Following Bataille, I have used the interpretive framework of taboo and transgression, the transactional nature of sexual arrangements and deployments of the body, in order to understand how eroticism functions in these films. Bataille's refusal to see sexuality in isolation from a complex of social and historical factors provides a necessary corrective to gender-biased accounts of women's representation in cinema. But Bataille also linked sensuality to the mystical experience and it is this aspect that is highlighted in Ishmael Bernal's unusual film, *Himala* (*Miracle*, 1982). While in two of the films discussed above, *The Home and the World* and *Yellow Earth*, there are distant intimations of transcendence – Bimala as mother-goddess of Bengal, Cuiqiao as the primordial Chinese spirit of endurance – *Himala* foregrounds the religious-mystical experience itself through a central female figure. *Himala* is part of what is known as the Philippine cinema's Second Golden Age that lasted roughly a decade beginning in 1975. More than any of Bernal's other films and those of the most celebrated Filipino director, Lino Brocka, this film clearly illustrates the relationship between eroticism and spirituality, and explores its implications for Filipino constructions of history and identity.

What Bataille finds common to sexual energy and the love of God is that "eroticism responds to man's determination to merge into the universe" (Bataille, 1993: 168). He even talks about the search for the other, although his searcher is invariably male. But what happens when the person who is absorbed by intimations of the sublime and feels enraptured by divine love is a woman? *Himala* is the story, based on an actual incident that took place in Cabra Island in 1967, of a young woman who claimed that she had seen the Virgin Mary. According to the film's screenplay writer, Ricky Lee, the island became commercialized as a result of her claim, an aspect which figures prominently in the narrative (quoted in Lim: 1). However, what is more germane to our purposes is the role that divine love and grace plays in the imaginative life of Elsa, the central character, and those around her. In a trajectory that replicates the throes of religious passion itself, Elsa's story allegorizes the uncertainties of Filipino cultural identity; her body and the violence it sustains represents the social body of this impoverished community.

Through Elsa's experience, the film takes a critical look at religious belief as a seductive, exploitative force, and so at the very nature of the mystical experience. Nora Aunor, with Vilma Santos, one of Philippine cinema's female superstars, plays the lead role in *Himala*, and through her, audiences confront their own fascination with human figures invested with near-divine appeal.

Himala's story revolves around Elsa, a young orphan girl who has been brought up by a kind woman and is given to dreams of spiritual grandeur. The action takes place in Cupang, an impoverished village that reflects the miserable lives of its inhabitants. The film opens with a series of short sequences that present the ambiguous nature of Elsa's mystical experience and local responses to it. Elsa has a "vision" of the Blessed Virgin on the day of a solar eclipse at the site of a bare and leafless tree on a lonely hilltop, signaled by a burst of light which falls on her uplifted face. Returning home, she confides in her mother, but is taken to the local shaman who delivers several lashes on her back to cure her of her delusions. Nevertheless, Elsa is back on the hillside where a friend finds her with bloody scratches on her arms and blood oozing through her fingers. Shocked and frightened, he brings back word to the other villagers. Elsa is then counseled by the local priest who lectures her on the dangers of inviting damnation on herself. But Elsa again prays at the hillside, and this time her mother and close friends pray alongside her. Now Elsa starts touch-healing and soon is importuned with long lines of the maimed and diseased hoping for a cure. Thus begins a massive upheaval in the life of the barrio. Tourists arrive, stalls are set up, and crowds come from far and near for Elsa's healing touch. Elsa's former employer sees the phenomenon as a commercial opportunity, and sells water Elsa has blessed while her followers, not to be outdone, charge a fee for her healing.

The turning point of this success story comes when, one day, as Elsa and her closest friend and follower, Chayong, are praying at the hill, they are found and raped by two drugged boys from the city nearby. Elsa is unable to invoke the divine intervention of the Blessed Virgin. When the two girls make their escape, they hide the true nature of the incident from everyone. But Elsa seems to lose her powers soon after. She fails to save a follower's children from death by cholera, her friend Chayong commits suicide, and Elsa finds herself pregnant. She is ridiculed and isolated and, eventually, decides to come clean. In a climactic scene, in which she addresses a large gathering on the hillside to say, "There are no miracles," she is shot through the heart and dies. Now martyred, she regains her stature and the town starts buzzing again.

Himala is marked by a fundamental ambiguity towards the nature of Elsa's claim, and thus towards mystical experience itself.[15] The question of the veracity of Elsa's vision is ultimately left unresolved, and her credibility is indeed undercut on several occasions: when her foster mother cautions her about her tendency to dreams of grandeur even as a young girl; when her friend Nimia confronts her with the question of what she has really seen after Chayong's death; and when, towards the end, Elsa confesses to the filmmaker-reporter that she is not sure if her mystical experience was genuine or not. Given these later scenes, one is left in doubt as to how to interpret the original episode at the beginning that showed a bright light momentarily shining on Elsa's face as she prayed during the solar eclipse, as also the mysterious bloody marks on her arms and hands noticed by a barrio native. Moreover, Elsa's "vision" includes an image of the Virgin Mary with blood on her chest, an image that foreshadows Elsa's own death at the end of the film. Once Elsa starts her "cures," however, the film foregrounds the public, commercialized nature of such spiritualism, with young boys blowing unused condoms for fun, stalls selling Elsa t-shirts, and crowds milling around. But the film's most pervasive and damaging metaphor for Elsa's mystical passion and its hold on the village is prostitution. Nimia is set up as Elsa's counterpart, her "Heaven" offering the pleasures of the senses to Elsa's spiritual comfort and cure. On one occasion, Nimia tells Elsa, "You are no better than I am; we are both prostitutes." Moreover, the reporter whose camera eye seems to provide a grounding in notions of objectivity and visual documentation in the film, is self-critical and disillusioned in the end, as he confesses to Elsa, "I violated you as much as anyone else!" In his relentless pursuit of Elsa in order to capture her every movement and glance on film, he turned her into an object for his own gain and visual pleasure.

Yet the film does not completely evacuate the realm of the spiritual. Inexplicably but happily for the inhabitants of the barrio, the rains come once Elsa is rumored to be pregnant, reigniting faith in her blessed state. The curse is finally lifted from that community, and a measure of joy erupts again. The orchestration of the final scene in which Elsa summons people to the hilltop for her revelatory speech is a powerful evocation of faith as a living force in many Third World societies. As the crowds assemble, all manner of diseased and decrepit bodies can be seen advancing towards Elsa in hopes of being cured by her or soothed by her words. All the more shocking to them, then, her admission that "there are no miracles," an admission that costs her her life. *Himala*, then, takes an unsparing look at the delusionary nature of faith in miracles and the mystical experience. It uses a 25-year-old woman, steeped in poverty, illiteracy, and social isolation as the contradictory icon of sublimated passion and repressed sexual desire. (The neighbors joke that Elsa is now too old to find a husband.) Elsa's rape is a supreme instance of her vulnerability as a woman and the emptiness of her spiritual pretensions. Through her, an entire cultural ethos is held up to critique and censure. At most, it can be said that the redemptive potential in this allegory consists in the willingness of the three central characters to face up to their own sense of degradation and take responsibility for their actions: Nimia leaves the barrio for Manila, with plans to start afresh; the reporter emerges out of his stint as the chronicler of the "himala" with a sobering view of his own omniscient gaze; and Elsa shows enormous courage in confronting the ghosts haunting her spirit and renouncing her privileged hold on the imagination of her fellow-beings. This film puts a spin on Bataille's notions of the link between death and sensuality in a way that he may not have envisaged.

Conclusion

In this study I have used Bataille to suggest that conceptions of the erotic are best articulated in terms of deeper social and psychic modalities, drawing examples from selected films that explore the boundaries between the sexual and the social/national. Female figures in these films are used to convey critical attitudes to history and society: "nationalist" configurations are represented through abnormal sexual relations, signified by an absence/failure of women's reproductive capacity. This dynamic of a charged sexuality lacking reproductive power may reflect the post-nationalist predicament of modernity as impasse, of life-in-death, of a future without vision. Undoubtedly these are bleak texts, with betrayal as a strong motif. If the bodies of women bear the brunt of the vicissitudes of history, it is the men who are actually sacrificed in history's slaughter-house. There may be a stern lesson here for all masculinist and narcissistic projects of nationalist redemption, even if women prove less than adequate to the task of creating society anew, for the erotics of history ironically signals the impossibility of access to the untranslatable language of sexual desire.

Notes

1 Irvin Schick's recent book, *The Erotic Margin*, is useful in this context.
2 In her excellent study of Spanish national identity as reconstructed through films, *Blood Cinema*, Marsha Kinder shows how this concern with history finds expression in the eroticization of violence.
3 Kinder's work on Oedipal mothers in Spanish cinema is worth noting here.
4 For obvious reasons, this last is not included in my paper, although Fassbinder's films lend support to the kinds of concerns and emphases I develop here.
5 A recent film, *Chinese Box* (1998), bears out this view as the Chinese actress, Gong Li, is made to represent "Chineseness" against Jeremy Irons' literally dying British colonial representative. While his is the consciousness that propels the film, her role is to appear beautiful and remote, with little or no access to (the English) language. She thus remains the eternally exotic "Other."

6 For Bataille, eroticism is the mark of inner desires on the pages of history and of history on our secret selves. Or as Homi Bhabha has written, "[I]n order to appear as material or empirical reality, the historical or social process must pass through an 'aesthetic' alienation, or 'privatization' of its public visibility" (Bhabha, 1992: 143).

7 For *Shame* ends with the terrifying image of its heroine as a nocturnal, marauding beast that calms its fires of sexual appetite by decimating men sexually. It is this characterization that leads Aijaz Ahmad to charge the author with misogyny and Sufiya Zenobia as being conceived in the worst traditions of woman as femme fatale, virgin-whore, castrating female.

8 At the same time, the films must also be seen as interventions in their own time and place. Ray's film, for instance, breaks the official taboo on kissing in post-independence Indian cinema while Chen's film is generally credited with inaugurating the Chinese New Cinema.

9 For a clear account of Tagore's role in the nationalist movement, his changing attitudes to Gandhian nationalism, see Dirks.

10 Compare the following remarks made by Anita Desai:

> It is clear that the figure of Bimala represents Bengal to Tagore. She is referred to frequently as "Mother" by one character or the other, suggesting that she is Durga, the mother-goddess and favorite deity of Bengal. Her husband offers her gold, jewels and tender love; Sandip offers his worship; and revolutionaries bow before her and touch her feet in obeisance. When Tagore writes of how her adoring husband begs Bimala to leave the zenana to which custom has kept her confined and come out into "the world", he seems to be coaxing Bengal out of the orthodoxy and superstition he so hated into the light of the modern age, to make her a fit deity for independent India.
>
> (Desai, 1985: 10–11)

11 It is interesting that the Indian filmmaker, Mrinal Sen, responded in almost the same terms when asked about the predominance of central female characters in his films. See "An Interview with Mrinal Sen" in Sumita Chakravarty, ed. *The Enemy Within: The Films of Mrinal Sen* (England: Flicks Books, 2000).

12 Rey Chow reads critics' responses as belonging to the binary of shi/xu, which contrasts depths with surfaces or superficiality (pp. 154–72). Her own ambivalent approach to the phenomenon of Zhang Yimou as Chinese filmmaker and her recuperative reading of his narrative and filmic approach to women's representation underscores the points I make about the "unspeakability" of certain textual formations.

13 It is also rumored that since Zhang and Gong Li were lovers, he was reluctant to "give" her other lovers.

14 Haili Kong writes:

> In *Judou*, Zhang Yimou boldly turns a beautiful four-hundred-year-old house in Shanxi into a visual maze where the living space is mixed with the working area, a small dye factory. The whole house is full of primitive machines and fabric banners that seem irrationally tall, complicated, and mysterious.
>
> (Kong, 1997: 103)

15 Filipino film scholar, Felicidad Lim, informed me that *Himala*, which has never been shown in the United States, was a commercial failure but a critical success in the Philippines. She also noted that her reading of the film as marked by ambiguity is in contrast to that of native Filipino critics, who saw Elsa as a complete fraud and the film as a critique of the Filipino people's obsession with miracles and superstitious beliefs. I am deeply indebted to Bliss (Felicidad) for making this film available to me and for helping me understand it. The decision to use it in the context of this study is, of course, mine.

Bibliography

Ahmad, Aijaz. "Salman Rushdie's *Shame*: Postmodern Migrancy and the Representation of Women", in his book *In Theory: Classes, Nations, Literatures*. London: Verso, 1992.

Alloula, Malek. *The Colonial Harem*. Minneapolis: University of Minnesota Press, 1986.

Bataille, Georges. *The Accursed Share*. Vols 2 and 3. New York: Zone Books, 1993.

Bataille, Georges. *Erotism: Death and Sensuality*, translated by Mary Dalwood. San Francisco: City Lights Books, 1986. Original publication date, 1957.

Bhabha, Homi. "The World and the Home." *Social Text* 31/32 (1992): 141–53.

Chow, Rey. *Primitive Passions: Visuality, Sexuality, Ethnography, and Contemporary Chinese Cinema*. New York: Columbia University Press, 1995.

Desai, Anita. Introduction to *The Home and the World* by Rabindranath Tagore. Harmondsworth: Penguin Books, 1985 (original publication 1919).

Dirks, Nicholas. "The Home and the World: The Invention of Modernity in Colonial India" in Robert Rosenstone, ed. *Revisioning History: Film and the Construction of a New Past*. Princeton: Princeton University Press, 1995.

Kinder, Marsha. *Blood Cinema: The Reconstruction of National Identity in Spain*. Berkeley: University of California Press, 1993.

Kong, Haili. "Symbolism Through Zhang Yimou's Subversive Lens in his Early Films." *Asian Cinema* 8.2 (1996/1997): 98–115.

Lee, Joann. "Zhang Yimou's *Raise The Red Lantern*: Contextual Analysis Through a Confucian/Feminist Matrix." *Asian Cinema* 8.1 (Spring, 1996): 120–7.

Lim, Felicidad C. "The Classical Realist Narrative And Its Subversion In The Heterogeneous *Himala*." Unpublished Paper.

Nowell-Smith, Geoffrey. *The Oxford History of World Cinema*. London: Oxford University Press, 1995.

Quing, Dai. "Raised Eyebrows for Raise the Red Lantern." Trans. Jeanne Tai. *Public Culture* 5.2 (1993): 333–7.

Rosenstone, Robert (ed.) *Revisioning History: Film and the Construction of a New Past*. Princeton: Princeton University Press, 1994.

Rushdie, Salman. *Shame*. London: Pan Books, 1983.

Schick, Irvin. *The Erotic Margin: Sexuality and Spatiality in Alterist Discourse*. London and New York: Verso, 1999.

Yang, Mayfair Mei-Hui. "Of Gender, State Censorship, and Overseas Capital: An Interview with Chinese Director Zhang Yimou." *Public Culture* 5.2 (1993): 297–313.

Zha, Jane Ying. "Excerpts From 'Lore Segal, Red Lantern And Exoticism'." *Public Culture* 5.2 (1993): 329–32.

Part III
Alternative cinemas in the age of globalization

Marvin D'Lugo has made many major contributions to the study of Spanish and Latin American cinemas. Yet one of his most challenging theses to-date can be found here when he contends that Third Cinema and the New Latin American Cinema in general were, in fact, only a historical phase in a broader pattern of *auteur* strategies that pre-dated the new cinemas of the 1960s.

In this context it should be noted that during the repeated crises within Latin American, African and Asian polities, waves of filmmakers either fled their homelands or, as in the less common case of Vietnam, emerged as did the Italian Neorealists from the ashes of destruction. The deeper motivations for the dis-locations of filmmakers from the beleaguered Third World, both voluntary and involuntary, are treated at some length by Hamid Naficy in *An Accented Cinema: Exilic and Diasporic Filmmaking*. Latin America, however, constitutes a special category even within this framework, for the self-same directors who theorized the transformation of society through the agency of the medium of cinema were also the earliest Third Cinema filmmakers to find themselves in the contradictory situation of gaining an international audience at the very moment they became outcasts in their own lands. As if in acknowledgement of the limits of their powers to influence the course of history in their attempt to overcome political force through popular action, Latin American *auteurs* resorted to a cinema of international co-production in which depictions of "national culture," according to D'Lugo, dialogize the very stereotypes and cultural clichés familiar to the international audiences of Second Cinema.

The situation of African cinema is no less riven by contradictions, not least those between film production in regions linguistically demarcated (as Francophone, Lusophone and Anglophone) as the result of a still oppressive colonial inheritance. Frank Ukadike, who addressed such issues in *Black African Cinema*, here treats the recent emergence of yet another postcolonial "cinema," in this case a video-film alternative that imitates Indian and American First Cinema, now that the disastrous policies of the IMF have rendered financing feature films impossible.

Despite the success of these video-films in creating an indigenous and increasingly sophisticated audience, their appeal according to Ukadike may be retrogressive (a "fast-forward to perpetual domination"). Nevertheless, he also notes that they have challenged the BBC-ish versions of English attempted by Nigerian feature films, that they have produced talented *auteurs* in Ghana, and that in general they have created a widespread appeal for topical forms of cultural exchange in West Africa.

These markedly different First and Second Cinema challenges to imported First Cinemas suggest an increasing cultural particularity in the now irreversible globalization process. They prove also that there is unlikely to be (and probably never was) a royal road to cinematic Xanadu.

4 Authorship, globalization, and the new identity of Latin American cinema

From the Mexican "ranchera" to Argentinian "exile"

Marvin D'Lugo

Of co-productions and cultural hybridity

Over the last two decades formulas for international co-productions with European producers and state agencies have increasingly dominated much Latin American film production.[1] These co-productions usually involve a dominant share of investment from European state television and quasi-state funding agencies, and more modest participation from various combinations of Latin American state organizations or individual producers.[2] For European investors, such collaborative schemes reflect a diversity of overseas interests in the region, primary of which has undoubtedly been the desire to exploit images of Latin America as exotic cultural objects. On the Latin American side, these collaborations appear driven by the imperative to reconstitute local markets after the long-term loss of more than half the Latin American movie-going audience during the 1980s.[3] Film authors have reemerged as key players in this Latin American audiovisual cultural scene of recent years. Struggling to survive creatively, compelled by circumstance to serve as mediators between the business and art of Latin American film, they find themselves forced to negotiate their own political and artistic visions in accordance with the commercial demands of global film finance arrangements.

Transnational projects in fact are neither new to Latin American cinema nor especially unique. From its origins, Latin American film production has been shaped as much by global or internationalist pressures as by local or nationalist goals. Paulo Antonio Paranaguá has recently called for a more complex reassessment of the geopolitical dynamics of Latin American cinema that acknowledges this regional cinema's historical positioning in a triangular relationship with both the US and Europe that has helped shape the essential global dynamics of local production (Paranaguá, 2001, pp. 12–13).[4] This essay seeks to historicize the interplay among local, regional and the global interests in Latin American cinema as a phenomenon that, though dramatically intensified around recent cinematic co-productions, also requires a closer scrutiny of the artistic practices that historically have shaped these co-productions, especially the exploitation of authorial cinema in the region. Such an inquiry will lead us to see the ways in which global processes affecting film production relate to the broader questions of cultural identity as impacted by mass media.

At the core of the historical and aesthetic questions guiding the development of Latin American cinema in global contexts is the nature of cultural hybridity that without exception seems to have characterized regional cinematic development. Though often dismissed simplistically as merely the mixing of local and foreign elements, characters, styles, and speech in particular films, hybrid culture, as theorized by Néstor García Canclini, involves a deeper interrogation of modes of cultural production. At its roots lies a textual process that involves the audience of such hybrid cultural productions in a rethinking of the hierarchy between center and periphery (García Canclini, 1995, p. 241), whereby territorial identities are blurred but, importantly, the focus is not on some meaningless blending, but rather a redressing of the powerful asymmetry of the core/periphery relation (García Canclini, 1995, p. 266). Out of the process of hybridization developed through the aggressive entrepreneurial schemes of multinational groups, a new type of Latin American film has emerged that does not adhere to the clichéd descriptions of neocolonial exploitation or, as recent popular discourse would have it, of globalization. Rather, the most serious and significant of these co-produced films challenge the assumptions of the core/periphery model by generating cultural texts that have as their underlying project the co-production of newly emerging cultural identities. In the context of global culture markets, as Stuart Hall describes it, "[t]he margins begin to speak. The margins begin to contest, the locals begin to come to representation" (Hall, 1997, pp. 53).

Roots of Latin American co-productions

In terms of film production and distribution, transnationality has usually meant the exploitation of Latin America either as a potential market for European-produced films or, at best, a condescending appreciation of the exotic stereotypes of the region embodied in those Latin American actors like Ramón Novarro, Dolores Del Río, Carmen Miranda, and more recently, Sonia Braga, who have made careers abroad. That asymmetrical relation has been restated time and again as a process of commercial dependency and industrial underdevelopment that views Latin America as a fertile market for the consumption of cultural products produced in Europe and the US (Paranaguá 1996, pp. 210–12; Getino, 1998, pp. 147–53).

During the silent period such patterns of dependency became firmly established (Getino, 1998, pp. 20–1). With the early sound period, however, relevant modifications of the paradigm began to emerge. In Mexico, Brazil, and Argentina the desire for local language and cultural themes helped forge "national" film industries around the impetus of sound technology, perhaps traceable, as Paranaguá argues, to the profound impact of the first talkie, *The Jazz Singer*, in 1927 (Paranaguá, 1989, p. 13; Monteagudo and Bucich, 2001, p. 11). It is, however, Hollywood's efforts to retain its commercial hegemony in the region through the failed "multiple version" model where, in fact, the first significant alteration of the national/transnational interface in Latin American cinema is to be noted. These productions involved various casts of different language speakers shooting versions of the same film for export to different countries.[5] Given the high number of Spanish-speakers throughout the world, the "Film Hispano," or Spanish-language production, was perceived as potentially the most marketable of these multiple language versions. These films, of which more than 100 were made by 1938 when the practice was abandoned, were shot either in Hollywood or Joinville, outside of Paris, with largely unknown pan-Hispanic casts. By design, they lacked the cultural specificity of any one region to facilitate the widest possible distribution.

In general, the model failed to attract audiences in Spanish-speaking countries due to Hollywood's inability to see the Latin American audience as more than a homogeneous mass undifferentiated by local culture (Paranaguá, 1996, p. 213). One singular exception to the wave of failed productions was the series of tango films made in Paris and later New York starring the already world-famous Argentine tango singer, Carlos Gardel.[6] In 1931, while on a European concert tour, Gardel was contracted by Paramount to make the first of what would eventually be four full-length sound features singing tangos (*Luces de Buenos Aires/ Buenos Aires Lights* [1931], *Espérame/ Wait For Me* [1932], *La casa es seria/ The House Is Serious* [1932], *Melodía de arrabal/ Melody of the Slums* [1932]). The success of these films in Latin America and Spain was followed by a US contract for Gardel which enabled him to make four more Spanish-language sound films in Paramount's New York studios (*Cuesta abajo/ Down Hill* [1934], *El tango en Broadway/ The Tango on Broadway* [1934], *El día que me quieras/ The Day You Love Me* [1935], *Tango Bar* [1935], as well as a featured appearance in the English-language *The Big Broadcast of 1936* which starred Bing Crosby).

There was little effort to develop these as artistic productions, their sole purpose being to cater quickly and cheaply to the Spanish-language audience that had once been a captive market for Hollywood products. Yet audiences reacted enthusiastically when the Gardel films were shown in Buenos Aires, for instance, and demanded an encore of the musical numbers. Gardel himself complained about the obstacles these production schemes posed for anything remotely approaching a true flavor of Buenos Aires or Argentine musical culture (Monteagudo and Bucich, 2001, p. 33). But cultural authenticity was not the motivation for such films. It was, rather, to exploit the potential for a musical form that capitalized on sound technology and on the international star status of the singer. Not inconsequential in this formula was the tango itself as a hybrid music and dance form that combined both European and Latin American elements and, in the decade preceding the advent of sound cinema, had become an international rage (Urra, 1999, p. 146; Taylor, 1976, pp. 284–8).

The Gardel films are thus a significant historical antecedent to subsequent development of a commercially viable transnational hybrid cinematic form in that they were the earliest demonstration of something that no local film producer of the period could provide, namely the magnet effect of both a cultural object – the tango – and a charismatic star – Gardel – who could appeal to both Latin Americans and to a wider audience outside the region. In doing so these films posed problematic issues of identity politics of Latin American cinema, as Paranaguá contends, involving questions of imitation versus cultural authenticity and the persistent attraction-repulsion of the Hollywood model of filmmaking (Paranaguá, 1996, p. 216). But these were questions scholars and others would only raise in subsequent decades. From the immediate perspective of local Latin American producers, the message of the Gardel films was that there existed Latin American musical traditions that seemed to embody the local culture but could also appeal to the global audiences.

The Gardel phenomenon may well have been the inspiration for the development of Latin American musical genre films beginning in the mid 1930s. This was a home-grown folkloric cinema that included Mexican *"ranchera"* musical comedies, Argentine tango films, and Brazilian *"chanchadas,"* distinctive musical genres of popular inspiration and narrative style. Though rooted in local cultural stereotypes, many of these films were able to circulate beyond national borders during the first decade of sound. The most conspicuous successes among these were the *ranchera* musicals that became popular throughout the region beginning with Fernando de Fuentes's 1936 *Allá en el Rancho Grande/ Over at the Big Ranch*. Unlike the Gardel films, these were locally produced films, albeit films that seemed to be inspired as imitations of Hollywood's musical genre (Monsiváis, 2000:, p.ms to create a more integrated regional film market than Latin Americans had yet experienced.

Another, more artistically powerful type of film that also demonstrated a similar transnational appeal, comprised those works that from time to time transcended their region of production by virtue of their dramatic force or some element of their content and were shown successfully at festivals in Europe or else distributed commercially there or in the US. These films were either the products of what would come to be identified with authorial cinema or works that helped to establish certain filmmakers with the aura of auteur. The earliest examples of this paradigm may be seen in Mexico in the films of Emilio "Indio" Fernández in the 1940s beginning with *María Candelaria* (1943), followed by Luis Buñuel's Mexican films of the 1950s. Argentina, which, during the first decade of sound films had been the largest producer of Spanish-language films in the region but ceded that position to Mexico in the 1940s (Schnitman, 1984, pp. 116–17), was represented by the early careers of Leopoldo Torre Nilsson and Fernando Ayala beginning in the late 1950s. This was followed by the government-funded *"nueva ola"* (New Wave) of the 1960s (López, 1985, pp. 54–7).

Like the musical genre films, these early expressions of Latin American film auteurism represent a significant backdrop against which to read subsequent strategies of co-productions in that they reaffirmed the potential of Latin American films to circulate locally, regionally and transnationally. Though generally conceived of as popular commercial fare, these films that touted the name of a recognizable and potentially marketable director eventually came to be seen as indicators of a practical strategy for local production to connect with foreign audiences and to develop potentially new prestige markets abroad. During that crucial twenty-year period Latin American films garnered a series of awards at European festivals beginning with a prize for Gabriel Figueroa's cinematography for *Allá en el Rancho Grande* at the Venice Film Festival in 1937, and continuing with prizes at Cannes for Emilio Fernández in 1946 and Luis Buñuel in 1950.

As prestige accrued to the Latin American cinema generally, the figure of the film auteur became more firmly aligned with certain national cinemas. The most prominent of these author-nation alignments was that of Luis Buñuel who, by virtue of his previous European career, was seen, almost from his arrival in Mexico in 1946, as an international figure. After the artistic triumph of *Los olvidados* at the 1950 Cannes Film Festival, his Mexican films easily found European and US distributors. He was regularly sought out by European producers and made four international co-productions for French and US producers, all shot in Mexico but with notable international casts.

The essence of Buñuel's success was the distinctive combination of a unique authorial identity, nurtured by newspaper profiles of his personal eccentricities, the presumed "Mexicanness" of various productions that seemed to play well at European film festivals, and the low budgets that made Mexico in general and Buñuel in particular attractive commodities for co-productions with European partners. Thus, even before it because fashionable to speak of auteurs, Buñuel had come to represent for many the ideal model of the filmmaker as cultural and commercial negotiator between Latin America and international commercial film interests. At the same time that his films brought international attention to Mexico and Latin America, his story served as an inspiration to aspiring filmmakers who saw in his particular triumph their own potential successes.[7]

Solanas's *Tangos*: the critique and affirmation of the authorial model

The figure of the commercially viable film auteur posed by the Buñuel model as a solution to the commercial marginality of Latin American cinema is not without its problematic features. Intended to function as a form of negotiation between local and global cultures and markets, it occupies a seemingly contradictory liminal position which is powerfully depicted in Fernando Solanas's 1985 Argentine-French co-production, *Tangos: el exilio de Gardel/ Tangos: the Exile of Gardel*. As his title indicates, Solanas intentionally positions his film within the history of the transnational scenario of local icons – Gardel and the tango – used as cultural capital for foreign markets. His objective is not only to capture a specific moment and condition in Argentine history related to the Dirty War, the six-year military dictatorship that ran from 1976 to 1983 involving the plight of Argentine political exiles, but also to pose as narrative problem the asymmetry of cultural and economic demands from international partners on the creative process of Latin American auteurs. *Tangos* thus affords us a unique view of the inherent attractiveness and contradictions of Latin American authorial cinema.

Solanas is no mere accidental auteur. Long before *Tangos* he had achieved a unique status in international film circles as one of the principal theorists of New Latin American cinema in the 1960s. He was a radical firebrand who argued against both national and authorial cinemas as being deceptive products of neocolonialist influence. Instead, he advocated a politically aggressive "Third Cinema," the development of which he theorized in an influential article, "For a Third Cinema," co-authored by Octavio Getino. By the 1980s, after his exile in France, he had become one of the principal advocates of international co-productions of authorial cinema that for some suggested a reversal of his earlier political stance. As a close examination of *Tangos* reveals, however, Solanas's sense of the problematic cultural politics of Latin American cinema in unequal global exchanges is still clearly in evidence (Ciria, 1995, pp. 204–5).

There is a scene late in the film in which that stance is pointedly dramatized as a group of Argentine political exiles in Paris stages a rehearsal of parts of their "*tanguedia*," a political tango show that, principally through dance, recounts aspects of the recent Dirty War. This particular rehearsal of the *tanguedia* has been arranged in an effort to persuade French backers to support this production. After seeing the dress rehearsal, however, the audience is somewhat baffled; one of them even complains that the *tanguedia* is simply "too Argentine," and therefore beyond the knowledge and interest of French audiences.

Importantly, the *tanguedia* alters the Europeans' notion of what the tango is as a dance by hybridizing the form, making it "political" in ways that coincide with the Argentine tradition but are at odds with the non-culturally specific foreign clichéd notion of the dance. In this way part of the self-consciousness of the film's theme is the negotiation of reinscriptions of local culture to promote the transnational. The dialogue between the show's creators and the on-screen audience of the rehearsal self-consciously replicates as plot the very problematic of Solanas's own film as it must struggle in aesthetic, cultural, and financial spheres to construct its foreign audience simply to be able to exist. To do this, Solanas, like the authors of the *tanguedia*, seeks to transform within *Tangos* the signs and artifacts of national culture into cultural capital in the global marketplace. To that end, the staged play-within-the-film combines in a single genre two of the most successfully marketed tropes of Argentine national culture: the tango, which since the 1930s has proven to be a marketable international commodity for Argentine films; and the Dirty War, a more recent cinematic construction of Argentineness.

Solanas's script gives narrative prominence to the two authors of the *tanguedia*, the unseen Juan Uno, who has stayed back in Buenos Aires in order to remain in touch with his native culture, and Juan Dos, who is in Paris seeking backers to stage the production. Juan Dos waxes euphoric about Argentine literary tradition as part of the inspiration for the *tanguedia* and rebuffs all efforts to make his production coherent. These features, combined with Solanas's insistence on narrating national history as dance and refusing to admit a simple narrative closure to the story of political exile, underscore the film's dense, self-referential layering of hybrid forms. Among these is the playful rewriting of the Hollywood genre of the backstage musical, a genre which the film satirizes while appearing otherwise to embrace (Ciria, 1995, p. 207). Solanas mixes the marks of the national with the global in ways that emphasize for the viewing subject the complexity of cultural hybridity in a transnational context. For him, as for other filmmakers sensitive to the problem of cultural identity in the context of globalization, hybridity is a form of negotiation. As noted by cultural theorist, Néstor García Canclini:

> In the exchange of traditional symbols with international communications circuits ... questions about identity and the national ... do not disappear. The conflicts are not erased ... They are placed in a different register ... the autonomy of each culture is rethought.
>
> (García Canclini, 1995, pp. 240–1)

Thus, the film ceases to be about a dance or a group of exiles and becomes an interrogation of the tensions between cosmopolitan and folkloric impulses that vie for dominance as Argentine cultural products enter a global market.

In analyzing the impact of globalization on film culture, Fredric Jameson describes "the disappearance of the specifically national cultures and their replacement, either by a centralized commercial production for world export or by their own mass-produced neo-traditional images" (Jameson, 1995, p. 3). Jameson perceives a certain category of film work that emerges as a response to this process, imbued with what he calls a "geopolitical aesthetic," that is, the deployment of mythic narratives through which filmmakers "allegorize our consumption and construction of the object works in terms of Utopian wishes and commercially programmed habits" with the goal in mind of refashioning national allegory, as he says, "into a conceptual instrument for grasping our new being-in-the-world" (Jameson, 1995, p. 3). Solanas's film, indeed, demonstrates that diagnostic machinery within the filmic texts as it continually poses questions about the place of national culture within the world system.

Globalization and the privilege of film authors

What made it possible for Solanas's film to circulate successfully in European markets was as much its constructed status as author cinema as its condition as a co-production. Yet, as the director well knows, so-called "author cinema" has long been a problematic category in Latin American film culture. In the sixties and seventies, filmmakers sought to re-articulate authorship often through a necessary collaboration with state agencies who fostered their work as part of a national cultural project. This was indeed the case with the efforts to "nationalize" Mexico's film industry through the state's financial support of filmmakers like Felipe Cazals, Jaime Humberto Hermosillo, Paul Leduc, and Arturo Ripstein during the Echeverría regime. A similar alignment of state-sponsored authorial cinema emerged in Brazil, under the rubric of *Cinema Nôvo*, and in Argentina with its "new wave."

In contrast to these moves, the theorists and filmmakers of the emerging "New Latin American Cinema," Solanas principal among them, sought to contest the aestheticism of European-style auteurism by "transferring the individual agency of authorship to mechanisms encouraging cooperative models" (Pick, 1993, p. 39) that combined artistic creativity with cultural and social militancy. Thus, as Zuzana Pick contends, the "Third Cinema" movement, as well as New Latin American cinema generally, saw a curious reaffirmation of the film auteur by men such as Fernando Birri and Solanas in Argentina, Glauber Rocha in Brazil, and Tomás Gutiérrez Alea and Julio García Espinosa in Cuba, all of whom envisioned some form of film authorship in opposition to neocolonial state authority. This was a notion of authorship mitigated by the practices and goals of production collectives rather than merely of the individual filmmaker's desire for self-expression.

By the mid 1980s, however, film authors whose earlier work and careers had been as divergent as that of Ripstein in Mexico, Solanas in Argentina, and Alea in Cuba, all positioned in similar ways as authorial icons representing their respective national culture within the global market. In each case, their well-established reputations as oppositional, anti-status quo, resistance figures had become refigured as national auteurs, principally through international film festivals which privileged the authorial as an expression of the national.[8]

Such refigurings of auteurism along nationalistic lines, though inevitable in the international film market culture, seemed a retreat from the political and ideological redefinition of a decade earlier, as indeed it was. Despite efforts to develop other marketable auteurs in Cuba, Alea remained throughout the 1980s, almost to the exclusion of all others, the principal Cuban transnational filmmaker. His films that were most commercially and critically successful abroad were those that depicted the ideological binds of socialism – *Hasta cierto punto/ Up to a Certain Point* (1986), *Fresa y chocolate/ Strawberry and Chocolate* (1992) and *Guantanamera* (1995). It was no coincidence that these were also the films that most explicitly reinforced for international audiences the largely erroneous romanticized figure of Alea, the heroic auteur as an agent of resistance to Cuban socialism.

A similar phenomenon occurred with Solanas, although less a coincidence than the effort by the filmmaker to promote the national politics of "redemocratization" through the self-conscious foregrounding of his own auteurist practices (Ciria, 1995, pp. 210–11). As *Tangos: el exilio de Gardel* (1985), *Sur/ South* (1987) and *El viaje/ The Journey* (1992) circulated through international film festival circuits, their screenings were regularly accompanied by the press image of Solanas as a heroic figure linked to Argentine culture through various national marks of national identity (the condition of exiles from the Dirty War in *Sur*, solidarity with the larger Latin American community in *El viaje*). By design, he fashioned his authorial persona as a voice of popular cultural values fighting against the excesses of reactionary politics and ideology.

Ripstein represents perhaps the most peculiar circumstance of the three. Once self-defined as the heir of Buñuel's iconoclastic cinema, he had undergone progressive transformations owing to the political and economic fortunes of Mexico's film industry since the 1960s. By the early nineties, he had emerged as a deterritorialized *auteur* whose films posed ever increasing critiques of Mexican film culture and society. Although supported by both Mexican and foreign (largely Spanish) producers, his critically acclaimed films could not sustain themselves commercially in Mexico. The essence of this dialogical authorial style, as brilliantly depicted in his 1996 film, *Profundo carmesí/ Deep Crimson*, is a critical debunking of the idols and icons of Mexican patriarchal society and cultural stereotypes, specifically those of motherhood and machismo, themes calculated to appeal to the transnational markets of auteur cinema.

Framed discursively, both in their production and exhibition by a market imperative, the works of these filmmakers thus came to embody the dialectical play of the local and the global. They emerge from a particular sensibility that spiritually coincided with the concept of exilic transnational authors, described by Hamid Naficy as "partial subjects and undecidable multiple objects, [who] are capable of producing ambiguity and doubt about the absolutes and taken-for-granted values of their home and host societies" (Naficy, 1996, pp. 124–5).

Consequently, the identity of the author in much recent author cinema is understood not so much in terms of self-fashioned identity in the romanticized mold of fifties and sixties auteurism, but as the result of a marketing strategy[9] with the precise aim of redefining the audiences and purpose of the national cinema in the face of the collapse of those local markets. This kind of authorship was to have an understandable attraction, both to agents of the national cinema (local producers, state agencies, cultural critics), as well as to certain international audiences. Not only does the evocation of a recognizable and esteemed filmmaker serve as an emblematic figure of local cultural pride, but also, as Timothy Corrigan has observed of the phenomenon, "the increasing importance … of the auteur [worked] as a commercial strategy for organizing audience reception, as a critical concept bound to distribution and marketing aims that identify and address the potential cult status of an auteur" (Corrigan, 1991, p. 103).

Less clear, however, is the significance of this kind of cultural production in the context of artistic creation and the position of artists caught between the interests of the state on one side and international commercial interests on the other. Again, García Canclini notes: "The artists and writers who contributed most to the independence and professionalizing of the cultural field have made the critique of the state and of the market the axes of their argumentation"

(García Canclini, 1995, p. 67). He goes on to argue that in the case of a growing number of Latin American authors and intellectuals, while their antistatist position remains firm, it is "joined with the defense of a conception at once traditional and modern, ambivalent, toward the autonomy of the artistic field" (García Canclini, 1995, p. 67). It is in the context of this ambivalence that we can view recent author cinema as efforts to define a form of cultural production and the place of the artist in it that is not a sellout either to the forces of commerce or to the state.

Modes of reterritorializing Latin American cinema

Implied in nearly all discussion of the economic state of Latin American national cinemas is the notion that there is somehow a coincidence of geographic space with the static populations defined by local cinematic production as national communities. Yet, geography is often a deceptive indicator of the true audiences of these national cinemas. As García Canclini suggests, there has been a continuing process by degree of deterritorialization and reterritorialization in Latin America media. He describes these two processes respectively as "the loss of the 'natural' relation of culture to geographic and social territories and, at the same time, certain relative, partial territorial relocations of old and new symbolic productions" (García Canclini, 1995, p. 229). Indeed, this migration of audience begs the question of the true nature of the national in terms of audiovisual cultures. In that same light, one needs also to recognize, as Richard Maxwell contends, that

> ... infranational and supranational economic regions have their own boundaries despite political nationalisms of whatever size ... capital produces its own media geography on its march for environments of the highest return ... The economic region has no provincial, regional, or national borders.
>
> (Maxwell, 1995, p. 151)

Understood in this context, national cinema is much less a sacrosanct expression of national culture than a particularized discursive formation, the product of a local film culture intended to represent that culture commercially not only within, but also beyond its own borders.

While seeming to exploit or promote the cultural capital of their respective national cinemas as globally marketable commodities, some Latin American film auteurs have over the last decade sought to resist mere standardization of global film patterns by channeling some of the reterritorial dynamics of which García Canclini speaks into a new form of identity politics. It is instructive to consider briefly the patterns of one such group of filmmakers who have worked in Argentine cinema, which arguably has shown itself to be the most highly developed area for such reterritorialized film industries. While the discussion of these recent tendencies appears to suggest an argument for a sacrosanct

Argentine "national" cinema, my objective is actually quite the opposite. In tracing the development of co-productions in the decade of Argentina's redemocratization following the Dirty War, we observe highly original and creative ways that individual filmmakers have sought to weaken the hold of what Andrew Higson has called "the limiting imagination of national cinema" (Higson, 2000, pp. 63–4). Implicit in their work is the sense that national cinema serves only to mask the commercial and cultural realities of global film culture "as modern communication networks operate on an increasingly trans-national basis and cultural commodities are widely exchanged across national borders …, dissolving rather than sustaining the concept of the nation" (Higson, 2000, pp. 66–7). Like the Solanas model established by *Tangos*, with its strong self-referential style, these films function with the double imperative of constructing new markets, but also of affirming a new position within which local culture is not an exclusionary term, but rather the basis of expanding cultural diversity beyond the narrow confines of a state-based national cinema. The examination of their strategies and approaches thus brings us closer to understanding the textual and contextual denseness that belies the simple label of international co-productions throughout Latin America.

"The universality of human-rights themes"

To compensate foreign audiences for their ignorance of local culture or history, Latin American filmmakers often return to recognizable genres, specifically imaginary as a rhetorical gesture that bridges the gaps in cultural knowledge. As Marsha Kinder has argued in the instance of Spanish cinema (Kinder, 1993, pp. 65–73), the melodramatic imagination is a highly malleable form of expression, cutting across various national cultures and allowing for a series of culturally-specific inflections with ideological functions that run the political gamut from reactionary fascist meanings to highly subversive counter-cultural forms. As Ana López argues, melodrama in Latin American contexts has been used cinematically to work through "the problematic of cultural underdevelopment as well as a series of specific gender empowerments" (López, 1993, pp. 150–1).

Luis Puenzo's *The Official Story* is clearly the most commercially and critically successful model of the ways in which genre substitutes for a culturally specific knowledge of local culture. This Argentine-US co-production follows a model popularized only a few years earlier in Costa-Gavras's mainstream American film, *Missing* (1982), in which the atrocities related to the 1973 Chilean military coup were framed through the melodramatic tale of a father's search for his missing son. That film marked the textual strategy and clearly established the mainstream market niche for films like *The Official Story*. Puenzo formalizes the strategy that will recur in a number of subsequent Argentine productions by transposing the local thematics revolving around the horrific acts of the military dictatorship of 1976–83 into a register of universal, humanitarian themes. His implicit project is to redraw the affective borders of the nation by aligning certain narratives with the ethical values deemed universal. In *The Official Story* it is the generals' trafficking in the kidnapping and adoption of the children of the "disappeared." Not unrelated to this linkage of culturally-specific material with universal themes is the effort to reshape cinematic narration along more accessible lines.[10] As some critics have noted, the goal of greater accessibility for the film is mirrored in its visual style and editing which are more reminiscent of television soap operas than of feature-length films (Beceyro, 1997, pp. 26–9).

A similar displacement of culturally specific themes by the broader genre rhetoric of melodrama, is one of the most notable features of María Luisa Bemberg's *Camila* (1984). The enunciative strategy of that film is to recast the story of nineteenth-century political repression under the Rosas dictatorship as a melodramatic narration of resistance by a young woman to patriarchal tyranny ideologically aligned with the state. The pattern here is to use melodrama which, besides its near-universal appeal, is also culturally-specific to the development of Latin American cinemas from a period even prior to the advent of synchronized sound (Monsiváis, 2000, pp. 66–7).

Lita Stantic's 1992 film, *Un muro de silencio/A Wall of Silence*, perhaps best sums up the logic of this strategy of universalization when one character, a British filmmaker, explains to her Argentine hosts that European audiences would be interested in a film about the "disappeared" of the Dirty War because of Europe's own history of Nazi concentration camps. Here, we see the humanitarian theme conjoined with a series of dialogues and incorporated newsreel footage to familiarize a non-Argentine audience with the complex historical background that led up to the Dirty War.

Such efforts serve a double pedagogical function. They orient international audiences through well-established rhetorical tropes that undermine the presumed exoticism and difference between Argentina and other Western societies. In addition, and of no less significance, the streamlining of often complex details of recent Argentine history creates an internal distance for national audiences that enables spectators to see their own culture from a position of renewed critical distance.

Authorial biography

Given the international audience's ignorance of the complexity of most Latin American history, the biographical figure of the film author often functions to confer a unity and coherence to international auteur cinema. Its source, to some degree, lies with the *politique des auteurs* promoted by the French New Wave with its emphasis on the personality of the auteur as decisive in the creation of the filmic work. Here the precedent of Buñuel in Mexico seems again relevant as a model of a filmmaker whose personality as defying bourgeois social norms was often read into his films. More recently this is strikingly the case in the filmic and biographic interplay of themes of gender politics in the works of María Luisa Bemberg. Having written a number of screenplays for films by Raúl de la Torre and Fernando Ayala before directing her first film at the age of fifty-eight, Bemberg had a relatively slim filmography consisting of only six feature-length films made between 1980 and her death in 1993. This abbreviated corpus, however, brought her resounding international success that exceeded that of most of her Argentine contemporaries. The reason, in part, may lie in Bemberg's development of a series of films that clearly linked the local social thematics with issues of the status of women (as embodied in her own situation) within Argentine society.

The first two films she directed, *Momentos/ Moments* (1980) and *Señora de nadie/Nobody's Lady* (1982), were made under the tight censorship imposed by the military regime. It was not until her third film, *Camila* (1984), with censorship restrictions having been eliminated, that Bemberg was to achieve astounding and far-reaching success. The Oscar-nominated film was, again, an Argentine-Spanish co-production, set during the terrible nineteenth-century dictatorship of Juan Manuel Rosas, that told the story of a young woman of the upper-class who transgresses societal prohibitions by falling in love with and running off with a young Spanish priest. The two are hunted down and executed. The film cleverly blends Bemberg's own feminism with the backdrop of violent political repression against the Argentine people. In no small measure, the film succeeded because of the clear link between its melodramatic tale and the recent history of political repression in Argentina (Ciria, 1995, p. 162). In interviews, Bemberg did not shy away from the notion that her films were at least spiritually, if not at times literally, autobiographical (Bemberg, 2000, pp. 218–20). Indeed, her screen work is populated by strong female characters often drawn from protected upper-class backgrounds, as is the case of Charlotte, the diminutive heroine of *De eso no se habla/ Let's Not Talk About That* (1993), or women who rebel against their social and marital status, as in *Señora de nadie* (1981) or *Camila* (1984), or women who find themselves trapped within prisons built by the constraining social and gender restrictions of conservative Latin patriarchal society, *Miss Mary* (1986) and *Yo, la peor de todas/I, the Worst of All* (1989).

In collaboration with her enterprising producer, Lita Stantic, Bemberg effectively moved toward co-producing her own films with foreign companies. The commercial promotion of her unique "celebrity" persona as a feminist filmmaker with a penchant for making films about women who defy patriarchy helped circulate a more heroic view of Argentine culture to counter the general image of a regressive and backward country forged by international media during and after the dictatorship of the military junta. Not only did this defiant, feminized view of Argentina find a sympathetic reception from liberal international audiences, but Bemberg's use of international actors in leading roles (Spain's Imanol Arias in *Camila*; Britain's Julie Christie in *Miss Mary*; Italy's Dominique Sanda in *Yo, la peor de todas* and Marcelo Mastroianni in *De eso no se habla*) also helped to expand the potential foreign market for her work. As John King reminds us, Bemberg was the first Latin American director to make "systematic use of non-Spanish speaking 'stars' " in her films (King, 2000, p. 25).

The conscious effort to move beyond the "natural" national audience of Argentine cinema is nowhere more apparent than in the film often called Bemberg's masterpiece, *Yo, la peor de todas*. An Argentine-French-Spanish co-production, with the Spanish actress, Assumpta Serna, and the Italian actress, Dominique Sanda, in leading roles, the film was Bemberg's first incursion into apparently non-Argentine material. A reconstruction of aspects of the life of Sor Juana Inés de la Cruz, the seventeenth-century Mexican nun who achieved notoriety as a poet, playwright, and intellectual, the film was based on Sor Juana's biography written by the revered Mexican poet, Octavio Paz. It told the story of the particular difficulties Sor Juana (Assumpta Serna) had with ecclesiastical authorities who persecuted her for what she and others saw as her status as a woman.

While seemingly a break in period and subject-matter, *Yo, la peor de todas* reveals Bemberg's strong authorial signature in its focus on the efforts to force the submission of women to patriarchal institutions, here represented by the Spanish Church officials of Spanish colonial Mexico. In this manner the issue of reterritorialization goes to the very heart of the film's conceptual center. While the story and its biographical subject are rooted in colonial Mexico, its parallels suggest a reworking of the very same national issues as those in *Camila*: divine love versus passion; the linkage of a tyrannical Church with the state that persecutes the individual. In this way, Bemberg was able to reinscribe the specific configuration of the Dirty War theme as well as to incorporate a broader attack on religious fanaticism into the narrative.[11]

In *Yo, la peor de todas*, certainly, the inclusion of an international cast tellingly opens up the narrative to another suggestive transnational reading that effectively erases any easy identification with a single national cinema or culture. The principal actors include one Catalan actress, two Argentines, and an Italian. Yet, binding these seemingly dispersed figures together is a story that works dialogically, emphasizing for Latin American audiences parallels with recent Argentine history at the same time that it gives centrality to the broader theme of the problematic status of women in patriarchal society. Bemberg's self-identification with feminism as the core of her cinema reveals with striking clarity the potential force of the authorial as a way of rechanneling the questions of gender and nationness within a wider commercial and discursive field.

Geographic repositionings

Lita Stantic's 1992 *Un muro de silencio/A Wall of Silence* serves as an even more emphatic model of the dynamic interplay of cinematic/cultural spaces in the global system as theorized by Jameson. An Argentine-Mexican co-production with Channel 4, London, the film marks the directorial debut of Stantic, a woman closely connected with Argentine film productions of resistance (Bemberg, Hector Olivera). A key figure in the territorialization of Argentine cinema over the past two decades, she has shown herself to be both independent –working beyond the alliances that have formed the usual male-dominated commercial patterns of Argentine film – and creative – continually seeking to redefine the progressive political position of Latin American film as a critical intervention in regional cultural politics.

Un muro de silencio is a striking demonstration of Stantic's formidable directorial talents. From its opening frame, the film effects a temporal distanciation by looking back on the Dirty War from a vantage of approximately a decade after the events it interrogates. The story focuses on two women. Silvia Massini (Ofelia Medina)[12] is the wife of one of the disappeared; she has now begun a new life with her adolescent daughter, Elisa, and her second husband, Ernesto. Kate Benson (Vanessa Redgrave) is a British filmmaker who has come to Buenos Aires to make a documentary about Silvia, based on the script by Bruno (Lautaro Murúa), a professor of political science with whom Silvia had earlier had an affair. Silvia refuses to see Kate, but, mysteriously, as the filmmaker rehearses scenes from Bruno's script, Silvia begins to relive moments in her own past life, which textually become intertwined with Kate's version. Thus, the two women who are seen "representing Argentine history" become psychic and narrational doubles.

Vanessa Redgrave in the role of Kate mirrors her off-screen celebrity persona as the defender of unpopular minority causes, such as those of the Palestinians and the IRA. That intertextual identity helps to naturalize the fictional character of Kate Benson, giving it an implicit moral authority never verbalized in the script but clearly the point of the actress's presence in the film. In the face of the "wall of silence" she encounters in her contacts with Argentines regarding their recent past, Kate is transformed into an agent of historical inquiry. She doesn't understand recent political history and must interrogate it in ways that cast the film in a pedagogical light, as one which educates its audience through that process of historical inquiry.

For the Argentine viewer, the Redgrave-Kate Benson character becomes the site for a peculiar kind of "re-learning" about the nation in which the very act of questioning poses a counter-narrative to the clichés of official cultural discourse about Argentine history. Because Kate is not merely an uninformed Argentine inquiring into her national history, as was the case with Alicia, the heroine of Puenzo's film, her presence effectively serves as a stand-in for the foreign audience of the film. This, however, turns out to be more than merely a convenient ploy to justify the global commercial aspirations of the film. Kate's questions also challenge the reified notions of a painful national history that goes unexamined in the minds of Argentines. The resistance to her inquiries attests to the ways citizens have been passively positioned to absorb a false sense of national community by virtue of the "wall of silence" that they have erected around the painful memories of the Dirty War. In effect, they have "learned" to accept as normative precisely the patterns of oppression and marginalization that are the unquestioned legacy of the military dictatorship. The presence of the foreign interrogator of local history thus creates a kind of distanciation/identification for the local audience that affirms a sense of democratization by refiguring the nation within a broader transnational community.

That process of bringing the viewer to both stand back from and also identify with the on-screen inquiring spectator-in-the-text is further problematized through the complex plot development of Kate's imaging of her double, Silvia, and Silvia's relation with her daughter, Elisa, the offspring of her union with her "disappeared" husband. The intricately constructed narrative of *Wall of Silence* emphasizes the doubleness of the characters of Kate and Silvia as "self-conscious" agents of historical interrogation and recollection, with Elisa as the subject of this new national discourse.

The point of the enunciative dynamic of *Wall of Silence* is for Silvia's daughter, Elisa, to confront the past in order to be able to face the future. At first, however, Elisa and her mother represent Argentine historical amnesia, the "national" disavowal of a traumatic past. As a benign, "feminine" force that identifies with but does not confuse herself with the Argentine generations, Kate enables Argentines to confront the past and move on; she is made to appear essential and necessary to the telling of their story. Thus, the narrative design of the film is crystallized in the pairing of characters, one to begin the film with a fundamental question and the other to end it. In the first narrative sequence Kate and Bruno visit the now abandoned building complex on the side of the Río de la Plata that served as a clandestine prison and torture site. Tellingly, the question posed by Kate and answered by Bruno at the beginning of the film as they toured one of the former sites of torture used by the military regime ("Didn't people know what was going on here?" "What they didn't know, they suspected.") is nearly exactly repeated when Elisa questions her mother as they stand near the same site in the final scene of *Wall of Silence*.

The echoing of Kate's question by Elisa suggests that foreignness or "other-ness" is not an immutable identity but rather a positionality defined within and against the shifting conception of the nation itself. Camera movement, particularly the slow tracking in the film's final sequence, which begins from a static camera placement in the space earlier identified as the clandestine prison for the disappeared, brings the audience to ponder, as the characters do, the full significance of the "Dirty War" in its relation to individuals. That slow and persistent approach of the camera to the place of the two women becomes a way of remapping the contemporary Argentine audience's placement as "outsider" to the site of interrogation within the cultural space defined by the film's narrative.

In that final camera movement, Stantic's goal is made clear: to transform the positionalities defined as "other" and "foreign" within the cultural politics of recent Argentine history into sites of interrogation and, ultimately, of national renewal. In this context of the malleability of identities in process, *Wall of Silence* opens up the Argentine subject to the possibility of a productive reading of the nation against the fixed core of beliefs that historically has situated Argentina as self-contained and geographically peripheral.

Indeed, one of the important dimensions of Stantic's film is its foregrounding of the emotional, cultural, and geographic sense of isolation felt by Argentines during and following the years of the dictatorship. It is a theme that, of course, resonates for a broader Latin American audience for whom the patterns of authoritarianism are well known. The politics of isolation, in fact, have become an essential leitmotif of the films of Adolfo Aristarain who has emerged in recent years as the preeminent contemporary Argentine film author. Aristarain's work, beginning with *Tiempo de revancha/ Time of Revenge* (1981), a political thriller that addresses the question of the Dirty War through veiled references, has relied on a plot structure that continually reinforces the protagonist's spatial isolation. In his later *Un lugar en el mundo/ A Place in the World* (1992), a co-production with Uruguay, Aristarain foregrounds the Argentine interior – a rural farm collective in Patagonia – in order to narrativize the struggle between individuals seeking to find a social, economic and ethical community and the opposing forces of modernization, tellingly embodied by a multinational corporation seeking to control that territory. While framing the narration within specific Argentine geographical and political contexts, the film nonetheless undercuts the limited frame of the national by linking the narrative to European multinational schemes involving Latin America while "Americanizing" his narration through the use of narrative devices and characters that evoke the formulas of Hollywood action genre films, characters evidently drawn from the western and film noir traditions (Getino, 1998, p. 123). The ultimate effect of these elements is to diminish the Argentineness of *A Place in the World* and to reposition the story within the larger epic terms of a transnational struggle for individual utopia in the face of encroaching globalization.

Aristarain's films since Argentina's return to democracy have consistently involved international co-production schemes that have established him as the most internationally marketable contemporary Argentine filmmaker. Perhaps the summa of his work, certainly his most lavishly praised film, is *Martín Hache/ Martin H*, an Argentine-Spanish co-production which embodies Jameson's geopolitical aesthetic in a clearly self-referential manner. In the story of Martín Etchenique (Federico Luppi), a self-exiled screenwriter living in Madrid, who is forced to take in his nineteen-year-old son, also named Martín and therefore nicknamed Hache (for Spanish "h," *hijo* or son), Aristarain has his protagonist ruminate about the nature of paternal and filial relations, filmmaking, and affiliation with one's homeland. Ultimately, the three themes coalesce for Martín, gradually leading the spectator to reflect on the ingredients of identity politics in ways that transcend the usual clichés and one's allegiance to one's homeland.

Through the elder Martín's uprootedness, especially his obviously successful transplantation in Madrid, and his comments that "Madrid is a good place to be," the film seems at first to buttress the ideology of the transnational culture that produced it. Yet, when one night in Madrid, Hache asks his father if he ever misses Argentina, the elder Martín becomes unhinged and responds with a tirade against national affiliations in general and Argentine identity in particular. He derides patriotism and, alluding to the Dirty War, calls Argentina's politics a trap that makes you believe you can change it, when in fact you can't.

As powerful as Martín's denunciation is, the criticism of national affiliation proves to be double-edged, for Martín is portrayed through his contacts with his closest friends and family who reveal their impression of him as a rootless and isolated figure whose critique of allegiance to the nation is merely symptomatic of his own personal displacement. He is criticized for his ambivalence by his lover, Alicia (Cecilia Roth), and his best friend, Dante (Eusebio Poncela). At the film's end, when Hache returns to Buenos Aires "to become something," he leaves a videotape for his father, explaining his reasons for wanting to forge his own life. The elder Martín acknowledges his loss, not only of his son, but of his roots, thus confessing nostalgia, not for people, but for places. In this regard, the film poses a contestatory theme in its affirmation of cultural roots and its rejection of the "borderless" global position that self-referentially defines the character and the film itself.

One of the truly distinctive features of *Martín Hache* is that thematically the film occupies the "slip-zone" of indeterminacy between denying validity to national roots and embracing one's *patria*. What emerges as the narrative process of the film, therefore, is not the clichéd Argentineness expressed in a tango lyric as nostalgia, but rather a process of rediscovery of one's place in the world that works for Martín as well as for the subsequent Argentine generation symbolically represented by his son, Hache.

The ease with which the action shifts from Buenos Aires to Madrid, then back to Buenos Aires, seems all part of a constructed geographic seamlessness in which Madrid is "relocated" only a frame away from Argentina; the shift between spaces thus appears both effortless and even desirable. The film appears to discard the larger national history framed by Solanas, Bemberg and others for a personal history, but, importantly, the process is developed whereby that national history is resemanticized within personal and therefore more universally humanistic terms. Here, for instance, while the space of the other is held in a positive light, eventually the film seems to fold back on the issue of the exile and affective loss when the elder Martín realizes that, despite his successful repositioning in European culture, the specter of his uprootedness follows him.

That same kind of ambivalence defines the film's apparent self-parodic style. Clearly recycling the formulaic cinema that sought to capitalize on the Dirty War theme, it even plays with the sound of tangos for a brief moment. As well, Aristarain adds a self-conscious parody of his own professional autobiography and allusions to the celebrity status of Federico Luppi, Argentina's internationally renowned actor, who plays the role of Martín. These are touches that underscore the film's discursive strategy of undermining nearly all of the hallmarks of global film aesthetics in its reaffirmation of the cultural roots of a national affiliation that must be balanced with broader global interests.

Co-producing cultural identity beyond the borders of the nation

To many audiences, the plotting of Aristarain's film, with its shifts from Buenos Aires to Madrid, may appear simply to be a convenient device to justify the commercial imperatives of an international co-production. The film's characters and discursive strategies, however, suggest a more serious effort to engage Argentine and global audiences in an interrogation of personal and collective identity. In attempting that transnational mode of address, however, Aristarain exposes the fundamental paradox that underlies not only his own film, but other attempts at serious co-productions over recent years. That paradox is embodied in the figure of the elder Martín Etchenique by virtue of his interstitial position between cultures. The unvoiced questions his presence provokes are these: Where does cultural identity lie? Is it in the place one has left or in the place one seeks to occupy? Is it merely economic expediency that leads individuals and cultural products to move beyond the familiar borders of the nation and to assume new roles? What is the place of tradition, of history, of memory, in the shaping of the new cultural order that emerges out of global economic synergy?

Cultural identity in recent decades, the film seems to say, has become a media-managed co-production. For Martín it is no longer possible to think of himself as simply an Argentine in exile, nor as a man without a country. In this sense, his identity as the alter-ego of his creator, Aristarain, is shaped under the sign of a more complex hybridity, one in which individuals are no longer afforded the luxury of imagining the "patria," the nation as a pristine home, but rather one that is marked and forever altered by the inevitable interaction with a broader economic and social world.

The story that Argentine filmmakers like Aristarain, Bemberg, Stantic, Puenzo, Solanas and others tell is increasingly one that constructs a new discursive place in the world, one which, as it contrasts with the mythic constructions of the homogeneous nation, understandably seems hybrid by contrast. In that same context, the function of the film author can no longer be that of an estranged Romantic creator at odds with his world, a position that Martín seems to relish throughout most of Aristarain's film. Rather, it needs to be as mediator between economic markets which are also cultural markets, between the narratives of the past understood around the fictions of the nation, and the emerging new narrative of a more utopian global community.

In addressing a European audience on some of these questions during a talk appropriately entitled "Being an Artist in Latin America," María Luisa Bemberg summed up the nature of that project for a whole generation of Latin American film authors:

> Precisely because of this planetary transmission of life-like and imaginary images, nations and individuals wish to escape the threat of uniformity

and want to be known by what makes them unique. The diversified people of the world want to be identified idiosyncratically.

(Bemberg, 2000, p. 217)

The tension between those planetary images and the idiosyncrasy of local identity continues to move film authors to seek ways to co-produce new Latin American cultural identities through collaborative practices that have as their ultimate goal not the erasure of the local but a meaningful relocation of it in the global community.

Notes

1 The number of co-productions vary according to sources and the often shifting definition of what constitutes a co-production for various national agencies. The Argentine Instituto Nacional de Cine, for instance, acknowledged fifty-seven co-productions between Argentina, the US, Europe and other Latin American film producers in the period 1983–92 (España, 1994, pp. 286–7). According to Luís Bonet and Albert de Gregorio, Spanish independent producers as well as state agencies entered into a total of forty-three co-productions with Latin American producers between 1982 and 1986 of which eleven were with Argentina and ten with Mexico (pp. 118–19). Other statistical sources, however, such as Argentina's Instituto Nacional de Cine, indicate an even higher rate of co-productions during this same period.

2 Alberto Ciria cites the principal state-funded agencies lending financial support to co-productions which includes Spanish Television (TVE), Italian State Television (RAI), Britain's Channel Four, Spain's Ministry of Culture through a formal agreement between 1986–96, the Fifth Centenary Foundation (Ciria, 1995, pp. 195–7). More recently, Ibermedia, an Iberoamerican consortium modeled after the European Community's Eurimages, has been active in supporting co-productions between Spain and Spanish-America. Much of the implementation for Spanish/Spanish-American co-productions has been carried out over recent decades through the work of two enterprising Spanish producers, Andrés Vicente Gómez and Gerardo Herrera, the latter having worked out co-productions between Spanish production entities and their counterparts in the region for films such as Peruvian director Francisco Lombardi's *La boca del lobo/ In the Wolf's Mouth* (1988) and *Caídos del cielo/ Fall From Heaven* (1990), and Tomás Gutiérrez Alea's *Guantanamera* (1995).

3 Octavio Getino cites sources indicating that in the decade of the 1980s, the audience for commercially distributed motion pictures in Latin America and the Caribbean fell from approximately 850 million spectators in 1979 to between 450–500 million a decade later. Country-by-country figures appear equally grim with Argentina, for example, showing a decrease of audience attendance from 61 million in 1984 to 22 million in 1988 (Getino, 1996, pp. 168–9).

4 John King's description of the extent of European and US participation in the development of film production in Argentina, Brazil and Mexico during the silent period add rich detail to Paranaguá's thesis. The extent of foreign activity ranges from the appearance of Lumière cameramen in parts of Latin America as early as 1896 to European film imports in Buenos Aires, Mexico and Sao Paulo during the years preceding the First World War. (See King, 2000, pp. 10–29.)

5 For a detailed discussion of multiple-language productions see Vincendeau, 1999, pp. 207–24.

6 Paranaguá lists the Mexican tenor, José Mojica, as the only other major singing star to achieve broad commercial success in the Films Hispanos. See Paranaguá, 1996, p 220.

7 As late as 1999, in a survey of Latin American critics asked to judge the most important Latin American films and filmmakers of the twentieth century, Buñuel was the most cited director and *Los olvidados* the second most cited film, after Alea's *Memories of Under-development*. See Galiano and Caballero, 1991, p. 41.

8 Along with the attention accorded to Latin American film productions at the Berlin and Venice Film Festivals, several other more specialized European venues have helped promote the commercial fortunes of Latin American cinema. These include the Category A San Sebastián Film Festival, which, since the early 1990s has devoted a special section to films "Made in Spanish," and the Iberoamerican Film Festival held annually in Huelva, Spain since 1979, which is devoted exclusively to Spanish and Portuguese language Latin American films.

9 See particularly, Thomas Elsaesser's argument formulated around the promotion of New German Cinema:

> In this sense, the author was indeed an institution, in so far as he functioned both as a principle of production coherence and, over time, with the increasing international fame of some of them, also became an "auteur" of the international art cinema. On the side of the author, self-expression became redefined as self-image, leading to a "marketing" of the name as itself the seal of quality and a brand name.
>
> (Elsaesser, 1989, p. 116)

10 Puenzo's career as a transnational filmmaker continued with *The Old Gringo* (1989), co-produced by Jane Fonda, followed by an English-language adaptation of Albert Camus's *The Plague* (*La peste*, 1992) which used a cast of American, Argentine and European actors to pose the human rights theme in the context of Latin American military dictatorships (see Ciria, 1995, pp. 217–23).

11 Julianne Burton-Carvajal cites a Bemberg interview in which she speaks of her effort after abandoning the idea of filming *Yo, la peor de todas* in Mexico to transform the script into "a more universal story of repression and brain-washing," using an atemporal, universal tone through which the film might attack fanaticism of all kinds. See Burton-Carvajal, 1997, pp. 75–92.

12 The role of Silvia is played by the Mexican actress, Ofelia Medina, best known for her performance in Paul Leduc's *Frida* (Mexico, 1983). Again, the logic of the international casting of the principal characters, as in Bemberg's films, provides a dialogical resonance to the film not otherwise evident in the script.

Bibliography

Beceyro, Raúl. *Cine y política*. Buenos Aires: Universidad Nacional del Litoral/Centro de Publicaciones, 1997.

Bemberg, María Luisa. "Being an Artist in Latin America," in John King, Sheila Whitaker, Rosa Bosch (eds) *An Argentine Passion: María Luisa Bemberg and Her Films*. London and New York: Verso, 2000, pp. 216–23.

Bonet, Luís, and Albert de Gregorio. "La industria cultural española en América Latina," in Néstor García Canclini and Carlos Juan Moncla (coordinators) *Las industrias culturales en la integración latinoamericana*. México: Grijalbo, 1999, pp. 87–128.

Burton-Carvajal, Julianne. "Firmar la vida: entrevista atemporal con María Luisa Bemberg," *Nuevo Texto Crítico* 19/20 (1997), pp. 75–92.

Cine Argentino anuario, 1996/1997. Buenos Aires: Instituto de Cine y Artes Audio-visuales, 1997.

Ciria, Alberto. *Más allá de la pantalla*. Buenos Aires: Ediciones La Flor, 1995.

Corrigan, Timothy. *A Cinema Without Walls: Movies and Culture After Vietnam*. New Brunswick, NJ: Rutgers University Press, 1991.

Elsaesser, Thomas. *New German Cinema: A History*. New Brunswick, NJ: Rutgers University Press, 1989.

España, Claudio (compilador/coordinator). *Cine argentino en democracia 1983—1993*. Buenos Aires: Fondo Nacional de las Artes, 1994.

Galiano, Carlos and Rufo Caballero. *Cien aòs sin soledad: los mejores películas latinoamericanas de todos los tiempos*. Havana: La Habana Editorial Letras Cubanas, 1999.

García Canclini, Néstor. *Hybrid Cultures: Strategies for Entering and Leaving Modernity*. Minneapolis and London: University of Minnesota Press, 1995.

Getino, Octavio. *Cine argentino: entre lo possible y lo deseable*. Buenos Aires: Ediciones Ciccus, 1998.

Getino, Octavio. *Tercera mirada: panorama del audiovisual latinoamericano*. First edition. Buenos Aires: Paidós, 1996.

Hall, Stuart. "Old and New Identities, Old and New Ethnicities," in Anthony D. King (ed.) *Culture, Globalization and the World-System*. Minneapolis: University of Minnesota Press, 1997, pp. 41–68.

Higson, Andrew. "The Limiting Imagination of National Cinema," in Mette Hjort and Scott MacKenzie (eds) *Cinema and Nation*. London and New York: Routledge, 2000, pp. 63–74.

Jameson, Fredric. *The Geopolitical Aesthetic: Cinema and Space in the World System*. Bloomington, IN and London: Indiana University Press, 1995.

Kinder, Marsha. *Blood Cinema: The Reconstruction of National Identity in Spain*. Berkeley, Los Angeles, London: University of California Press, 1993.

King, John. "María Luisa Bemberg and Argentine Culture," in John King, Sheila Whitaker, Rosa Bosch (eds) *An Argentine Passion: María Luisa Bemberg and Her Films*. London and New York: Verso, 2000, pp. 1–32.

King, John. *Magical Reels: A History of Cinema in Latin America*. London and New York: Verso, 1990.

López, Ana. "Tears and Desire: Women and Melodrama in the 'Old' Mexican Cinema," in John King, Ana M. López, Manuel Alvarado (eds) *Mediating Two Worlds: Cinematic Encounters in the Americas*. London: BFI Publishing, 1993, pp. 147–63.

López, Ana. "Argentina: 1955–1976: The Film Industry and its Margins," in John King and Nissa Torrents (eds) *The Garden of Forking Paths: Argentine Cinema*. London: BFI, 1985, pp. 49–80.

Maxwell, Richard. *The Spectacle of Democracy: Spanish Television, Nationalism, and Political Transition*. Minneapolis and London: University of Minnesota Press, 1995.

Monsiváis, Carlos. *Aires de familia: Cultura y sociedad en América Latina*. Barcelona: Editorial Anagrama, 2000.

Monteagudo, Luciano, and Verónica Bucich. *Carlos Gardel y el primer cine sonoro argentino*. Huesca: Filmoteca de Andalucía, Chicago Latino Film Festival y Festival de Cine de Huesca, 2001.

Naficy, Hamid. "Phobic Spaces and Liminal Panics: Independent Transnational Film Genre," in Rob Wilson and Wimal Dissanayake (eds) *Global/Local: Cultural Production and the Transnational Imaginary*. Durham, VA and London: Duke University Press, 1996, pp. 119–44.

Paranaguá, Paulo Antonio. "América Latina, Europa, y Estados Unidos, relaciones triangulares en la historia del cine," *Journal of Film Preservation*, 62 (April, 2001), pp. 9–15.

Paranaguá, Paulo Antonio. "América Latina Busca su Imagen," in Carlos F. Heredero and Casimiro Torreiro (coordinators) *Historia general del cine X Estados Unidos (1955–1975). América Latina.* Madrid: Cátedra: Signo e imagen, 1996, pp. 205–393.

Paranaguá, Paulo Antonio. "The Sound Era in Latin America," in Patricia Aufderheide (ed.) *Latin American Visions.* Philadelphia: The Neighborhood Film/Video Project of International House, 1989, pp. 13–19.

Pick, Zuzana. *The New Latin American Cinema: A Continental Project.* Austin, TX: University of Texas Press, 1993.

Schnitman, Jorge A. *Film Industries in Latin America: Dependency and Development.* Norwood, NJ: Ablex Publishing Corporation, 1984.

Taylor, Julie M. "Tango: Theme of Class and Nation," *Ethnomusicology* 20 (1976), pp. 273–91.

Urra, Jorge Luis. "Cine Argentino: Recuento sin nostalgias," in Carlos Galiano and Rufo Caballero (eds) *Cien años sin soledad: las mejores películas latinoamericanas de todos los tiempos.* Havana: Editorial Letras Cubanas, 1999, pp. 141–61.

Vincendeau, Ginette. "Hollywood Babel: The Coming of Sound and the Multiple-Language Version," in Andrew Higson and Richard Maltby (eds) *"Film Europe" and "Film America": Cinema, Commerce and Cultural Exchange 1920–1939.* Exeter: University of Exeter Press, 1999, pp. 207–24

5 Video booms and the manifestations of "first" cinema in anglophone Africa

N. Frank Ukadike

Until the 1960s, almost all the films shown in Africa were of Euro-American or Asian origin. During the pioneering decade of African cinema, the aspirations of the pioneers coincided with those of the 1960s tri-continental revolutionary movements[1] and ideologies which were channeled toward decolonization and liberation. In the arts, liberationist literatures, often pervaded with an orthodox Marxist philosophical rhetoric, impacted on the evolution of revolutionary cinema which thus developed as an antithetical structure to counter dominant cinemas, particularly Hollywood. Operating from geographically divergent zones, the cinema in the Third World – including, of course, the third or fourth world within the first world – the documentary film practice of Latin America and the engaged or the questioning cinema of Africa adopted denunciative cinematic structures. Although different techniques were applied to render the narrative structures culturally and politically specific, the unifying factor for achieving this goal, in its varying practices, was the creation of cinematic art based on the philosophy that film and politics are inextricably interwoven. As I shall show, this position is diametrically opposed to what is happening in the video-film world, which I have termed the manifestation of a "first" cinema in anglophone Africa.

In broader ideological terms, in African cinema there has been a deliberate attempt to use the film medium as a "voice of the people;" there has been a persistent mandate to interrogate narrative structures so as to develop new strategies for genuine indigenous film practice; and politically and aesthetically, there has been relentless experimentation with film form aimed at achieving an indigenous film culture distinct from the dominant foreign commercial cinemas. I shall show why the latter, in particular, is the most contentious of all the integral components of the business of film/video making and exhibition, arguing that it is indeed this factor that has contributed enormously to the current state of affairs brought about by the globalization of free market enterprise – a system which is now embraced worldwide with endless negotiations and renegotiations geared to protect and maintain the exclusionary prerogatives of dominant cinemas.

In Africa, specifically in the francophone areas, the audacity with which African identities, politics and social life have been shown on film reflects the rhetoric of difference permeating ideological discourses, and the sociopolitical dynamics impacting upon the cultural production. The francophone pioneers of African cinema took a didactic stance, feeling compelled to create an "African" style of expression as an educational tool. The most apparent manifestation of use of the motion picture to induce awareness of African consciousness occurred from the 1960s through the 1980s. In the 1990s, however, commercial factors have offered severe challenges to the old order. Elsewhere, I have identified the digressionary tendencies of the African cinema of the 1990s, which stem from the new breed African filmmakers' inclination to create a full-fledged cinematic industry that focuses on entertainment more than education.[2] It comes as no surprise, then, that Chris Kabwato's argument that the primary interest of the paying audience is to go "to the cinema to be entertained first and [perhaps] through entertainment be educated"[3] reaffirms the prevailing audience mood in contemporary Africa. However, to achieve this goal means that a film must appeal to the audience, and for the young video practitioners it also means commanding the space to promote their works.

The new phenomenon of video-films, as they are popularly known, crystallizes a unique cultural art while remaining true to its primary objective – commercial viability. The explosion of video production and its popular appeal in the anglophone countries of West Africa attests to the manifestation of what might be called a real "first" cinema, a cinema which competes with the so-called "First Cinema" of the West on its own terms. Video's triumph does not necessarily imply the displacement of the celluloid film medium, but rather the transcendence of limitations imposed by the conventions of celluloid filmmaking. For example, this new boom has created thriving local industries and market-oriented economies within the media sectors and has rapidly expanded the parameters for defining national film and video cultures and audience tastes. Indeed, from the late 1980s to the present period we are witnessing an unprecedented video boom – even *The New York Times* has devoted almost a whole page to this recent phenomenon.[4] And in a special news segment which followed soon thereafter, CNN commentators were stunned by developments in this burgeoning industry which has the potential of becoming the most consequential cultural art production of Ghana and Nigeria at the start of the present century.

In treating the development of such a hybrid phenomenon, we should keep in mind Homi Bhabha's notion that "appropriation is negotiation, and negotiation is what politics is all about." He goes on to state that "political negotiation is a very important issue, and hybridity is precisely about the fact that when a new situation, a new alliance formulates itself, it may demand that you should translate your principles, rethink them, extend them."[5] In applying Bhabha's concepts of negotiation to the understanding of the situation of video-film production in the anglophone region, I will argue that video has changed the industry's outlook not because of its merit but because of the manner in which the producers negotiate the parameters of the hybrid spaces in the popular imagination in conjunction with the question of video marketability and reception, marketing strategies hitherto not attempted by its predecessor, the celluloid film. Video evolved in ways that were unanticipated and peculiar to the economic setting of post-independence sociopolitical structure, and like many technologies it displays the ability to construct and transform meanings and practices that render it economically viable in a period of severe economic turbulence and fiscal austerity.

In Ghana and in Nigeria, from the late 1980s to the present, a plethora of video-films have been produced. By 1987 the video "boom" in Ghana had begun to challenge dominant (Ghanaian) cinematic practices and film culture. In this same period in Nigeria video also posed a formidable challenge to the thriving but highly segregated film genre, the "filmed theater," an offshoot of the Yoruba popular Traveling Theater tradition, the "*Alarinjo*." Paradoxically, video art forms in Ghana and Nigeria have proliferated with the implementation of the "Structural Adjustment Program" (SAP) imposed by the International Monetary Fund (IMF) in an attempt to revamp the economies of both countries. (The policy has failed spectacularly in Africa and elsewhere in the "Third World," including Russia which has joined the "club.") During this period, as a result of currency devaluation, the Ghanaian cedis and the Nigerian naira became valueless in international monetary exchange, thus making hard currency inaccessible to filmmakers for the importation of filmmaking equipment, the purchase of raw filmstock and the accomplishment of postproduction tasks. Filmmakers soon discovered that it was more productive to use the video format. Ghana and Nigeria each now produces at least two feature-length video-films every week. This contrasts sharply with the production in Ghana of only six celluloid feature-length films in the 1980s and none in the 1990s. Similarly, there has not been any significant feature film made in Nigeria that has appealed to the general populace since *The Death of a Black President* in 1983 – although the Yoruba films mentioned above still flourish.

It is the hardship resulting from the current economic quagmire which has forced almost all Ghanaian and Nigerian filmmakers into producing video-films; and although this new phenomenon has succeeded in creating its own popular audience, it has also raised a number of questions regarding production values and artistic and aesthetic concerns, as well as posing formidable challenges to film viewing habits. However, the lively stories appeal to the public who shape popular culture, and as the videos are being exported to the growing African populations resident in Europe, the USA, and Canada, they are beginning to penetrate classrooms and reach non-African audiences. This is a remarkable development since in anglophone Africa, Ghana and Nigeria specifically, celluloid cinema has never been used to address the contemporary historical and sociocultural dynamics of the people as do the new video works, and as the sub-canonical francophone films widely used in the US classrooms have done in the explication of the francophone experience. Video production portrays local African experience in a number of genres: comedy, satire, musical, adventure and horror movies are gradually creeping into the fold.

As a result of this local intervention in the global film market there is a growing need for a framework of analysis for what has emerged as a major cultural art of the twenty-first century. Since technology and the economic determinants of video-film production are mutually constitutive and, as such, are locked up in a circle of inexorable dependence, I am interested in how dependency theory could be applied to the discourse of the new African video-films. As Albert Memmi has noted, "the colonial system manufactures the colonialists, just as it manufactures the colonized,"[6] an idea which helps to explain the prevailing consumer culture and the culture of poverty in Africa today when, as a result of powerlessness, the West has found a new way of recolonizing the continent through, for example, the forced Structural Adjustment Programs which have ushered in the video boom which now threatens to obliterate celluloid film production and potential competition with Hollywood and other Euro-American media products.

The obvious dilemma that a relatively expensive technology poses is this: could Africa ever afford to compete with a well-established commercial film industry in the developed world? The alternative that video provides is symptomatic of how oppressed peoples employ a form of "bricolage" to survive with dignity, but they are resorting to video also as a way of withdrawing from the mainstream. Again Memmi's insight is invaluable. He notes that "all impossible conditions call for a radical solution, all absolute misfortunes demand an absolute revolt."[7] Echoing the earlier assertion made by Bhabha regarding negotiation, politics and hybridity, one critic has stated that "the years of SAP have produced a new generation of artists whose bitterness and impoverishment have created a new aesthetic of hunger and rage."[8] To what extent, therefore, has this level of deprivation dislocated cultures, economies and traditional notions of self-sufficiency? If this new phenomenon is sustained by high-powered improvisation, how has this strategy impacted upon aesthetics and the traditional notion of art in Africa?

In Kwaw Ansah's view the current video trend is a "stopgap measure,"[9] after which, as the economy improves, producers will revert to celluloid film-making. This is optimistic: video is providing employment for people and creating an immediate source for fame and fortune for the few individuals who have access to funding sources and the technology of production. Given this reality it is difficult to imagine the end of the phenomenon unless, of course, the producers run out of ideas or the audience revolts. The situation becomes even more complicated with the advent of satellite television, pay-per-view cable television and the internet, the so-called information super highway, which have the potential of threatening the local cultures and social structures of the consumer nations of Africa. These neocolonial trajectories of cultural imperialism, economic alienation and political ambiguity are further problematizing the postcolonial situation in Africa.

At the same time the technology of video, while participating in the economic regimes of capitalism, has enabled social mobility within African cultures. For example, women are fully participating in the production, directing, editing and acting for the video-films, and given the fact that women producers are emerging rapidly. A crucial question arises, then, as to whether the economic coordinates of the emerging industry permit these filmmakers to counter the negative images of women found in some of the male-directed videos? Moreover, many of the new video-film entrepreneurs have risen from the "low ranks" of their societies, thus also implicating questions of social class in this burgeoning social phenomenon.

Traditionally denied access to the medium of film, African women have been increasingly taking control of the camera in recent years. Female video makers are exploring cultural conventions and innovative strategies that challenge Eurocentric and male chauvinistic assumptions/readings of black female subjectivity. One of the most innovative video-films by an African woman that emerged from this practice is Veronica Quashie's *Twin Lovers* (Ghana, 1996). The film is about the consequences of urban life, the lure of the city, promiscuity among young people, and the menace of "sugar daddies." The film revolves around the central character Juliet, who at about the age of 22 is still a virgin until she meets Kobbie – not by choice, but in the company of socializing friends. Her friend Doreen slips a narcotic into her drink making it possible for Kobbie to lure her home to be raped. Kobbie is a rich engineer and, as a notorious Casanova, he uses his charm and other dubious tactics including intimidation and deceit to achieve his goal. As a village girl, Juliet is pure, but the city full of vices, to which she went for education, destroys her ambitions. Now pregnant, she is terrified that her father will kill her if she fails to perform the puberty rite, a ritual of honor that makes parents proud. In tranquil villages where tradition is upheld, sex and pregnancy before marriage are abhorred. Here, the film reminds us that villages are where cultures and traditions are preserved in modern Africa, while the city is a confluence of foreign influences. This emphasis on purity and culture also explains why in those days in Africa, civil servants who lived in the cities would go home to their respective villages to marry, ignoring the young city women, who were thought to be contaminated.

At one level, the film could be read as an indictment of social service systems, of corruption and unemployment in the cities. At one point Juliet laments not being able to find a job because "every job in this city has a certificate attached to it." Her quest also illustrates, as she later learns, that as a woman, having a job does not solve all problems. Sometimes it compounds them. In her new job, she learns about the relationship between her boss and Barbara, her counterpart. Barbara is the boss's concubine and when she gets pregnant, he opts for abortion in the same way Kobbie denies paternal responsibility for Juliet's child. But why have such women lost their dignity, respect, and security? The film blames the patriarchal system that has entrenched male dominance in almost all facets of life. *Twin Lovers* shows how in the new women films thematic and aesthetic prerogatives are determined by specific social, political, and gender objectives rather than as conventional spectacles for commercial benefit.

Since the inception of African celluloid filmmaking, indigenous themes have sustained the narrative patterns of African films; they have highlighted not only the contradictions between Western values and African cultures but have also utilized narrative styles based on hybrid paradigms that mix the dominant cinematic codes with the conventions of other types of indigenous cultural expression. Yet with few local exceptions African cinemas have not produced an economically viable industry. Recognizing the disastrous effects of this moribund market, as well as the need to capture a larger audience, the videomakers have turned toward local but universalized themes which, when rendered as drama and comedy, allow the African video-film to draw bigger crowds into the movie theaters than its celluloid predecessor. What is fascinating in the video themes is that even when they are rendered in aesthetically sloppy structures, as they indubitably were in the first video-films, they are still able to galvanize such massive audience appeal.

In my book *Black African Cinema*, I have argued that universalized themes and aesthetics have their pros and cons.[10] For the anglophone videos, the target audience is the local population; this is where the video-film has transcended the inability of the celluloid film to cultivate its own audience/film culture, its own version of universalized aesthetics and themes notwithstanding. Deploying alien conventions, sometimes using them regressively to make video-films appeal to the largest common denominator of the audience, may ensure recuperation of capital investment, but it is also tantamount to mimicry of the West, thus eroding knowledge, imagination and skilled direction, and negating the varied ways in which the artistic production of culture contends with claims of power and authenticity. The point is that mimicry does not operate as a response to repression, or as a means of reasserting identities as did militant literatures with their "ability to move human mind and spirit beyond so-called reality and into realms formal history has no capacity to recognize."[11] In this context, mimicry has rather become a fast-forward to perpetual domination. Echoing Anyidoho's view quoted above, Werewere Liking reminds us of the perfidious ramifications of unquestioning imitation: "What is needed is to educate oneself and nurture the faith in one's inner divinity, to stop running behind other people's destiny, for our own destiny is running after us."[12]

On the other hand, the video revolution in Ghana must be viewed in the context of its peculiar origins as the result of the entrepreneurial acumen of a few individuals with no technical training whatsoever. There were several pioneers, each claiming to be the first innovator. William Akuffo and Richard Quartey made *Zinabu* in 1987 with an antiquated home video camera. Although the film itself had low production values and was amateurish, it made history in terms of illuminating the potential for video-film viability and other possibilities of the new medium. As Seth Ashong-Katai, one of the best directors of the now defunct Ghana Film Industries Corporation (GFIC),[13] put it, "People paid to see [this film], some out of curiosity and some out of the desire to see a Ghanaian film."[14]

The same year saw the emergence of Sidiku Buari, better known as Sid, a man of many talents, an ex-Olympic athlete, musician and businessman who owns a recording studio and a *bureau de change*, the Cedi Top Forex Bureau. He is considered to be the first to commercialize video-films.[15] He came into the video business by accident when he realized that the recorded images he made with an old amateur video camera to match the text of one of his songs, *AAYALOLO* (We Are On the Move), which was very popular in Ghana at that time, also captivated the audience. Critics agree that "as a film [it] was a disaster," but it became a box office hit anyway for "people liked it because they could see themselves and places they knew."[16] Kofi Middleton-Mends, Head of Directing at the National Film and Television Institute (NAFTI), believes that video production started with NAFTI due to financial constraints and the prohibitive cost of raw filmstock which forced upon the institute the use of video equipment donated by German Parastatal. According to him, as early as 1982, NAFTI students were already making story films on video. At this point Sidiku Buari intervened with a brilliant idea: he consulted with NAFTI authorities who provided students who helped him shoot *AAYALOLO* and he then launched an effective entrepreneurial marketing strategy. This, he claims is the story of how the video revolution was launched.[17]

Another pioneer is Socrates Safo whose training in filmmaking consisted of watching numerous films when he worked as a janitor in a movie theater to support his training as an auto mechanic. With the help of his auto mechanic friends, he shot an experimental but commercially successful first feature-length video, *Ghost Tears*, which is believed to be one of the six highest-grossing features of the period. The success of this movie spurred a successful career in the video business leading to the production of five movies in five years and the cultivation of a video audience and video counterculture that is now growing in Ghana.

It is important to state that what the new videos lacked in technical and aesthetic quality, they made up for in good storytelling technique. Video pioneers Richard Quartey, Sidiku Buari, Socrates Safo, and, especially, William Akuffo, have all been credited with writing captivating screenplays.

The reason for the increased appetite for locally made movies is best expressed in the words of Tom Ribeiro, an independent director: "First [Ghanaians] used to enjoy Cowboy films. That died off. Then kung fu pictures. That died off. Then just killing, killing, killing. And we think, is that all Americans know?"[18] Consequently, the entire range of Ghanaian production, from full-length feature films to the new video movies and the experimental shorts made by the students of NAFTI, has a popular following. So it stands to reason that since the early 1990s, theaters in the major cities of Accra, Takoradi, and Tamale have exclusively played Ghanaian video movies.

Audience admiration for foreign films seems to have fizzled out from the late 1980s to the present, echoing the widespread African sentiment regarding foreign films whose content seldom has positive connections with the people of the continent. As demand for local products grew, so too emerged a profusion of video works. Hitherto African cinema had always had a small audience, even locally, where Indian and American popular movies dominate. That is no longer the case in Ghana. As the technical quality of the video-films improves, as audiences make increasing demands for quality (leading to a marked evolution in both acting and scripting), the success of these films has become so great that according to *The New York Times* article cited above, "Hollywood may rule the rest of the world, but here [in Ghana] it has been trounced by Ghanawood."[19]

Successful Ghanaian video-films have spawned sequels such as William Akuffo's *Zinabu* II, III, and IV. Triggered by the immense success of the first *Zinabu*, these films treat witchcraft and the eternal confrontation between good and evil. Tragic love is the theme of both *Ghost Tears* and *Abiiba* directed by Socrates Safo and Eben Owusu Ansah, respectively. Romance is the most admired genre because of the similarity of their plots to the love stories often told during regular evening story telling when families reenacted folktales which find their way into television dramas, comic strips and newspapers and tabloids. Ghana is also a society where newspaper columnists enjoy exposing the extramarital affairs of government officials. Hence, as Daniel J. Sharfstein rightly observed, a typical film by the originator of the Romance genre, Safo, deals with the woes of unfaithful husbands, their mistresses usually placing a heavy financial burden on the men because of their spending sprees, eventually reducing them to abject poverty. As a result, when they somehow fail to become mentally deranged or made objects of ridicule, they either die or are left alive to be haunted forever by menacing ghosts.[20]

Genre experiments have proliferated. Dubbed "Ghana's first hip-hop film," Bampoe-Addo's *Abrantee* portrays youthful exuberance and love. *Tricky Twist* and *Matters of the Heart* are popular comedies starring the well-known comedy actor Augustine Abey.[21] While Bismark Nunoo's *Phobia Girl* and *Sam B's Deliverance* have explored the metaphysical/supernatural, in Sidiku Buari's *Ogboo I* and *Ogboo II* characters are transformed into animal figures and vice versa. Although these films are extremely melodramatic and replete with technical problems, *Ogboo*, for example, displays commendable experimental breakthroughs which are surprisingly psychedelic. In an interesting scene when almost everyone has been converted into an animal except Sidi the hero and one of the surviving policemen, we witness a cleverly contrived action marked by deliberate distortion of perception. It is a scene between an eagle and a snake, in which the eagle flies down (as a policeman watches in surprise and fear) and lands on a black snake. The snake then wraps around the eagle as the eagle looks at it, motionless but for its powerful wings. In a closer shot, we see how the eagle devours the snake. The message is obvious, depicting the necessary savagery of nature: we must eat to survive, even though the "kill" can be brutal and unpredictable. The eagle symbolizes strength, freedom and efficiency. The black snake can be related to the evil side of humans. The scene is a parable about nature and humanity, yet it can also reflect how evil should be treated. Cinematographically, the eagle's mysterious descent upon the snake is technically a puzzle. One is left wondering how the director accomplished this mythic Lukas-like special effect with the limited resources the overall production had at its disposal.

Videos that probe societal mores and contradictions more directly also abound. *Baby Thief* by Seth Ashong-Katai examines traditional customs that force Abla to steal a baby to help maintain the royal status of her husband. The ever-growing desire of young people to immigrate in search of greener pastures is depicted in *Uptown, All that Glitters Is Not Gold*. With 90 percent of its action transpiring in the United States, *Uptown*, Ghanaian slang for America, features a multi-ethnic cast of Ghanaian, Nigerian and American actors. In this humorous film, Kotey, played by Patrick Anin Addo, aspires to go to the United States to ensure a prosperous future and to further his education. Contrary to what he thought was going to be a dreamland, the country is alienating and teaches him to be distrustful of others. His luggage is stolen on his first day of arrival; soon thereafter he encounters a seductive pretty white lady, but finds himself propositioned by a gay man.

In terms of depicting serious societal issues with a rejuvenating cinematic aesthetics, Kwaw Ansah's brilliantly photographed and well researched *Harvest at 17* and *Crossroads of People, Crossroads of Trade* have set standards for other video makers to emulate. *Harvest at 17*, Ansah's first experimental video, vividly captures the problem of teenage pregnancy, a universal theme but given a convincing Ghanaian setting. *Crossroads* deals with black emancipation and accomplishments, tracing 500 years of the economic and cultural history of Ghana and connecting it with the African Diaspora. The release of this masterpiece, specifically commissioned by the Smithsonian Institution and the Ghana Ministry of Culture, was used in the opening of the Pan-African Festival of Arts and Culture (PANAFEST, 1995) and effectively concretized the video revolution in Ghana. *Crossroads* demonstrates the dexterity of a master craftsman, the award winning filmmaker of *Heritage ... Africa* fame. The film creatively blends a collage of still photographs, animation and live action in a unique way, capturing the "pivotal events of [black] history including the development of kingdoms and empires, the development of trade routes and major trade activities, the Trans-Atlantic Slave Trade and the survival aspects of [black] culture in the African Diaspora."[22]

Crossroads also reminds us about the nature of "social interaction" and the ingenious techniques African people have devised to cope with obstacles and hardships as they have moved into the industrial age. That the film is able to encapsulate five centuries of history into a short screen time of 45-minutes calls attention to its superlative manipulation of cinematic conventions. The expertise with which this tapestry of history is controlled and the fluidity of its narration also accounts for the film's educational quality – teaching without being overtly didactic,[23] and entertaining without trivializing serious diasporic issues. Commenting on the intricate nature of the narrative structure and the ingenious scripting and direction, James Anquandah, Head of the Department of Archeology at the University of Ghana, Legon, who is also the consultant on content for the film, commended *Crossroads'* "ability to show the continuity between the past and the present, the way [the director] linked local situations and local history with the Diaspora," and he added that its director is "someone who has the perception and the capacity to read between the lines of history and culture."[24]

In Ghana, as in Nigeria, language has been a major issue for video-film producers. Kofi Yirenkyi's *Sika Samsum* and *Kanana*, shot in Twi, a local Ghanaian language, were risky since most TV programs are made in the English language. The indomitable director, Kwaw Ansah, opting not to marginalize his films, noted that "Ghana has 12 different languages" and using any of them means applying subtitles which are "distracting." According to him, English enables him "to cover about 70 per cent of the population" and also to market his films in English-speaking countries.[25] This probably explains why although Yirenkyi's stated aim was to use the vernacular to free the actors "from the inhibitions of foreign language"[26] he soon abandoned the use of any of the local languages, choosing instead to shoot his next video feature, *Heart of Gold*, in English. In sharp contrast, in Nigeria the plethora of genres are either set in local languages with English subtitles or in pidgin English. They are partly successful because of their local flavor – the dialogue is simple to grasp, the locations are familiar, and the stories touch on every aspect of the "national character," an often-used term which refers to the ways of life, politics and culture of all the more than 200 ethnic groups of the federation.

There are three categories of Nigerian video-films which can be grouped geographically: those produced in the North reflecting the Hausa, Islamic and other cultures of the northern states; the Igbo films produced in the southeast, which utilize the tradition of Igbo theater practices; and the Yoruba films, produced in the southwest, which, like the others, mirror the ethnic tradition of the Yoruba traveling theater. The most prolific and most developed are the Igbo and Yoruba video practices. As in Ghana, the Nigerian video scene is dominated by "emergency" directors and producers (Nigerian slang for upstarts), whose agenda is simply to make money. In the Yoruba videos, most structures are inundated with the fantastical, supernatural dimensions of the Yoruba cosmology. Its origins are traceable to the popular Yoruba traveling theater, whose remarkable tradition of excellence and professionalism neither the video-films nor the Yoruba celluloid films are able to match. However, like the traveling theater whose exponents and popular performers command enormous crowds, so also the video-films possess Yoruba audience appeal, as some of them make use of popular theater actors and the Yoruba language. With the low cost of video subtitling, some of the videos are subtitled or dubbed in English to make them cut across ethnic lines, whereas the Yoruba celluloid films, though well received among the Yorubas, were shunned in other regions where the language is not spoken.

The relationship of the video-films with the celluloid films and the theater tradition is an area for further exploration in order to address the complex patterns of Nigerian spectatorship. The puzzling question is, however, whether this tradition is capable of attaining the status of an economically viable industry in its present form of organization. A critical evaluation of the video practices must consider the overreaching influences that are responsible for the growth or retardation of the emerging trend, specifically regarding how the conventions of the folktale and traditional storytelling techniques are deployed and even such questions as how the videos replicate the themes of romance, love, song and dance reminiscent of the Hindi musical romance melodramas (which have had a long-lasting effect upon Nigerian film audiences).

In terms of its own historical development, however, video-film production proliferated in Nigeria with the release of a highly successful revolutionary work in the Igbo language, *Living in Bondage*, about a powerful secret organization, the Ogboni Society. A series of Igbo films shot in the Igbo language and originating from the Igbo theater followed. This is rather interesting considering the stiff competition with dominant Yoruba films, which had monopolized the Nigerian film business for a long time. With video movies, Igbo drama, long plagued by a "lack of permanent structure," as Johnson Kalu puts it, is transcending its community status as sporadic "pieces of entertainment for guests," or as "cyclic/festival performance and ritual displays," to become a vibrant cultural art in Nigeria. In this new arena, Kalu also notes that the Igbo drama has become "a piece of art containing the mythical, the psychological desires and aspirations of the Igbo people in a contemporary setting," cautioning, however, against parading mediocrity as genial art as the video boom proliferates.[27]

This concern for quality has been partly resolved in Ghana, ironically, by its trendy audience which, in the process of watching films, has matured to become critical of mediocre videos. This process has been accelerated by the enlistment of the services of GFIC and NAFTI trained professionals and technicians by the businessmen-cum-producers who without formal training of their own could not have hoped to meet audience expectations. There is no equivalent of NAFTI in Nigeria, so trained technicians are rare commodities. However, the government has recently built ultramodern filmmaking facilities at the Nigerian Film Corporation (NFC) complex in Jos where it is possible to make films from their initial conception to the finished product, according to its former Managing Director, Brendan Shehu.[28]

Apart from the popular Yoruba theater and the Yoruba tradition of filmed theater, numerous popular Nigerian television dramas, like *Checkmate*, *Mirror in the Sun*, *Ripples*, and *Cockcrows at Dawn*, have been criticized for the manner in which they are steeped in the Queen's English and in elite settings that have always alienated the less educated. In sharp contrast, with characters who understand the culture and language of the people, the Igbo video drama has broken the wall that divided viewers of the Nigerian [film and television] drama. The Igbo video drama is indeed helping in the development of the Igbo language, education and orientation.[29]

Yet the use of Igbo language has not necessarily restricted cultural hybridity. *Taboo*, directed by Vic Mordi, which depicts the issue of arranged marriage, recalls the romance themes and sexual titillation of the popular Indian films. Character movement, singing and dancing illustrate how the conventions of the typical Indian romance film can be blended with the Igbo theater conventions. What is interesting about *Taboo* is how its hybrid structure does not diminish the understanding of the portrayal of serious cultural issues, as in the depiction of the caste system where the focus is the "impossibility" of an individual of an upper class family to win permission to marry a person of a much lower class, the *Osu*. In some Igbo cultures, the *Osu* is a slave, an outcast who is not allowed to marry a member of a "superior" class irrespective of how beautiful or how popular the *Osu* might be. Music and dance never obfuscate the detail of the conflict and resolution, nor the moral force of the entire drama.

As in the Ghanaian and Yoruba video-films, Igbo video-films highlight the numerous vices prevalent in society. Even when witches and witchcraft are featured, it is done in the context of normal everyday conversational patterns where people express their opinions freely: they talk about teenage pregnancies, infidelity among married couples, drunkenness and other issues. As the Ghanaian columnist Baba Abdulai has observed, the advantages of replicating these vices on film stem from the fact that it not only encourages discussion of the issues but also contributes to redressing those tendencies that are considered inimical to society.[30] *Dirty Deal*, produced and directed by Kenneth Nnebue, and *Circle of Doom* by Vic Mordi, are about the notorious crime syndicate dubbed "419"; and *Diet of Lies* by Chris Oyams pokes fun at sugar daddies who entice young girls with false promises for sexual purposes. Consultation by barren couples with the river goddess (Mammy Wata) for help to bear children is the theme of Zeb Ejin's *Nneka, the Pretty Serpent*. Numerous other features deal with syncretic religions; Christian and Muslim conflicts; inheritance and the lack of property rights whereby women suffer because of their marginal status in society; social decay as a result of misplaced priorities, deceit and ill-gotten wealth. Thus video-films have become a medium that compels people to accept criticism of their traditions, and often to laugh at themselves while at the same time being entertained.

It is also noteworthy that popular themes still abound. This is not to say that the videos are devoid of authenticity but rather that there is an inclination to satisfy the audience with a variety of perspectives on well-known social problems. The notorious crime syndicate dubbed "419" is already dealt with in *Dirty Deal* and *Circle of Doom*, but in *The Stalk Exchange 419*, it is deployed with new significance. The producers also lure the public by embellishing video jackets with colorful photographs and catchy blurbs. The writing of the jacket information has become an art of its own with each producer vying for the most enticing style, à la Nigeria. The synopsis on the cover of the video cassette of *The Stalk Exchange 419* reads:

> The deal was worth $264 million … and it was going to be the easiest money anybody ever made. Smooth talking Jakinde "Jak" Lawanson has

a sure-fire way of selling this bogus deal to a bunch of greedy and unsuspecting foreigners. All they have to do is come to Nigeria and meet the man behind the deal, Dr. Egoma Onwuelingo. And thereafter, send a worthless shipment of car and airplane parts to Lagos. With "Dr. Lingo" in charge of inspections the deal would be a cinch, right? In this film directed by Don Okolo (*Material Witness*, 1994, *The Kangaroo*, 1995) it is total deception, where you are stalked before you are mercilessly devoured.

It is noteworthy that almost all the video-films display Ghanaian and Nigerian contemporary living tinged with ostentatious allure. In Nigeria, for example, video has become a fertile ground to display the current quest for wealth. Here you are not going to find lots of naked village-maiden breasts (as in francophone films), but rather high-profile upper class, middle class and lower middle class people, especially businessmen and women "who have made it." The concern to emphasize good living mirrors the aspirations of the majority of Nigerians and the images are presented to the audience members for them to reflect on the causes underlying the inequalities and prevalent societal decay. In the Igbo videos we find displays of luxurious houses, real ones rather than camouflaged luxurious hotel rooms and buildings of Lagos often used in other video-films. In the guise of such social criticism, the films also indulge in a preference for posh fast cars over the familiar dilapidated death-trap taxis plying the roads everywhere, and the Lagos of the imagination is infested with the latest models of Acura, Infiniti, Jaguar, Mercedes and Rolls Royce. Expensive clothes and imported wines all supposedly emphasize misplaced priorities, materialism and the get-rich-quick mentality of the fast age. At first, this trend for showing the good life promoted mediocre acting and technical infirmities (numerous bad video-films are still abundant), but video practice is gradually developing into a sophisticated art of entertainment and information, even as the demand for fun and the mad rush to get-rich-quick continues unabated.

If we take all these contrasting tendencies into account, it is readily apparent that video-filmmaking in Ghana and Nigeria uses a wide variety of themes and techniques to inform, entertain and sell, thereby developing a thriving market-based cinema and contributing to a new development in popular culture. This cinema, which eschews studio sets and embraces improvisation, recalls two parallel developments in the early history of Third World cinemas: the birth in the 1930s of the Brazilian musical genre, the *Chanchada*, and the development of the musical romance melodrama as the dominant cinema of India. The intriguing aspect of these two traditions is that both were culture-based and generated tremendous audience appeal. The *Chanchada* films were saturated with local language, popular songs, screwball comic plots, and well-known comedians.[31] Similarly, in India, the introduction of sound to cinema ushered in an unprecedented exploitation of local language, music and song in films, and thus gave birth to what is now believed to be the world's most popular film genre, the Indian musical. In both cases, their success is attributable to audience loyalty and strict adherence to the tastes of local culture, although in the case of India some critics have dismissed the films as "inconsequential" amateurish bastardizations of Hollywood musicals. However, the cultural specificity of the two film traditions spurs audience participation, both through the audiences' identification with the themes and vignettes of contemporary life, and by displaying, in an entertaining way, strategies for coping with post-colonial exigencies that foreign films are incapable of comprehending.

The factors described above have similarly lead to the proliferation of video-film production in anglophone Africa. Even when the films contain images of "destitution," they constitute, I would argue, not anthropological cliché but a form of documentary reality – Third Cinema's strategy of constructive analysis whereby images function as polyvalent signifiers, pointing to the struggle against traditional and post-colonial constraints. From this perspective, the audience members enjoy laughing at themselves or being angry with the perpetrators of their marginalization, and debating the consequences.

As video-film compels us to reassess the dynamics of African cinema, it also draws our attention to the limitations of dominant critical theories and demands a reconsideration of our polemical and pedagogical assumptions. The usual way of analyzing films – consideration of narrative technique, visual presentation and ideological orientation – may still apply. But just as West African countries are moving aggressively towards a market-based economy, so video-film culture is evolving along an unconventional path to its own autonomy. The nature of its uniqueness, its differentiation from mainstream cinemas, does not merely consist of an opposition to dominant cinematic forms. Collectively, the response of African filmmakers to the remaining post-colonial obstacles is a fighting stance against all factors retarding development, but this strategy is neither prescriptive nor binding and does not emanate from the conflict between "dominant" and "alternative" forms, but from change imposed by the prevailing circumstances and the difficulty of circumnavigating the perplexities of Africa's persistent post-coloniality. Thus the cinematic (and now video-film) discourse on post-colonial identities is primed less by a nostalgic reconstructive notion of history than by the complex, lived ramifications of present post-colonial dispositions.

I argue that this discourse depends on reconstituted frames of reference; it lies on the one hand in the confluence of the pan-Africanist ideology of post-colonial development and on the other in neo-capitalist or market enterprise theory, both of which must be accounted for in the reorientation of the discourse on post-coloniality, film and culture. The progressive nature of such a frame of reference results from viewing film and cultural discourse not through dogmatic or universalist tenets but in a relative, global context. Thus, the video-films have challenged us to acknowledge that it is only in witnessing the course of a nation's social and cultural development in the context of critical theory that we can apprehend an analytical outline of any society's individual cinematic aesthetic.

To sum up, I would emphasize that among recent cultural innovations the video-films undoubtedly present the most consistent attempt at mapping a commercial African cinema culture. But while the video-films may be generally understood as stepping stones or building blocks for a renascent African cinema, their success needs careful qualification. To be sure, it does not herald a transcendence of the limitations of African cinema; at best, it is a maneuver against the representational authority of celluloid filmmaking. At another level, it marks the proliferation of artistic expressions no longer bound by extant distribution/exhibition systems. This shift, aided in part by new technologies of representation, thrives on integrating social discourse in its narrative, just like celluloid films, but with the frugality and immediacy of the video format. It is in this way that the desires and anxieties of post-SAP communities assume marketable forms. It is in this way, as well, that these video-films speak *for* and *to* their burgeoning market/audience. As has been indicated, certain conditions have fostered this apparent break-through. But while these video-films vary in technical merit and conceptual sophistication they share a commonality to the extent that they are governed largely by what may be termed *the logic of the popular*. Within this logic, the mundane takes on discursive or representational importance, insofar as the textual coherency of these videos is anchored in the topical, the scandalous, and the cliché of contemporary society. It is important to note, as well, that video-films' popularity and "populist" leanings stem from contradictions and tensions within the definition of African cinema. This is so because these videos are grounded in an unapologetic commercial culture and seem quite indifferent to the social responsibility agenda of contemporary African cinema. There is another way, too, in which video-film phenomena embody the many responses of Africans to post-colonial commercial cultures. The video-films are popular to the extent that they have not only sustained the loyalty of the core cinema audience in their respective societies – mainly, urban and working class aficionados of Kung Fu, Hollywood, and Indian imports – but have also made advances in new audiences from the middle class *nouveaux riches*.

What does all this mean? First, we have to look at these video-films in relation to the construction of African subjectivities. In other words, it is important not just to focus on how circumstances shape the emergence of these videos but the definitions of African selves that emerge from them. This is quite important given the discursive dispositions of African cinema. While the majority of video-films do not show much technical virtuosity, they have instituted considerable shifts in the discourse of African cinema and raised important questions about types of film the African, as an autonomous subject, wishes to make. This is more significant if we note that production funds for these videos, unlike that of cinema, are solely indigenous. Be that as it may, arguing that the success of video-films is proof of what films Africans want or the direction African cinema *must* take is premature. The ethical and aesthetic standards of these video-films, whether in terms of production values or narrative conceptualization, cannot resolve these issues. The sustainability of the video-film boom would, in large part, depend on what structures they institute apart from the capricious tides of public taste and how the existing networks of distribution/exhibition accommodate or appropriate this new phenomenon. The irony of the situation, however, is that the success of video-film harbors dilemmas for the African cineastes who share the belief that cultivating the various publics for African cinema is a *sine qua non*.

Acknowledgement

This research was assisted by a grant from the Joint Committee on African Studies of the Social Science Research Council and the American Council of Learned Societies with funds provided by the National Endowment for the Humanities.

Notes

1   For a brief discussion of the 1960s tri-continental revolutionary movements which impacted upon the development of Third World cinemas, see Roy Armes, *Third World Film Making and the West* (Berkeley: University of California Press, 1987).

2   See Nwachukwu Frank Ukadike, *Black African Cinema* (Berkeley: University of California Press, 1994).

3   Chris Kabwato, "Eisenstein? Which Eisenstein?" *Zimbabwean Film Bulletin*, November/December 1996, p. 6.

4   Daniel Sharfstein discusses the Ghanaian video-films in his article, "Move Over, 'Forrest Gump'; in Ghana It's 'Sugar Daddy'," *The New York Times*, Sunday April 23, 1995, pp. 13, 23.

5   Homi K. Bhabha, "The Third Space: Interview with Homi Bhabha," in Jonathan Rutherford (ed.), *Identity: Community, Culture, Difference* (London: Lawrence and Wishart, 1990), p. 216. Also cited in Mark A. Reid, *Post-Négritude: Visual and Literary Culture* (New York: State University of New York Press, 1997), p. 22.

6   Gary Wilder, "Irreconcilable Differences: A Conversation with Albert Memmi," *Transition*, no. 71, 1977, p. 60.

7   Albert Memmi, in ibid. p. 60.

8   Jonathan Haynes "Mobilizing Yoruba Popular Culture: Babangida Must Go," a paper presented at the ASA Conference in Chicago, 1988. His use of the term "aesthetic of hunger" conflicts with Glauber Rocha's original conception of the term. However, the difference enables us to reflect on the politics of representation as dictated by either political and cultural determinants, or by the economic and socio-political realities of a given time. Hence, Hayes's term highlights the "shoddy" (his term) Nigerian films and video aesthetics made more scandalous and less socially-relevant by artists who practice for short-term gains, or, as others have observed, by sacrificing artistic maturity for perpetual mediocrity See p. 20 of his article "Structural Adjustments of Nigerian Comedy". On the contrary, Rocha's term was understood as constituting a politically-charged indigenous aesthetic which, in the parlance of Third Cinema ideology of the 1960s and early 1970s, was termed deconstructive, instructive and decolonizing.

9   Françoise Pfaff, "Conversation with Ghanaian Film Maker Kwaw Ansah," *Research In African Literatures*, vol. 26, no. 3, p. 190.

10 For a fuller discussion of universalized themes and universalized aesthetics, see chapter 5 of my book, *Black African Cinema*, op. cit.

11 Kofi Anyidoho, "Art in a Society in Transition," *African Quarterly on the Arts*, vol. 1, no. 4, p. 80.

12   Werewere Liking, "An African Woman Speaks Out Against African Filmmakers," *Black Renaissance*, vol. 1, no. 1, Fall, 1996, p. 176.
13   The Ghana Film Industries Corporation was sold by the Ghana Government to the Gama Film Company Limited, a Malaysian Company, that now operates TV3, a radio station, and maintains a video production unit. Some of the directors, writers and technicians of the defunct GFIC have been integrated into the new system while others have left in protest.
14   From an interview conducted by this author in Accra at the Ghana Film Industries Corporation in 1996.
15   Dietrich Berwanger's account, "Making Films and Money in Africa: Yoruba Films in Nigeria and Video Films in Ghana," is in *TTC News* (a newsletter, published by the Television Training Centre, Berlin), 1994 pp. 1–8 (whole issue).
16   Ibid. p. 2.
17   Conversation with this author at the National Film and Television Institute, Accra, 1996.
18   Sharfstein, op. cit., p. 13.
19   Ibid.
20   Ibid.
21   I obtained the above infromation from Nii Laryea Korley in conversation at the Ghana Film Industries Corporation, 1996, and from his illuminating article "The Video Boom," *Ecrans d'Afrique* (Africa Screens) no. 7, 1994, pp. 66–70.
22   Nii Laryea Korley, "The Video Boom," op. cit., p. 68.
23   Nii Laryea Korley, "Crossroads," *The Statesman*, December 18, 1994, p. 10.
24   Ibid.
25   Pfaff, op. cit., p. 190.
26   Quoted in Korley, "Crossroads", p. 10.
27   Johnson Kalu, "A Critique of Igbo Films," *Saturday Champion*, August 19, 1995, p. 20.
28   For Brendan Shehu's detailed assessment of the Nigerian Film Corporation, see his interview in Nwachukwu Frank Ukadike, *A Questioning Cinema: Conversations with African Filmmakers* (Minneapolis: University of Minnesota Press, forthcoming).
29   Kalu, op. cit., p. 20.
30   Baba Abdulai, "Video Films to the Rescue," *Weekly Spectator*, Saturday April 8, 1995, p. 6.
31   For a discussion of this aspect of Brazilian film see Robert Stam, "The Shape of Brazilian Film History," in Randal Johnson and Robert Stam (eds), *Brazilian Cinema* (New York: Columbia University Press, 1995), pp. 15–52.

Bibliography

Abdulai, Baba, "Video Films to the Rescue," *Weekly Spectator*, Saturday April 8, 1995, p. 6.

Anyidoho, Kofi, "Art in a Society in Transition," *African Quarterly on the Arts*, vol. 1, no. 4, p. 8.

Ayorinde, Steve, "Associations Firm Up Control On Video," *The Guardian*, July 10, 1997, p. 31.

Berwanger, Dietrich, "Making Films and Money in Africa: Yoruba Films in Nigeria and Video Films in Ghana," *TTC News* (a newsletter, published by the Television Training Centre, Berlin, 1994, pp. 1–8.

Bhabha, Homi K., "The Third Space: Interview with Homi Bhabha," in Jonathan Rutherford (ed.) *Identity: Community, Culture, Difference* (London: Lawrence and Wishart, 1990).

Haynes, Jonathan, "Structural Adjustments of Nigerian Comedy: Baba Sida." *Passages* 8 (1994): p. 20.

Kabwato, Chris, "Eisenstein? Which Eisenstein?" *Zimbabwean Film Bulletin*, November/December 1996, p. 6.

Kalu, Johnson, "A Critique of Igbo Films," *Saturday Champion*, August 19, 1995, p. 20.

Korley, Nii Laryea, "The Video Boom," *Ecrans d'Afrique* (Africa Screens) no. 7, 1994, pp. 66–70.

Korley, Nii Laryea, "Crossroads," *The Statesman*, December 18, 1994, p. 10.

Liking, Werewere, "An African Woman Speaks Out Against African Filmmakers," *Black Renaissance*, vol. 1, no. 1, Fall 1996, pp. 170–7.

Pfaff, Françoise, "Conversation with Ghanaian Film Maker Kwaw Ansah," *Research In African Literatures*, vol. 26, no. 3, 1997, pp. 186–93.

Reid, Mark A., *Post-Négritude: Visual and Literary Culture* (New York: State University of New York Press, 1997).

Sharfstein, Daniel, "Move Over, 'Forrest Gump'; In Ghana, It's 'Sugar Daddy'," *The New York Times*, Sunday April 23, 1995, pp. 13 and 23.

Ukadike, Nwachukwu Frank, *Black African Cinema* (Berkeley: University of California Press, 1994).

Wilder, Gary, "Irreconcilable Differences: A Conversation with Albert Memmi," *Transition*, no. 71, 1977, pp. 158–77.

Part IV
The relocation of culture
Social specificity and the "Third" question

The Third World was, in a sense, born in Indonesia, where at the Bandung Conference of Non-aligned Nations President Sukarno made it the rallying cry for resistance to neocolonialism, adding fresh impetus to Lumumba's Pan-Africanism, inspiring Fanon and Cabral to theorize the postcolonial moment at the borderlines of emancipation, and giving voice to decolonization struggles in North Africa and Indo-China. Nevertheless, as Krishna Sen now argues, various historical conjunctures resulted in the paradox that Third Cinema had, at best, a very marginal impact on oppositional discourses in Indonesian Cinema.

During the Sukarno period "resistance" to First Cinema was state-sponsored (and thus far from oppositional) and followed rubrics established by Soviet Socialist Realism and Chinese "revolutionary romanticism." The subtle subtext of this argument suggests the paradigms of Socialist Realism (the dominant mode favored by the state-sponsored cinemas resembling those advocated by Teshome Gabriel), with their near-exclusive concentration on the content of films, institute an inescapable and unsustainable contradiction with the formal opposition to the language of First Cinema, a practice insisted upon by Solanas and Getino.

Sen's chapter also engages Benedict Anderson's optimistically benign conception of nation, for, as she points out, Suharto's Indonesian nation fast took to functioning like a non-inclusive, repressive state. Indeed, the infant Marxist filmmaking practices that had arisen during the fallen regime were put to the sword in Suharto's uniformitarian New Order, while at the same time a deep ambivalence persisted regarding the chief cultural export to Indonesia of the now "friendly" US government. Thus, for Indonesian film-makers "nationalism" has had a far more corrosive and homogenizing effect on the local than globalism. Localism, in such a situation, argues Sen, can thus extend Fredric Jameson's conception of "national allegory," perhaps proving that what hurts most about history is its tendency to compound paradoxes.

It is something of a paradox also that the two chapters of *Rethinking Third Cinema* which contribute the most to theorizing conceptions of location in cinema are also the chapters which are the most "local" in choosing to explicate individual film texts. Rey Chow's contribution is unusual in many respects. A cultural critic noted for her analysis of China's encounter with the "West" through the media of literature and cinema, and for her work on diaspora, she here adopts a form of critical engagement seldom undertaken by Third Cinema critics; namely, a close, textual reading that does not shy away from critical methodologies developed in other fields and in other contexts (recall, in this regard, the celebrated debate between Gabriel and Burton). Central to Chow's argument is the question of "home"; is the filmmaker's home a geographical location (such as birthplace), a shared cultural tradition (community or nation), the site of inscription of the primal scene (i.e. a corner of consciousness), or, as Lacan would have of a writer's language, the mirror of the screen itself where, and where as Christian Metz argues, spectators see reflected conscious and unconscious acts of condensation?

Third Cinema theorists, in (understandably) privileging certain discursive formations, have sometimes missed deeply revelatory moments of discursive intersection. Sen and Chow suggest complex circuits of perception of self/ other, community/nation, then/now, here/there. Were Third Cinema theorists to incorporate the methodologies suggested by them, the critical under-development of which Third Cinema has been accused would soon pass into memory.

6   What's "oppositional" in Indonesian cinema?

Krishna Sen

At a time when the border-zones of the Indonesian nation are being violently tested by ethnic, religious and regional differences, when in fact it has contracted in relinquishing the world's newest nation, East Timor, it may be foolhardy to speak at all of something called Indonesian cinema. But the institutional organization of films produced and consumed in Indonesia is such that it is impossible to discuss these except as "national cinema". Moreover, the current contestations over what constitutes the Indonesian nation allow us to raise new questions about domination and resistance in its film culture – questions which the Third Cinema movement inserted irrevocably into all theorising about films in the "non-western" world.

Here I focus on two moments of enormous ideological contradiction in Indonesia: the first half of the 1960s, prior to the fall of post-colonial Indonesia's first President, Sukarno; and the second half of the 1990s building up to the fall of the second President, Suharto. Third Worldist discourses have a long history in Indonesia. Sukarno's radical nationalism was in part legitimised by a close association with the Third World "Non-Aligned" movement. Sukarno's rhetoric included a quite explicit demonisation of Hollywood within its more general attack on "cultural imperialism." And yet Indonesian radicalism and "Third Cinema" (both as movements and as sets of ideas) seem to have by-passed each other. Re-reading two important moments of Indonesian film history in relation to Third Cinema theorising I suggest that the globalist paradigm of Third Cinema theorising does not quite capture the radical drives within Indonesian cinema. Instead, Indonesian cinema's radicalism needs to be defined in terms of the political constellations within the nation and cannot be read off in any generalised way in relation to Hollywood, global culture or capitalism.

Hollywood and the Third World in Third Cinema

The high tide of Third Cinema both as an analytical position and as a film movement has passed. What had started in the 1960s as a set of radical manifestoes and low-budget experimental films of a small group of Latin American filmmakers became by the 1980s an academic project of defining a cinema of opposition, otherness and alterity. These later accounts of Third

Cinema remained locked in what this cinema *was not* as every attempt to spell out what it was brought to the fore the problem of diversity that no single description could accommodate and exclusions that no account could avoid. Academic writing also tended to separate Third Cinema from the Third World. In his review of the concept of Third Cinema, Paul Willemen asserted, for instance, that "The notion of Third Cinema" was "most emphatically not Third World Cinema" (Willemen 1989, p. 3). The move suited Willemen's purpose in the late 1980s of "endeavouring to make more breathing space within the UK for the emergence of otherness as a challenge to English ideology" (p. 29). However, both historically (that is, when one returns to Latin American roots of the concept) and in Gabriel's early attempt (1985) to theorise it, the concept of "Third Cinema" attempts to name a tri-continental phenomenon which depends on the notion of the "Third World."

Glauber Rocha, Fernando Solanas and Octavio Getino and following them Teshome Gabriel, all start from the notion of the Third World, drawing on the revolutionary discourse of Che, Fanon and others which had already marked the "Third" as a space of counter-imperialist collectivism. Glauber Rocha's now classic account in 1967 reads:

> For the Third World Filmmaker, commitment begins with the first light, because the camera opens on to the Third World, an occupied land … .
>
> These films from Asia, Africa, and Latin America are films of discomfort. The discomfort begins with the basic material: inferior cameras and laboratories, … .
>
> The tools belong to Hollywood as arms belong to the Pentagon. No filmmaker is completely free. Even when not the prisoner of censorship or financial commitments he [sic] remains a prisoner until he discovers within himself the tri-continental man.
>
> (Johnson and Stam 1995, p. 77)

For Gabriel the "third" phase of Third World cinema is attained when the industry is under national (or even government) control and filmmakers insist on "viewing film in its ideological ramifications" (Gabriel 1985, in Pines and Willemen 1989, p. 33):

> Film as an ideological tool. Here a film is equated or recognised as an ideological instrument. This particular phase also constitutes a framework of agreement between the public (or the indigenous institution of cinema) and the film-maker. A Phase III film-maker is one who is perceptive of and knowledgeable about the pulse of the Third World masses. Such a film-maker is truly in search of a Third World cinema – a cinema that has respect for Third World peoples.
>
> (Ibid., p. 34)

There are problems with such an internationalised description of national cinemas, which Willemen (1989) has taken up, and to which I will return later. I want to turn first to Indonesian cinema's Third-Worldism which pre-dated Rocha's positing of a tri-continental filmmaker, and which was grounded in the many claims of global anti-colonial solidarity in Sukarno's Indonesia, especially his bid for leadership of the Non-Aligned movement.

Hollywood vs Third-Worldism in Indonesia: 1960s

In April 1964 Indonesia hosted the Afro-Asian film festival, designed to exclude all nations in the region allied to the United States. Here the idea of a Third World-centred challenge to Hollywood's industrial and aesthetic dominance was widely canvassed. A month later, one of the nation's foremost poets wrote in the Communist Party daily *Harian Rakyat* (*People's Daily*):

Action For Boycott

I boycott American films
For the victims of imperialism
I boycott American films
For South Vietnam ... .

I boycott American films
Because the Black American is my friend ... .

My comrades everywhere
Whom I defend as an Afro-Asian writer
I boycott American films
Because I want space
for the films of my country,
and for the films of the "new emerging forces".

Unlike Rocha's theorisation, anchored in an analysis of cinema itself, the foregoing emerges not from analysis of cinema, but from an attempt to locate cinema within a national political scheme.

In 1957, Sukarno, Indonesia's first President (after independence from Dutch colonialism in 1949) overthrew the multi-party democracy and estab-lished what he called "Guided Democracy."[1] In practice his government was to become increasingly anti-Western on the one hand and authoritarian on the other. Several political parties were banned, his critics often silenced and even occasionally jailed. The Communist Party, which had polled 16 percent of the votes (fourth largest) in Indonesia's first election in 1955 expanded over the rest of the decade and provided part of Sukarno's mass support base. The early 1960s were marked by a massive economic downturn and state-sponsored radical nationalism. In his speeches to the United Nations in 1960, and to the Non-Aligned nations at Belgrade in 1961, Sukarno made his own claim to the leadership of the "new emerging forces" (Legge 1972, p. 333). Conceptually fluid, Sukarno's "new emerging forces" (or NEFO as it appears in most Indonesian media of the time) encompassed "the Asian nations, the

African nations, the Latin American nations, the nations of the socialist countries, the progressive groups in the capitalist countries" (Speech 7 January 1965, cited in Legge 1972, p. 345).

Cultural life and cinema in particular were deeply marked by Sukarno's obsession with national political rhetoric. By the early 1960s all filmmakers and indeed the entire intelligentsia of the nation had divided into "left" and "right" – the former centred around the Communist Party, increasingly aligned to the President, the latter a mix of liberal and Islamic parties with growing support from governments of western capitalist nations, particularly the US and the UK. Through the early 1960s as Sukarno confronted Anglo-American power in Asia, and periodic bans were imposed on the films of those nations, Lekra (Lembaga Kebudayaan Rakyat, Institute of People's Culture), the key cultural mass organization of the Communist Party of Indonesia (see Foulcher 1986), attempted to articulate a cultural critique and a model for revolutionary culture including a film culture of opposition to Hollywood cinema.

A cinema of opposition?

Bachtiar Siagian was the most prolific and prominent member of Lekra (which in the Indonesian context can be read as a short-hand for left-radical), a film director and film theorist in the 1960s. There are two threads to his anti-Hollywood argument: economic and ideological. The economic critique depended first on documentation of the large and increasing numbers of American films coming into Indonesia since the end of the Second World War and, second, on the institutional arrangements through which AMPAI (American Motion Pictures Association in Indonesia) controlled film distribution in Indonesia.

The ideological critique usually went thus:

> Within the imperialist strategy of the US, Hollywood cinema is an important medium for preparing the psychological conditions for implementing their political concepts, while their military power acts as an instrument of pressure to enforce that political concept.
>
> ... its main target is our revolutionary mentality ... . American films provide examples and suggestions of the individualist way of life as a reflection of the society and culture of decadent capitalism.
>
> (Siagian 1964, p. 16)

But the development of a revolutionary aesthetic to guide the work of filmmakers and other cultural workers proved more complex than the polemical rejection of Hollywood cinema. Lekra theorists played out various versions of Soviet "socialist realism" and later the Chinese notion of "revolutionary romanticism."[2] Most of the attempt to define a cinema of revolution remained locked in discussion of appropriate subject matter. Only in his long piece (published in six parts in the Indonesian Communist Party's daily) on Chinese cinema, does Siagian explore the processes of a film's signification beyond just its subject matter.[3]

Asked by Chinese colleagues to review their cinema in 1962, Siagian starts his piece with an acknowledgement that his own mode of spectatorship has been formed by the experience of Hollywood cinema, which he cannot necessarily set aside in his responses to China's "socialist realist" works. Siagian then goes on to explore the relationship between film and the structure of the society in and for which it is made: "Socialist Realist films are the superstructure supported on [the base of] a socialist society … where the system of production and relations of production open up new perspectives on life." Socialist realist cinema he says, therefore, cannot be learned second hand from books "but through a development of social practice." Chinese socialist films he adds are made possible, indeed made necessary, by the new "material" and "new personality" that the Chinese revolution brought into existence (see Siagian 1962: part 1).

The point here is not that Indonesian cinema's oppositional work is better understood in relation to the theorisation of socialist realism than in relation to "Third Cinema." The question is whether the films and writings of Bachtiar (and others in that period) critiquing Hollywood can be seen as "oppositional" when this was in fact officially sanctioned, politically dominant (though not nationally popular) Indonesian cinema in the early 1960s. In the framework of a global film culture into which the notion of Third Cinema is inscribed, the work of Siagian and his Lekra colleagues needs to be seen as "oppositional" at least in the limited sense of attempting to imagine for Indonesia a model of cinema other than those produced by Hollywood. But in the national Indonesian political frame, this cinema was, at least for a brief period, aligned to the state under President Sukarno as he authored and authorised nationalist, anti-Western cultural discourse. This alliance with state power does not disqualify this cinema from Gabriel's notion of Third Cinema, but it equally does not sit comfortably with elaborations such as Willemen's, where in the final analysis Third Cinema is recognized as such by its sense of "non-belonging, non-identity with the culture one inhabits, whether it be nationally defined, ethnically or in any other way …" (Willemen 1989, p. 28).

In 1960s Indonesia, not only were Hollywood films banned, but also the work of Indonesian filmmakers who were politically opposed to Sukarno, or who incorporated into their films any overt critique of him. A small number of these filmmakers were deeply influenced by Hollywood cinema and consciously modelled their work on it. Usmar Ismail, whose films have been most clearly identified with an anti-Sukarno liberal-democratic politics, not only had some months of training in Hollywood funded by an American scholarship, but he has also written in some detail to describe the ways in which he learnt and incorporated the style of Hollywood cinema in his own work (see Sen 1994, pp. 27–49). Ironically, in the political constellation of the moment, Hollywood may thus even be seen to have provided some of the language of political opposition in Indonesia.

Hollywood strikes back

Immediately after the Afro-Asian film festival in Jakarta, the Action Committee for the Boycott of Imperialist American Films, PAPFIAS (as the acronym reads in Indonesian), was formed. Political graffiti (cited in *Harian Rakyat*, 2 July 1964) expressed the importance of the film boycott in Indonesia's overall opposition to the US:

> Boycott American Films
> Chuck out Jones [the US Ambassador]
> Crush the US Fleet [US Seventh Fleet in the Indian Ocean]

On 17 August 1964, the Ministry of Trade asked the American Motion Pictures Association to stop trading in Indonesia, which was seen effectively as a ban on American films. Within days, however, the Film Council under military control was urging movie theatres to continue to screen American films as long as these had been imported and censored in accordance with existing laws. Nonetheless, for the following 12 months, few American films were imported into or distributed in Indonesia.

This state support of left-wing cultural work was short-lived. A coup attempt by young officers in the early hours of 1 October 1965 set in motion a chain of events that led to the fall of Sukarno and the destruction of the Communist Party and associated political and cultural forces. The army under then Major General Suharto crushed the coup, which they blamed on the Communist Party. The so-called New Order was established when Suharto took command of national security and, in the following months, of the nation state itself.

If Sukarno had tended towards authoritarianism this was nothing compared to what followed. For the next 33 years, the Suharto regime legitimised its authoritarian rule by demonising Communism. The party and its mass organisations were banned. Books and films by "fellow travellers" burned and banned. Hundreds of thousands of suspected leftists were murdered or imprisoned. Bachtiar Siagian was incarcerated for 13 years. Even as the military alliances were being cemented, the anti-American film policy was officially reversed in 1966. In the following year 400 Hollywood films (more films than had been made in the US in any one year) were imported into Indonesia and the numbers rose every year until the early 1970s.

I came to Indonesian cinema in the early 1980s, a period regarded by many political observers as the high tide of Suharto's New Order. By this time not only was Hollywood cinema unassailable in the market place but a generation of spectators and filmmakers had grown up with Hollywood as the dominant textual system against which all other films were to be judged. As I have suggested in my previous work, "a significant part of Indonesia's cinematic heritage was destroyed in the civil war and counter-revolution of 1965–6" (Sen 1994, p. 49). In 1980–1, my year as a post-graduate on field research on Indonesian cinema, I uncovered few and always highly negative references to filmmakers who worked within or with the support of left-wing organizations. In the first full-length book on the history of Indonesian cinema, author Salim Said provided a characteristic New Order view:

> Thinking that it had a friend in President Sukarno ..., the PKI (Indonesian Communist Party) ... felt that the time they had long awaited and prepared for had arrived, that is the time for an offensive.
>
> The PKI started the offensive not without serious calculations. Its first target was the cultural sector. Especially film.
>
> (Said 1982, p. 60)

In the film archives, poorly funded in any case, there remained only shreds of two films by known Lekra filmmakers. A very small amount of leftist literature on cinema was held in a restricted collection, access to which required special permission from the director of the archives. No one working in the archives, or any of the established filmmakers themselves, knew the whereabouts of Bachtiar Siagian or other filmmakers who had been released from prisons in the late 1970s. But small groups of university students and young artists who had grown up in the New Order and who were looking for alternatives to the severely restrictive cultural practices in Suharto's Indonesia had started to make contact with released Communist prisoners. The interest of these students and cultural activists was not so much in the works and ideas of these filmmakers – there was after all no way to recover those films – but rather in that these former prisoners represented in their very being the repressed "other" of New Order Indonesia's culture and politics.[4]

It was in this socio-political climate that Bachtiar's work was re-discovered. I have argued elsewhere that Bachtiar's films, more than his writing, challenged Hollywood cinema's dominant form and content. He had tried to shift the standard point of film aesthetic reference in Indonesia, where Hollywood equalled "good" and Bombay marked its opposite "commercial," "lower class" cinema (see Sen 1994, pp. 11–49). It is easy to map Bachtiar's work ideologically and institutionally onto what Teshome Gabriel calls the "third phase" of development of Third World cinema (p. 46). But we can only reconstruct his films indirectly from written shooting scripts and reviews. None of his films have been available for viewing since 1965. Film work of the left was eradicated far more perfectly than many other kinds of cultural texts. Music was remembered by students and played privately in homes. It was never possible to burn left-wing books in every private collection. But in a pre-video era, the limited numbers of film prints were easily obliterated by wholesale destruction and the ravages of time. In the 1980s some of the poets and novelists released from prisons were able to write and publish again. The legal ban on employing former political prisoners in the media was, however, strictly enforced in the film industry.[5] When Bachtiar did get piece-work writing scripts under an assumed name for low budget films, the producer asked for an explicit assurance that there would be absolutely nothing in the script to give away the identity of the writer!

I have tried elsewhere to piece together an account of left-wing film praxis in pre-1965 Indonesia from scripts, reviews, other writings and interviews (Sen 1985). However, without the films, it is all but impossible to examine these in relation to Gabriel's central argument about Third Cinema's distinctive organisation of time and space. As such the almost perfect "otherness" of left-wing cinema in post-1965 Indonesian culture, its complete repression, puts it beyond the reach of text-based film theory altogether.

The "nation" question in Third Cinema

If self-conscious ideological opposition to Hollywood was the first marker of Third Cinema, then an identification with national liberation (however variedly defined) was the next most common theme, at least in the early writings on the subject. The idea of the nation in this discourse, however, always rubs up against globalized Third World identification. On the one hand, the tri-continental definition of a radical film aesthetics defies national boundaries. On the other hand, as Willemen points out, "if any cinema is determinedly 'national' even 'regional' in its address and aspirations, it is Third Cinema." (Willemen 1989, p. 17) Similarly, as Aijaz Ahmad comments about one of the more influential left critical approaches to cultural texts, "[Fredric] Jameson insists over and over again that the *national* experience is central to the cognitive formation of the Third World intellectual, and that the narrativity of that experience take the form exclusively of a 'national allegory'." (Ahmad 1992, p. 109) Starting from a very different position, Ben Anderson, perhaps the most influential recent analyst of nationhood and of Indonesia, also sees the nation as the epicentre of cultural imaginings. In a piece best known to Indonesia specialists, but first published in the same year as his now classic *Imagined Communities*, Anderson argues against "the contemporary conflation" of a "popular, participatory nation with an older adversarial state" (Anderson, 1983, p. 119). He suggests that states have "genealogies older than those of the nations over which they are now perched" (p. 94) and elaborates on that separation between state and nation in the context of the history of Indonesia. He argues that the struggle for independence and the years that followed represented the defeat of the colonial state by a newly imagined nation. Suharto's New Order, however, "is best understood as the resurrection of the state [founded in Dutch colonialism] and its triumph vis-à-vis society and nation" (p. 109). At the end of the century, nearly 40 years after the victory of the "adversarial New Order state" over the "participatory Indonesian nation," both state and nation in Indonesia face their greatest challenge since 1965. Since the fall of Suharto, the separatist war in Aceh (on-going since early 1990s) has gathered momentum, as has the separatist movement in West Papua. Religious strife between Muslims and Christians in Maluku have left thousands dead and displaced, confounding all attempts by the state's agencies to bring an end to the war. In this context it seems worth asking whether the site of resistance to the state in Indonesia can still be located in the "national" community, or should we be looking in another space? East Timor has devolved altogether.

An aside in Arjun Appadurai's much cited essay "Disjuncture and Difference in the Global Cultural Economy" is a useful starting point:

> it is worth noticing that for the people of Irian Jaya, Indonesianization may be more worrisome than Americanisation, as Japanization may be for Koreans, Indianization for Sri Lankans, Vietnamization for the Cambodians, Russianization for the people of Armenia and the Baltic Republics.
>
> (Appadurai, 1990, p. 295)

The source of cultural threat, then, is not the triumphal bearer of global capitalism, the United States, alone, but depending on your location the nearest cultural strongman. My particular point, though, refers only to his first example: the fear of Indonesianization for the people of Irian Jaya. The Irian instance seems to me to be very different from the rest,[6] in that Irian Jaya is part of the Indonesian nation – at least at the level of formal national and international politics. The people of Irian Jaya ("West Papua" prior to its incorporation into Indonesia in 1962 and again now in the post-Suharto period) may or may not imagine themselves as belonging in the Indonesian nation; they are nonetheless daily addressed by the dominant electronic media as such. The people of West Papua and indeed people in many other parts of Indonesia (whether or not there is a current separatist war in progress) experienced the state as the agent of Indonesian nationhood – not just state television and radio, but also centrally issued textbooks, state laws that made raising of the national flag and singing of the national anthem compulsory in all schools, and the standardised *batik* uniform of all civil-servants were all mechanisms through which Indonesians were daily interpellated into the Indonesian nation. The hand of the state in the construction of the Indonesian national culture in the Suharto years does not need to be analytically uncovered: it was there for all to see. Newspapers and films were censored, television until 1987 was entirely state owned, and private radio and television stations had to broadcast the state station's news bulletin several times a day. Anderson's state (bad, old, adversarial) versus nation (good, new, participatory) dichotomy, though theoretically elegant, was not experientially available to many Indonesian citizens.

In the early 1960s, as I have suggested earlier in this chapter, the Indonesian nation, aligned to the state, became the symbol of radical opposition to global capitalism. At the end of the New Order in the late 1990s the Indonesian nation, enmeshed in the New Order state, was no longer available as a redemptive category in any straightforward way. Wilson and Dissanayake have identified the loss of simple dichotomies as part of the postmodern condition in the opening of *Global/Local: Cultural Production and the Transnational Imaginary*:

Postmodern cultural-workers, on the verge of becoming "symbolic engineers" and critical self-consciousness of global capital, stand at the cross-roads of an altered and more fractal terrain everywhere we guess at century's end: a new world-space of cultural production and national representation which is simultaneously becoming more *globalized* (unified around dynamics of capitalogic moving across borders) and more *localized* (fragmented into contestory enclaves of difference, coalition and resistance) in everyday texture and composition.

(Wilson and Dissanayake 1996, p. 1)

What space was left, then, where at the end of the 1990s Indonesian filmmakers could "engineer" symbols of radical opposition?

Willemen makes a passing reference to the "regional" address of Third Cinema, which is not developed in his essay as a point of difference from the nation. I will not address here the deep-seated regional diversities which are clearly marking the current political scene in Indonesia. I want to focus on one film, *Surat Untuk Bidadari* (*Letter for an Angel*), which constructs a *concrete* (one that we can touch and traverse and see) local communal identity in opposition to the *imagined* (or *imagineered* through textual strategies) national Indonesian one. For the rest of this chapter I want to unpack this "local" to understand its complex relation to the world and the nation.

One needs to be careful, of course, to avoid "putting abstract globality into binary opposition with a concrete localism … [which] often leads to dubious politics – as in the new consumerist cultural studies (John Fiske, Henry Jenkins, and others) where local users subvert dominant ideology to their own immediate ends" (Polan 1996, p. 258). Of course the same is true of an unproblematic binarism between an "imagined" national and a "concrete" local . What I am trying to get at, however, is not some inherent reality of the "local" as subversive or oppositional to global or national culture, but the availability of the "local" to be mobilised as such in the cultural discourse at the end of the New Order in Indonesia, in ways that the "national" was not. As Arif Dirlik has argued,

the postmodern repudiation of Enlightenment metanarratives and the teleology of modernity has allowed the reemergence of the local as a site of resistance and the struggle for liberation. It is the struggle for historical and political presence of groups suppressed or marginalised by modernization … that has dynamized this postmodern consciousness and has produced the contemporary notion of the local, which must be distinguished from "traditional" localism if only because such struggles are themselves informed by the modernity that they reject. This is the local that has been worked over by modernity. It finds expression presently in the so-called "politics of difference" that presupposes local differences (literally and metaphorically, with reference to social groups) both as a point of departure and as a goal of liberation.

(Dirlik 1996, p. 35)

It is on to this reading of localism as politics of difference that I want to map Garin Nugroho's *Surat Untuk Bidadari* (*Letter for an Angel*, 1993).

National cinema in Indonesia in the 1990s

Cinema in Suharto's New Order was allowed little space for experimentation (see Sen 1994). The relatively small size of the industry, censorship, the monopoly on distribution in the hands of Suharto-cronies and the historical definition of Indonesian cinema as the diet of the poor and the uneducated all acted against experimentation. The art film circuit in Indonesia is tiny and Indonesian films have no space within it. The handful of Indonesian films that have gained some international recognition have not only failed in the popularity stakes, they have also frequently failed to get mainstream critical acknowledgement in Indonesia (best represented by the Annual Film Festival Awards, *Citra*).

A plethora of regulations have forced cinema into a national strait-jacket and have circumscribed whole bodies of ideas from Indonesian cinema. All references to conflicts of race, religion and class were banned. Almost any ideology one could name was banned: Marxism, Leninism, Maoism, Imperialism (see Sen 1994, pp. 69–70). Indonesian films were quite literally forced to speak the national language, that is, films were not allowed to use regional languages or even dialects of Bahasa Indonesian (the national language) as the principal diegetic language. All producers of films had to be located in Jakarta and all films had to go through systems of national control. It was in this context that Garin Nugroho's film *Surat Untuk Bidadari* could recuperate the local (not any particular local, but a local-qua-local) as the site of opposition. If we read *Surat* against the highly restricted formal political language of the New Order, we find that Anderson's classic "imagined community" evolves into the repressive, unrepresentative state, and an alternative to the national space has to be imagined to ground the opposition to the repressive New Order state.

Surat Untuk Bidadari was an unusual film in many ways. Nugroho had risen to prominence with his first feature film *Cinta Dalam Sepotong Roti* (*Love in a Slice of Bread*) winning several awards at the 1991 Indonesian film festival, including the coveted "Best Film" *Citra*. He went on to receive the "Best New Director" prize at the Asia-Pacific Film Festival in Seoul in 1992. Garin Nugroho stated explicitly that he had set out to make a "European" film in the Indonesian language. To what extent he had reassembled stylistic codes of New European cinema in the Indonesian film ecology would constitute a separate study altogether. The point here is that Garin was expressly seeking a relationship to world cinema as a way out of some of the constraints of Indonesian cinema.

Love in a Slice of Bread did relatively well at the box office as well. This combination of popular and critical acclaim brought the new director funding for his second feature, *Surat Untuk Bidadari*, from the state film company

PPFN, troubled at that time by the downturn in Indonesian film production,[7] and the newly established "educational television" channel, TPI, owned by President Suharto's daughter Tutut. Internationally, *Surat Untuk Bidadari* proved to be Indonesia's single most successful film of the 1990s, receiving three international awards in 1994, one at the Berlin Film Festival, the Caiddi d'Oro award for the "best film" at the Twenty-fourth Taormina Film Festival in Italy, and the "Young Cinema" Award at Tokyo. However, *Surat Untuk Bidadari*, unacceptably experimental for the distributors, never had normal commercial release in Indonesia. It was also rejected by the Film Festival jury, although Indonesia's longest standing literary journal *Horizon* commended the film highly for its artistic courage.

Surat Untuk Bidadari is set in a remote village in Sumba, an economically backward eastern island, with no particular tourist appeal, with nothing to recommend it other than its marginalization by the global capitalism that has more firmly incorporated the western parts of the Indonesian nation. It is a place that feminist anthropologist Kathy Robinson would call a "step-child of progress" (Robinson 1986). The story is of a pre-teenage boy Lewa seen through his eyes and his camera. Lewa is motherless and is orphaned early in the film. With the camera that he has acquired from a visiting fashion-shoot crew, he proceeds to search for a "mother image," which in part takes the form of taking photographs of women's and girls' breasts. His only willing models are a pre-pubescent girl from a neighboring village and, almost at the end of the film, the village beauty, Berlian Merah (Red Gem). Their collaboration (or Lewa's entrapment of them?) sets him on a collision course with the law – first with the "traditional" law of the land when the neighboring villagers declare war, and in the final sequence of the film, after Lewa murders Berlian's brutal husband, with national law.

It would be easy enough to map this story on to an Oedipal rubric. What drives the narrative is Lewa's desire for his mother, projected (displaced) onto the bodies of other women. His Polaroid camera, a prosthesis for his eyes, puts him literally in touch with the maternal bodies. The story is completed when Lewa kills Kuda Liar (Wild Horse), the village strongman, who has murdered Lewa's father and brutalised the two women Lewa loves best, Berlian and Lewa's teacher, known simply as Bu Guru ("Madame Teacher"). The "law" of the fathers – "traditional"/local and "modern"/national – will not tolerate Lewa's desire. In the closing scene Lewa is without his camera, incarcerated, motionless and refusing to look at Berlian, who has come to visit.

It is not this universalised story, but the imagery through which the Oedipal imaginary unfolds, that tells the story of a very specific time and place and constitutes a very particular political intervention. The story could be told (as I have done above) without the global icons – Madonna, Elvis and the downed Second World War aeroplane which recur in scene after scene. It is through these "unnecessary" (from the point of view of the Oedipal story) signifiers that we can read the film as a political allegory underlying the psychoanalytical scenario. In a sense such a reading gets very close to Jameson's argument about the politics in Third World texts. But this political signification is very different from the "national allegory" that Jameson identifies in his reading of "third world texts" in his 1986 *Social Text* article. In *Surat* the nation is marginalised, visible only on the edges of the text as the cultural discourse of a repressive state.

Generically part ethnography and part fantasy, the film broke most norms of Indonesian filmmaking. Nugroho went to Sumba with a storyline about a young boy's search for identity, but without a fixed script or cast. The fiction was written into an ethnographic film that he shot entirely on location in Sumba, with long scenes of local rituals. There are only three professional actors in the film, as most of the rest of its large cast, including the boy hero Lewa, were drawn from the local village populations. The hereditary village chief (*"raja,"* literally king) was played by a real *"raja"* from the area. Several scenes contain dialogues which are partly in Sumbanese dialects – some characters including Lewa's father speak exclusively in Sumbanese. No other film in the New Order had used local casting to nearly this extent. While in the 1990s a small number of popular television series and films were starting to use Javanese and the Betawi dialect of Indonesian, this was the first Indonesian film since independence to make substantial use of a minority language from an outer island. The ethnographic turn of the film is in part characteristic of the early phase of Third Cinema as described by Gabriel. It was also in some ways reminiscent of some of the work of Bachtiar Siagian and others in the pre-1965 period. But Nugroho's work redirects the ethnographic towards a narrative closure that is quite different from Siagian's.

Films depicting regional cultural forms in part by using locally-specific images and casts had all but disappeared after 1965. Jakarta-dominated since the 1940s, the film industry became in the New Order (like Indonesian industrial capital more generally) entirely concentrated in Jakarta, the city, which also dominated as the setting for the films. At least three-quarters of the films in the last 30 years are either implicitly or explicitly set in Jakarta and its surrounds. Most of the rest are set in rural or mythical Java. Since the late 1970s a small but growing proportion have been set in "foreign" locations, usually in large cities in Europe, America or Southeast Asia. Films set on other islands of Indonesia were extremely rare during the New Order period, even more so when they constitute anything other than an extended setting for visiting Jakarta protagonists.

In the 1950s, arguably the most innovative period of Indonesian national cinema, Bachtiar Siagian and D. Djajakusuma,[8] starting from very different aesthetic positions, had experimented with both the incorporation of regional content into feature films and the use of non-professional casting from populations of regions where the films were set and shot. But Nugroho's film is not a direct descendant from either of these engagements with the local. Unlike Siagian, Nugroho is not seeking out regional stories of the Indonesian nationalist movement. Like Djajakusuma's most famous work, *Harimau Campa* (*Tiger of Campa*, 1953), *Surat Untuk Bidadari* shows the violence at the heart of a local community. But in *Harimau*, the hereditary violence in local culture is reformed by the emergence of the modern nation. In *Surat* the institutions of the nation state do not offer any solution. Also unlike the older film, the "local" and the "traditional" are not identical nor there to be found in their purity.[9] Foreign symbols littered Nugroho's location shooting sites: the Batman t-shirt (worn by Lewa) and the Elvis portraits painted on minibuses were ethnographic material the director found on the island and incorporated into his particular take on the local and the global.

In between scenes of ritual practices (filmed in a documentary mode), the film explores the life of Lewa in a small village community. The other central figures in the film are the village mad-man "Malaria Tua" (Old Malaria – who suffers from chronic malaria), Berlian Merah (Red Gem), the village beauty who becomes the prey of the villainous village strongman Kuda Liar (Wild Horse), and the well-intentioned young school teacher (called just "teacher" throughout the film) who has come from outside the village, who is also later raped by Kuda Liar. Early in the film, Lewa meets the crew of a fashion shoot on the edges of the village and acquires a Polaroid camera in exchange for a piece of "traditional weaving" needed as a prop for the shoot (until this point Lewa has worn it carelessly wrapped around his waist). This is the only moment of exchange between the village and the outside. This exchange on the free market, on the border of the village, for mutual benefit, unpremeditated, almost incidental, is quite unlike the instrumental textbook through which (later in the film) we see the state transporting national cultural artefacts – the image of what Indonesia is/ought to be. For the rest of the film the camera becomes Lewa's tool in his opposition to this transplantation of national imagery.

This nation first intrudes upon Lewa's life when his school teacher, using the prescribed textbook, tries to teach the class to read. The class read aloud the caption "ini ibu" (this is mother) under the line drawing showing a woman in Javanese clothes, projected as "national costume." But the alien image does not fit Lewa's imagination of his dead mother. He runs out screaming "this is not mother. The book lies." His father, an unschooled horse herd cannot answer whether or not the picture in the book looks like Lewa's mother. Lewa goes to look at the rusting bus in the gorge in which his mother was killed. He finds pasted on the bus a poster with a picture of pop star Madonna. Later he returns with his newly acquired Polaroid to take his first photograph. He sticks the photo in place of the "mother" in his textbook and the following day at school happily reads out "ini ibu." He has constructed a mother from an image which is simultaneously local (found on a rusting bus in his own surroundings) and global (of an international star), in defiance of the "national" construction. But he is immediately confronted by the next image, the national urban male in slacks and shirt with the words "ini bapak" (this is father). Lewa once again runs out of the class screaming "this is not my father's face" – an ironic play on the much repeated official slogan "Indonesian faces in Indonesian cinema." Lewa tries to find his father to take his photo to correct the book, but his father has just been murdered by Kuda Liar's thugs. During the elaborate burial ceremony which occupies the villagers' attention, Lewa steals the body, drags it to the edge of the village, where his father spent most of his time, and takes a photograph to place in his school book.

A second Western pop icon comes into play through Kuda Liar, a devoted fan of Elvis Presley. Kuda Liar imitates Elvis' hairstyle and costumes, in combination with items of traditional clothes. Elvis songs blare out of his car speakers and pictures of Elvis are pasted all over his room and car. But there are older foreign symbols too that are part of the local village – Lewa and Malaria Tua spend their happiest hours playing on an old war plane downed during the Second World War. And there is Lewa's friend "Kakek Jepang," Japanese Grandpa, left over from the same period, though it isn't clear whether he is Japanese or a former collaborator who speaks Japanese. Late in the film, and only fleetingly, Lewa attempts to hide from pursuing men from a neighboring village by donning an Australian Ned Kelly[10] bucket on his head! This unusual cultural referent, one with barely any currency at all in the global cultural image bank, underscores the messiness of Lewa's surroundings where foreign objects have no particular source and signify no particular economic or cultural power. Indeed these symbols are so enmeshed in the life of the village, that they are never identified as "foreign" in the film. The history of the Japanese war plane is never mentioned. Madonna is never identified as anything but an image on the bus. Even Gorbachev, peering out of a magazine which has arrived from outside via the village postman, is simply explained away as a "powerful man" (not as "Soviet" or Russian or even white).

The signifiers of the outside world co-exist alongside parochial signifiers – traditional clothes, rituals, village wars and the structure of legitimate rural authority still epitomised by the *raja* – without seeming to disrupt local cultural practices. The icons of global culture, like the local practices, are not in themselves either good or bad. The criminal Kuda Liar is an Elvis devotee, but for Lewa as pop icon Madonna is more acceptable as a mother-image than the Javanese woman of the national school curriculum. The West, alternately valorised and demonised in Indonesian political discourse, has no fixed meaning at the end of the Suharto regime. By contrast, the institutionally imposed "national" culture poses the real threat to the local. Lewa's problem starts when the "national" image of the family, men in slacks, women in kebaya, children in neat dresses, confronts his own lived realities of dead mother, illiterate father and life on horseback amongst hill tracks.

The nation intrudes more brutally after Lewa slays the drunken Kuda Liar with an arrow through his heart. Unlike all murders committed in the village by Kuda Liar and his men, the killing of the criminal brings the law of the nation into the village. A prosecutor and judge arrive, speaking in formal official Indonesian never used in the film until this point, to establish law and order in the village. Though villagers turn out in force to support Lewa, the court finds evidence of the boy's delinquency in his photographs of women's breasts, his attachment to Berlian Merah and of course his killing of Kuda Liar. Lewa is sentenced to time in a detention centre. In the last scene he lies still in a windowless room facing a wall, refusing to acknowledge Berlian Merah who has come to visit. This is the first time we see Lewa inside a closed room, the first time in the film we see him still and speechless. As in the archetypal New Order text, here too the state institution has finally established order out of Lewa's chaotic search for identity and justice. But this order saps the spirit of youth, it breaks the ties of local culture. The threat to local, even "traditional" culture comes not from global cultural forms brought in by the media and the markets (Elvis records, Madonna prints on buses, Polaroids from the fashion industry), it comes from the more motivated incursions of the nation state. Indeed, global icons like the Polaroid and Madonna become weapons in the local's struggle for survival against homogenized images of national identity imposed by the national centre. Lewa experiences the nation only as a punitive force.

The diegetic "locale" of the film is constructed very differently from the way we have come to understand the construction of national or even ethnic identity. The Sumbanese dialect, and the titles of the local dignitaries indicate that the film is set in the province of Sumba. Other ethnographic evidence such as the ritual practices and some items of clothing would only be recognised by a handful of anthropologists. There is no reference in the film to a Sumba identity, no reference to the island as a whole, or to any other national or ethnic identity. The only space that film constructs is of a village bounded by the highway and the gorge on one side, the river on the other, and hill all around. The community here live in physical proximity, they are *known* to each other.

It is worth recalling at this point Anderson's justification of why a nation *must* necessarily be imagined: "It is *imagined* because the members of even the smallest nation will never know most of the fellow-members, meet them or even hear of them, yet in the minds of each lives the image of their communion" (Anderson 1983, p. 6). It is common in Indonesian cinema for one village to act as a metonymic reference to the nation. What sets Nugroho's film apart is that this village is a material foil to the imagined nation. That nation, with its never-knowable constituents, is distanced, de-familiarised by the operation of this text, never allowed into Lewa's and his village's sense of "communion." The nation is this film's alien "other." By contrast, many of the objects that come from beyond the village, and which in an Indonesian national discourse would be foreign, are made familiar, even familial. A global pop-icon becomes the hero's mother. Lewa's Batman t-shirt, the Polaroid extension of his eyes, his Ned Kelly mask, even his Elvis-enemy do not represent incursions from another place, they are de-territorialised signifiers whose meaning depends absolutely on localised readings. The court and the school textbook by contrast do arrive from a particular, faraway place, and with destructive power. It is the powerfully intrusive nation that cannot be assimilated into Lewa's localised self or into the maps of his locale.

Closing questions

The finest contribution of the Third Cinema concept is perhaps two-fold. First, it "constitutes the necessary first step in ... expelling the Euro-American conceptions of cinema from the centre of film history and critical theory" (Willemen 1989: 17). Second, the very notion of Third Cinema demands socio-political contextualization of films in a way that textual approaches to cinema do not. These impulses that underlie all theorisations of Third Cinema are perhaps more abiding than the more prescriptive criteria such as the countering of Hollywood codes, or identifying with Third World or national liberation movements.

When we move beyond texts and take into account the political economies within which filmmakers operate from day to day, we find that there is no necessary correspondence between "oppositional" in one's lived social and political sphere and anti-Hollywood in the cinematic sphere. My own reading of Indonesian cinema in the 1960s suggests that Hollywood in fact may have provided some of the language for those filmmakers who did not want to be co-opted into legitimising Sukarno's growing authoritarianism under the guise of anti-West nationalism. Again in the 1990s, at another moment of cultural and political watershed in the Indonesian archipelago, Hollywood was insignificant as a target of opposition. As Garin Nugroho's film suggests, the lines between what is and is not "foreign," what does or does not belong to a particular geo-political site, are too difficult to draw. When a Dutch-Indonesian film *Max Havelaar* (1976), which tells the story of colonial corruption, is banned in Indonesia for being both imperialist and leftist (!) does it not confound all conventions of right/left (or colonial/nationalist or reactionary/ radical) divisions in politico-cultural debates? When a Dutch documentary about a banned Leftist-nationalist Indonesian writer, Pramoedya Ananta Toer, is banned in Indonesia but celebrated by specialist audiences around the world, how do we ever put it into any tripartite typology of cultural work? On the other hand, released from its topographical moorings, the idea of a Third Cinema may remain relevant as the "third space" which "displaces the histories that constitute it and sets up new structures of authority, new political initiatives, which are inadequately understood through received wisdom" (Bhabha 1990, p. 211).

Acknowledgement

I am grateful to my graduate students Laura Lochore and Denise Woods for reading through the paper at very short notice.

Notes

1 For a discussion on Sukarno's rule see for instance Legge (1972).
2 For details of Lekra's theory of literature see Foulcher 1986.

3 As will become clear later in the chapter, I had access only to a limited amount of Bachtiar's writings. My comments thus apply only to that body of his writing which I was able to find.

4 Bachtiar Siagian and fellow filmmaker Basuki Effendy had started recovering some of their old writing and film scripts after release, which they generously shared with me. I took copies of these to the Indonesian film archives, Sinematek, where they were received with quiet interest and held in the "restricted collection." That was also the fate of my PhD thesis in 1987, because of the single chapter that attempted to revise the New Order's account of the Left in cinema.

5 This effectiveness can only be understood if we look at the institutional restrictions imposed on film production in the New Order period. See details in Sen 1994: chapter 3.

6 Irian Jaya may have some parallels with Soviet Armenia, but at least in theory the Soviets were autonomous nations.

7 According to Department of Information figures 112 films were produced in 1990–1, 41 in 1991–2 and 28 in 1992–3.

8 D. Djajakusuma was associated with anti-Communist sections of the film community in the 1960s. However, he himself was relatively apolitical even in the politically highly charged years of the early 1960s. Siagian's appropriations of regional cultures is discussed in some detail in Sen (1985).

9 For summaries of films mentioned here see J.B. Kristianto, *Katalog Film Indonesia 1926–1995*, Jakarta, P.T. Grafiasri Mukti, 1995.

10 Ned Kelly is an Australian Robin Hood character, a highway robber who confounded the British colonial police. The Kelly gang is often portrayed with buckets as masks.

Bibliography

Ahmad, Aijaz, *In Theory: Classes, Nation, Literatures*, London, Verso, 1992.

Anderson, Benedict, *Imagined Communities: Reflections on the Origin and Spread of Nationalism*, London and New York, Verso, 1983.

Anderson, Benedict, "Old States, New Society: Indonesia's New Order in Comparative Historical Perspective," in *Language and Power: Exploring the Political Cultures in Indonesia*, Ithaca and London, Cornell University Press, 1990.

Appadurai, Arjun, "Disjuncture and Difference in the Global Cultural Economy," in Mike Featherstone (ed.) *Global Culture: Nationalism, Globalisation and Modernity*, London, Sage Publications, 1990, pp. 295–310.

Bhabha, H.K., "The Third Space," in J. Rutherford (ed.) *Identity, Community, Culture, Difference*, London, Lawrence and Wishart, 1990.

Dirlik, Arif, "The Global in the Local," in Rob Wilson and Wimal Dissanayake (eds) *Global/Local: Cultural Production and the Transnational Imaginary*, Durham, NC and London, Duke University Press, 1996, pp. 21–45.

Foulcher, Keith, *Social Commitment in Literature and the Arts: The Indonesian "Institute of People's Culture" 1950–1965*, Clayton, Victoria, Centre of Southeast Asian Studies, Monash University, 1986.

Gabriel, Teshome, *Third Cinema in the Third World*, Ann Arbor, University of Michigan Research Press, 1982.

Gabriel, Teshome, "Towards a Critical Theory of Third World Films," in Jim Pines and Paul Willemen (eds) *Questions of Third World Cinema*, London, BFI Publishing, 1989, pp. 30–53.

Jameson, Fredric, "Third-World Literature in the Era of Multinational Capitalism," *Social Text*, Vol. 15, Fall. 1986, pp. 65–88.

Legge, John D., *Sukarno: a Political Biography*, Baltimore, Penguin, 1972.

Polan, Dana, "Globalism's Localisms," in Rob Wilson and Wimal Dissanayake (eds) *Global/Local: Cultural Production and the Transnational Imaginary*, Durham, NC, Duke University Press, 1996, pp. 255–83.

Robinson, Kathryn, *Stepchildren of Progress: The Political Economy of Development in an Indonesian Mining Town*, New York, SUNY Press, 1986.

Rocha, Glauber, "The Tricontinental Filmmaker: That Is Called the Dawn," in Randal Johnson and Robert Stam (eds) *Brazilian Cinema*, expanded edition, New York, Columbia University Press, 1995, pp. 76–80.

Said, Salim, *Shadows on the Silver Screen: A Social History of Indonesian Film*, Jakarta, Lontar Foundation, 1991(originally 1982).

Sen, Krishna, "Hidden From History: Aspects of Indonesian Cinema 1955–65," *Review of Indonesian and Malaysian Affairs*, Vol. 19, No. 2, 1985, pp. 1–55.

Sen, Krishna, *Indonesian Cinema: Framing the New Order*, London, Zed, 1994.

Siagian, Bachtiar, "Berberapasegi Perfilman Tiongkok Sosialis Pt. 1," *Haryan Rakjat*, 6 October 1962.

Siagian, Bachtiar, *Ichtisar Sedjarah Perfilman di Indonesia. Komite Nasional Indonesia FFAA3*, Jakarta, 1964.

Willemen, Paul, "Third Cinema Questions: Notes and Reflections," in Jim Pines and Paul Willemen (eds) *Questions of Third World Cinema*, London, BFI Publishing, 1989.

Wilson, Rob and Wimal Dissanayake (eds) *Global/Local: Cultural Production and the Transnational Imaginary*, Durham, NC and London, Duke University Press, 1996.

7 The seductions of homecoming

Place, authenticity, and Chen Kaige's *Temptress Moon* [a]

Rey Chow

> That sentiment accompanying the absence of home – homesickness – can cut
> two ways: it can be a yearning for the authentic home (situated in the past or
> in the future) or it can be the recognition of the inauthenticity of all homes.
> (George 1992, p. 75)

Even though it has been an overwhelmingly successful phenomenon world-
wide, contemporary Chinese cinema is often greeted by Chinese-speaking
audiences with hostility. It is as if the accomplishments of this cinema have an
impossible task in returning home. The simple fact that it has traveled abroad
and been gazed at with interest by "foreigners" is apparently enough to cause
it to lose trustworthiness as wholly and genuinely Chinese. The films of the
two most well-known directors, Chen Kaige and Zhang Yimou, for instance,
have continued to be attacked for their tendencies to pander to the tastes of
Western audiences eager for the orientalized, exotic images of a China whose
history they ignore or falsify. This problematic, which is the problematic of
authenticity, is familiar to all those engaged in cross-cultural studies. [1] In the
late 1990s, when filmmaking and film watching are obviously global events
involving ineluctable interaction with the "foreign," how might a film intervene
in the tenacious and persistent demands for authenticity? I believe that Chen's
1996 film *Feng yue* (*Temptress Moon*) can in many ways be seen as such an
intervention, [2] the director's own cultural complexes notwithstanding. A
discussion of this may begin with the significance of place in the film narrative.
Place, as we shall see, is not only the setting that shapes characters in action;
it is also the locus of specifically filmic significations of "home" and authenticity.

The flight from home

Topographically, *Temptress Moon* shifts back and forth between the countryside
of Jiangnan (the location of the wealthy Pang clan) and the metropolis of
Shanghai, which was among the earliest Chinese cities to be opened to foreign

a Reprinted with permission from *Narrative*, Vol. 6, No. 1 (January 1998). Copyright 1998
by The Ohio State University Press. All rights reserved.

trade in the mid-nineteenth century (as a result of the Opium War of 1839–42). In the film, visual and architectural details combine to convey the sharp differences between the two locations as "tradition" and "modernity" respectively. The Pang family house, situated by a river, is a well-endowed ancient estate with its air of unbreakable heritage and kinship order; the solemnity and reticence typical of tribal bondage find their expression in darkish interiors with their austere, muted décor. Shanghai, by contrast, is a world of bright and gaudy colors, loud and vibrant foreign dance-hall music, fast-moving vehicles, and ruthless, mercenary human relations. Contrary to the mood of languid eternality that shrouds the old books, arcane utensils, and antique furnishings in the Pang household, Shanghai's Westernized domestic spaces are characterized by a much less permanent, because much newer, sense of time. In an apartment rented for the purpose of an illicit relationship, for instance, a vase of roses, a rocking chair, a window pane, a closet mirror, and the occasional music of a piano from afar all suggest the aura of a larger culture in the process of change. For those living in the countryside, meanwhile, everything from the city, including clothes, shoes, and hairstyles, and personal possessions such as pocket watches, slippers, razors, soaps, hats, and photographs alike, take on the historic fascination of "modernity," the legend, the sign that separates Shanghai from the rest of China's hinterland.

It is in Shanghai that we meet the adult figure of the leading male character, Yu Zhongliang. Zhongliang is by profession a special kind of gigolo. A key member of a Shanghai mafia in the 1910s, Zhongliang's work involves the seduction and blackmail of rich married women who fall for him. Using the pseudonym "Xiao Xie,"[3] Zhongliang would entice a woman into a secret affair; after the affair has gone on for a while, a typical scene is staged by the mafia: while Zhongliang is making love with the woman during one of their trysts, gangsters of the mafia would burst in on the scene, blindfold the woman, and threaten to report the affair to her husband unless the woman agrees to pay them a large sum of money. In the process, the woman would be told that her lover "Xiao Xie" is dead. After she is thus psychologically destroyed, Zhongliang would leave quietly with his cohorts and move on to the next target.

Zhongliang's professional success is the result of his familiarity with topography of another kind – a particular strategic spot on a woman's body. Typically, as he gains intimacy with a woman, he would kiss her on one ear, nibbling at the ear until the earring comes off. The earring, like Diderot's "bijoux indiscrets," is therefore the site of a female sexual confession.[4] For the mafia, this "memento" of a single earring exists as a repeated symbol of Zhongliang's invincibility. Although every case of extortion is carried out with the announcement that "Xiao Xie" is dead, in the next shot Zhongliang is usually alive and well, speedily departing from the scene of destruction for the next scene of conquest. Zhongliang's ease at the two sub-places that govern his life in Shanghai, married women's earlobes and the boudoirs of clandestine affairs, makes him indispensable to the mafia. Dada (or Boss), the head of the mafia, openly speaks of Zhongliang as someone he cannot do without.

To the audience, however, the smoothness with which Zhongliang moves about in Shanghai carries a different set of connotations. When the film begins, years prior to his Shanghai career, Zhongliang has just arrived at the residence of the Pangs in the countryside of Jiangnan after the death of both his parents. His only relative is his sister, Xiuyi, who is married to the young master Pang. Despite being officially the brother-in-law of the young master, Zhongliang is in effect treated as a servant. Between the lowly task of serving opium to his decrepit and perverse brother-in-law, and the intimate, incestuous affection of his sister, the young boy is plunged into a confusing encounter with the adult world. The twin experiences of a cruel adult male and a desirous adult female culminate in a scene in which Zhongliang's brother-in-law orders him to kiss his sister, who, sitting alongside the bed, acquiesces smilingly by opening her arms toward the boy. Fearful and reluctant, Zhongliang approaches the older woman while holding the opium-serving tray, his hands shaking violently. Amid the unforgettable noise of the opium utensils tossing against one another, his gaze is arrested on one of Xiuyi's earrings.

The place that is supposed to be a home for the displaced orphan child thus serves, in terms of narrative structure, as the unbearable site of infantile seduction (in the etymological sense of the word "infant" as *in-fans*, the state of speechlessness).[5] Like many first encounters with sexuality, the meaning of his experience of the sadomasochistic relationship of the two adults eludes Zhongliang and leaves him speechless. Architecturally, the traumatic nature of this seduction is mirrored by the circular, labyrinthine structure of the Pang estate, where a seemingly infinite series of doors and chambers, each connected with yet indistinguishable from the others, precludes any clear notion of entry or exit. Unable to comprehend (that is, to fully enter or fully leave behind) this primary encounter with sexuality, Zhongliang retains it through a certain repeated pattern of behavior. Having illicit relationships with married women that begin with the stealing of a single earring becomes his symptom and trademark, which turns a painful remembrance virtually into an industry. Although Zhongliang is a successful seducer, therefore, his success is presented from the beginning as a facade – a cover-up and a displacement of the trauma of *his own seduction*.

Meanwhile, there is another incident which makes it impossible for him to remain with the Pang family. Acting from resentment, he uses his opportunity of serving opium to poison his brother-in-law with a dose of arsenic, which causes the man to become brain-dead. For fear that his murderous act would be discovered, Zhongliang escapes. This escape clarifies the teleological tendency of the narrative of *Temptress Moon*. As an adopted home for Zhongliang, the backward, decadent countryside of the Pangs is significant as the site of a sexual primal scene that has shaped his character *negatively*. In order to be, Zhongliang must leave. His existential autonomy, in other words, will have to be established as a flight from the shock that is supposedly "home." But where will he flee from there?

Zhongliang intends to head for Beijing, the site of the historic, student-led May Fourth Movement of 1919, which sought, among other things, to revolutionize and modernize the Chinese written language and culture. To make sure that the audience understand this point, Chen Kaige inserts a scene in which Zhongliang, like other passengers, is hurrying along the railway, shouting: "Is this the train to Beijing?" Crucially, however, this intention is intercepted when Zhongliang, robbed of all his luggage before boarding the train, is picked up by Dada's gangsters and transported to Shanghai instead. Rather than Beijing, the enlightened capital city of modern China, in which he might have been able to receive a proper education, Zhongliang is literally abducted into a new home, the depraved underground world of Shanghai,[6] where he soon emerges as the favorite son. He is so at home in this Westernized, commercial city that Dada, who may be regarded as Zhongliang's adopted father, says to him: "You belong to Shanghai; Shanghai cannot do without you."

The escape from "home" leads not to liberation and enlightenment but rather to another type of entrapment. In the decadence of Shanghai, Zhongliang remains enslaved to an autocratic, violent, and immoral patriarchal community. His two masters, the poisonous Pangs in the countryside and the poisonous mafia in the metropolis, echo each other in the control they exert over him, and his life in Shanghai, despite its glamour and success, becomes a symmetrical double to his life in Jiangnan. We may even go so far as to say that, in fact, it is precisely as he becomes existentially autonomous and seemingly acquires agency as an adult human being that the shadow of the past begins to loom the darkest. He may have physically left "home," but psychically "home" has never left him.

This unfinished relationship with home is evident, for instance, in Zhongliang's affair with a nameless woman. In one scene, in which he is waiting for her in her apartment at Tianxiangli (Heavenly Lane) in Shanghai, we as well as he are transported by hallucinatory images from his current surroundings back to his former home: first, the woman's picture, which bears a striking resemblance to Xiuyi; then a flashback to the scene of Zhongliang's childhood seduction; finally, the woman herself appearing, putting her hands over Zhongliang's eyes from behind – a gesture that once again reminds us of the games Xiuyi used to play with her younger brother. This attachment to a figure who visually conjures the past constitutes an obstacle in Zhongliang's job: despite Dada's urging, Zhongliang is unable to bring himself to destroy this woman. He tries to delay her destruction by prolonging their relationship. In this postponement, this reluctance to execute, we recognize the prelude to his ultimate return home.

The homecoming ... as you wish

Dada's new target is Pang Ruyi, Xiuyi's sister-in-law, whom he wants Zhongliang to seduce. After Xiuyi's husband becomes brain-dead and leaves the clan without a male left to succeed the old master, the Pang elders decide to appoint Ruyi as the head of the clan. Since Ruyi is female, they also appoint Duanwu, Ruyi's younger cousin from a poor, distant branch of the family, as her male companion.

Upon receiving instructions for his new task, Zhongliang's first reaction is a firm refusal: "As you know," he says to Dada, "I will never go to the town of the Pangs." The next thing we know, he is there against his conscious will.

Strictly speaking, Ruyi is merely the latest in Zhongliang's series of targets, but what distinguishes her from the other women is precisely her topographical location. The fact that this wealthy and powerful woman lives in his former home means that his seduction of her is inevitably commingled with a fateful revisit to the scene of his own seduction. In the course of the film we are made to understand that Ruyi is topographically distinctive in another sense. Unlike the women in Shanghai, Ruyi is a virgin, a "place" yet untouched by the rest of the world because, having been raised in an opium-filled house, she remains unwanted by most families looking for a prospective daughter-in-law. Despite her "poisonous" history, moreover, Ruyi comes across as a beautiful person with a refreshing, untainted sense of personal integrity.

Like her name, which means "as you wish" in Chinese, Ruyi likes to act according to her own wishes, which are, contrary to her conservative up-bringing, entirely independent and liberatory. After becoming the head of the clan, for instance, she orders the retirement of her father's concubines, much to the anger of the clan elders. Then, after meeting Zhongliang, she is direct in her expression of interest in him: one day, she even asks him to teach her how to ride a bicycle. This occasion gives Zhongliang the opportunity to become intimate with her, but when he kisses her on the ear and comes away as usual with one of the earrings, Ruyi reacts by taking off the other earring and offering it to him as well. This unusual event, which epitomizes Ruyi's difference from all the other women Zhongliang has conquered, does not escape the notice of his cohort, who asks: "How come there are two earrings this time?"

If the possession of the single earring is Zhongliang's means of surviving the trauma of an illicit sexual experience, which he must nonetheless keep repeating – through the screening work of fetishization and continual repression – in order to attain a false sense of equilibrium, this equilibrium is now disturbed by the voluntary gift of the other earring by an unsuspecting Ruyi. By giving him the other earring, Ruyi offers Zhongliang something he had never found at home – a love which does not carry with it the connotations of enslavement, illicitness, and humiliation. As such, Ruyi's boldness and spontaneity stand as a force that has the potential of pulling Zhongliang out of the stupor that is his entire existence so far. Through this "virgin territory" that is the independent-minded woman at home, Zhongliang could have found redemption. Yet in spite of this, he remains unmoved. In a scene following the offer of the second earring, we find him displaying disgust at Ruyi, who, being in love, has secretly gone into his room to look at his belongings. Instead of reciprocating her attention, Zhongliang merely feels resentful and loses his temper. Accusing her of a lack of respect for his privacy, he reminds her bitterly of the class hierarchy that used to separate them – that he was, at one time, a servant at her house.

The seduction of the seduced

The strong, innocent woman who offers him true love thus remains, topographically, a goal that Zhongliang has the potential of reaching but somehow misses. Instead, he continues to aim consciously at the Ruyi that is his professional target – the rich woman to be cheated, blackmailed, and then abandoned. As in the case of his journey toward Beijing, however, Zhongliang's conscious move toward Ruyi is diverted en route, bringing about an unexpected turn in his plan. This turn occurs when Ruyi asks Zhongliang to meet her in the family boat-house by the riverside one evening. For her, it is a rendezvous with a new found love; for him, it is an opportunity to carry out his duty and finally have sex with her. As they begin to make love, Zhongliang, confident that Ruyi is inexperienced and that he should take control, suddenly hears her confess: in order to please him (who she believes likes women more than girls because of the picture of the nameless woman she has seen in his belongings), she says, she has already had sex with Duanwu. She has deliberately gotten rid of her virginity so that he would love her.

Zhongliang's face at this point has nothing of the look of someone who is happy at discovering that he is being loved. Instead, it is contorted with anguish. Since the film narrative does not offer any explanation, we must use the clues we have to speculate. Ruyi's independent behavior overwhelms Zhongliang, we might say, not because she has casually given her virginity to someone whom she does not really love nor even because she has performed a selfless deed for his sake. Rather, it overwhelms him because she has unwittingly plunged him into the abyss of his own past. For, in sacrificing her virginity, her *integrity*, for him, is Ruyi not exactly like the other women, and ultimately like Xiuyi? And, is Ruyi's incestuous relationship with Duanwu not a frightful mirror image of Xiuyi's incestuous relationship with Zhongliang years ago? With the blinding intensity of the unanticipated *déjà vu*, Ruyi's confession strikes Zhongliang as if it were *his own* flashback, his own involuntary memory: though (and perhaps precisely as) a picture performed by *others*, it forces him to recognize himself. Like the character Cheng Dieyi in Chen's *Farewell My Concubine* who is finally tamed by the sight of a performance of the story he has been resisting, Zhongliang is finally tamed and, instead of seducing others, becomes seduced once again into playing the role that is his fate.[7]

If this chance (re)seduction of Zhongliang, which constitutes the major narrative turning point, can be described as the ultimate meaning of his home-coming, what is the relationship between seduction and home? Etymologically, "seduction" refers to a leading astray, the opposite of going home. As the paradigm of Odysseus demonstrates, a man must, in order to return home, be determined to stave off seduction – to refuse to succumb to the sirens. In *Temptress Moon*, importantly, this classic opposition between home and seduction has broken down. Consciously, indeed, home is what Zhongliang resists and rejects, and yet in his negative, flighty mode as a professional seducer, he seems nonetheless to keep turning back, to keep clinging to something he does not fully comprehend. And, as he tries to ignore his own feelings about "home" and ventures forth with the task of seduction in cold-blooded indifference toward everyone at home, including the innocent woman who loves him, what he stumbles upon is none other than the "homely" (intimate), yet also seduced (gone-astray), part of himself.

Seductions of the former home involve the memory of and attachment to the entire scenario of Zhongliang's early encounter, a scenario composed by particular configurations of relationships in their enigmatic violence and intensity. Such violence and intensity have remained unrecognized, we may say, until Zhongliang sees it in the form of an other, an image presented by another person. If this *imaging* of how "others do it" may be described as a visual guide to home, then homecoming itself is, strictly speaking, a seduction of the already seduced. Working by the force of memory, which erupts at the sight/site of that which has already been experienced once before, this homecoming can be extraordinarily powerful. In fact, it is lethal.

What is most interesting about this double seduction – this state of being seduced encountering itself at the sight/site of an other – is that it no longer revolves around one particular character. At the point of Zhongliang's discovery of Ruyi's relationship with Duanwu, the story line of *Temptress Moon* is no longer narratologically reducible to the relationship between the "leading" characters, Zhongliang and Ruyi, but must instead be understood as a series of compound relationships involving differentiations on multiple planes and scales, including the sexual, familial, class, rural, metropolitan, modern, and feudalist. Such differentiations, moreover, exceed any restrictive hierarchical arrangement. A schematic would help clarify their superimposed nature as follows:

> Zhongliang and Xiuyi : Duanwu and Ruyi : Zhongliang and Ruyi
> Zhongliang and Xiuyi : Zhongliang and women in Shanghai : Zhongliang and woman at Tianxiangli
> Zhongliang and the Pangs : Zhongliang and the Shanghai mafia
> Zhongliang and the Shanghai mafia : Duanwu and the Pangs

In these relationship-series, every character becomes the narrative hinge for the emergence and development of another character, and every relationship becomes the double of another relationship. The subjectivity of a character is, hence, no longer a matter of his/her inner world but is the result of his/her interactions with others. Accordingly, the significance of each character no longer has an independent value but can only be established through his/her entanglement with other characters. While this may be obvious, it is also worth emphasizing in consideration of our persistently essentialist ways of thinking about characterization (as real-life persons). In *Temptress Moon*, since "meaning" cannot stabilize such multi-layered relationships, characterization takes on a topographical or even archaeological significance: characters themselves become intersecting places or crossroads, digs or ruins, all with multifaceted messages. In the case of Zhongliang, for instance, "character" is the meeting of a "prehistory," in which lie the remnants of a traumatic experience, which he does not understand and cannot express, and a "posthistory," which is a belated, deferred re-imaging, in the form of an other (scene), of that prehistory. If the ineluctability of this meeting is an ineluctable return home, then homecoming itself is always (the repetition of) a going-astray, a departure that has already taken place.

The man in flight, the women bound, and the country-bumpkin-turned-*nouveau-riche*

As the film approaches its end, Zhongliang is unsettled by his own feelings for Ruyi but must still fulfill his duty to Dada. Dada has meanwhile sensed that Zhongliang has changed. In order to prevent further harm, he decides to stage a scene in which Ruyi will discover for herself Zhongliang's identity as a gigolo. Dada is convinced that, once Ruyi sees this, she will no longer love Zhongliang, and Zhongliang will have to become once again his professionally cool and efficient self. This exposure of Zhongliang happens in Shanghai. By intricate arrangements, Ruyi is indeed forced to witness Zhongliang's act from the window of an apartment opposite his in Shanghai: he is making love to the woman at Tianxiangli for the last time, with the gangsters breaking in in their usual fashion, with threats for the woman, and so forth. Only this time, the woman, who refuses to be blindfolded and insists on confronting Zhongliang, commits suicide upon learning the truth.

Contrary to Dada's expectations, Ruyi's love for Zhongliang remains unshaken. Even so, she is unable to hear from Zhongliang what she wants the most – the verbal affirmation that he, too, loves her. Heartbroken, Ruyi returns to the countryside and prepares to marry another man. Upon knowing that Ruyi is to get married, Zhongliang hurries back to his former home once more and confesses that he does, in fact, love her. He even proposes that the two of them elope to Beijing "for real this time." Ruyi refuses to change her mind. In despair, Zhongliang replicates the other episode that resides in the "primal scene:" just as he used arsenic to poison his brother-in-law, so he now prepares a dose of opium mixed with arsenic for Ruyi, who consumes it unawares and becomes brain-dead as well. This act of poisoning completes the saga of Zhongliang's homecoming. As he tries to escape again from the countryside, he is gunned down by Dada's gangsters. If his initial arrival at the Pangs' family residence – by boat at night, through water – is a kind of birth, then the countryside now serves also as his tomb.

Throughout the film, Zhongliang's character is portrayed with a compelling depth, which is the result, ironically, of his need from the very first to escape. Like many writers of the May Fourth period (the landmark period in which Chinese literature became "modern"), Chen relies for the construction of male subjectivity on what may be called the paradigm of fright-and-flight.[8] Hence, just as in his preceding film *Farewell My Concubine*, *Temptress Moon* is full of instances of exaggerated music and sound, body movements, close-ups, and strained dialogues, which together with the cinematography (by Christopher Doyle) of fast-moving shots and changes of shots amplify the effects of a psychologically persecuted male character who seems always on the run.[9] In narratological terms, Zhongliang is hence constituted – visually and aurally as well as through the plot – by *patterns of departure* that help convey all the questions of his identity – "what is Zhongliang running from?", "Where is he going?", "Whom will he meet on the way?", and so forth. This negative pose of a male character on the run is a kind of "resistance" that, ultimately, delivers him home against his will. At the same time, if such a male "psyche" is the legacy of a mainstream modernism that defines itself in opposition to the *socius*, then what is revealed in the seductions of Zhongliang's homecoming is perhaps the unviability of this dissident masculinity as inscribed in the paradigm of fright-and-flight, a paradigm which is being subverted by the network of characters and relationships that sprawl around Zhongliang like a labyrinth. In the light of this unwilling captivity – and demise – of the Man in Flight, the women characters become very interesting.

Unlike Zhongliang, the women characters are all place-bound, both in terms of their physical and their mental locations: Xiuyi is stuck in the country-side and in her bond to a brain-dead husband; the women of the metropolis are trapped by the Shanghai way of life and by their own illicit sexual desires; even Ruyi, who is the most independent of all, remains a prisoner of her home and her heart. (Even though she is about to get married at the end, she consumes opium one more time simply because it has been prepared by Zhongliang, the man she once loved.) However, if these women are ultimately victimized in various ways by their topographical and bodily confinement (a loveless marriage, psychological destruction, suicide, and brain-damage), the bold defiance of patriarchal culture expressed by each of them nevertheless signifies a different concept of flight and departure that may, in due course, not have to lead back to the "home" that is the original place of captivity. As I have commented elsewhere, Chen is typically ambiguous and ambivalent in the manner he handles questions regarding women. Here, as always, he has left the implications of the women characters' fates in the form only of a suggestion, a possibility in all its open-endedness.[10]

Indirectly, Zhongliang's homecoming is what causes the power of the Pang clan to pass to Ruyi's servant-companion Duanwu. Like Zhongliang, Duanwu has been exploited by an older female for sexual purposes, but unlike Zhongliang, he seems to be unperturbed by this "initiation." He remains loyal to Ruyi until they reach Shanghai, where he discovers, he says, the war between the sexes. After Ruyi fails to confirm that Zhongliang loves her, Duanwu rapes her. Later, as they arrive home, he even exposes her relationships with both him and Zhongliang to the man she is about to marry. At the end, as Ruyi becomes permanently brain-damaged by arsenic, Duanwu logically succeeds her as the head of the clan. Like most characters in the film, that of Duanwu is far from being well-developed (his transformation in Shanghai, for instance, lacks persuasiveness), but he is thought-provoking as a type. What Duanwu stands for, in contrast to Zhongliang, is a new type of man – a new class perhaps – who has been abused but who somehow manages not to repress and internalize such abuse; instead, when the right moment occurs, this type of man would turn the violence he has experienced to his own advantage by directing it at fresh victims. Lacking the sensitivity and self-doubt, and hence vulnerability, of Zhongliang, Duanwu makes it to the top through petty cunning, hypocrisy, and opportunism. His success is, Chen's film seems to say, the vulgar success of the country-bumpkin-turned-*nouveau-riche*.

Filmmaking as homecoming

For a filmmaker, the paths of seduction lie not only in narrativization or characterization but also in film language itself. Is the movie screen not the ultimate place of an irresistible allure? If China and Chinese history are the home to which Chen attempts to return, what might be said about this particular homecoming that is filmmaking?

The story of *Temptress Moon* takes place at a crucial moment in the historical meeting between East and West – the 1911 Revolution, after which China shifted from the Imperial to the Republican era. Having been documented, described, debated, narrativized, and fantasized countless times, this moment can indeed be rewritten – schematically, of course – as a certain "primal scene" in which violence and progress converge, and in which the traditional, imperial patriarchal society gives way, albeit sluggishly, to a Westernized, feminized, and modernized state, henceforth to be ruled by the will of "the people." A contemporary Chinese director's revisit of this, modern China's critical historical moment, much like Zhongliang's revisit of his former home at the Pangs, cannot be naïve or simplistically nativist. This is probably why, besides the convoluted narrative and the superimposed effects of characterization, Chen's film is also remarkably reminiscent of other films about modern China. To that extent, *Temptress Moon* stands as an assemblage of allusions, often calling to mind previous films that one has seen.

Witness a striking example of pure screen resemblance: in the scene in which Duanwu is to receive the honor of being appointed as the companion to Ruyi, who has just been made the head of the clan, the young boy is shown to be running into the ancestral parlor while the entire clan stands in observation of the ceremony. In a great hurry, Duanwu throws his proper clothes on while running. In the context of the story of *Temptress Moon*, this demonstration of haste is rather illogical – there is no reason why Duanwu should need to be rushed in the manner he is – until we realize that the scene is probably an allusion to a scene in the older Chinese director Li Hanxiang's *Huoshao yuanming yuan*.[11] In Li's film, which is set during the reign of the late Qing Emperor Xian Feng, there is a scene featuring Prince Kung, one of the emperor's brothers, who has to be recalled from his duties afar to attend

Xian Feng's funeral. Since, by historical account, clothing for different imperial occasions was greatly ritualized, and since the prince was recalled in haste, the character in Li's film is shown to be throwing on the proper funereal garb befitting the brother of the emperor as he dashes into the ancestral parlor. Chen probably so liked the compelling ambience of that scene that he had to recreate it in his own work, even when it is not contextually necessary.

But the film which has left its marks most vividly on Chen's is, interestingly, not one made by a Chinese director – Bernardo Bertolucci's *The Last Emperor* (a film in which Chen was an extra, playing one of the anonymous guards standing at the entrance to the palace). It is from this film that Chen has made copious imaginative borrowings, from the construction of characters and narrative episodes to the use of architecture, interior décor, lighting, and individual screen images. For instance, just as the bulk of the story of *The Last Emperor* is historically situated in the transition period between the Qing Dynasty and the Republic of China, so the story of *Temptress Moon* begins with the 1911 Revolution, when the Qing Dynasty officially ended, and lasts until around 1920.[12] The poignancy of this epochal moment is in both cases portrayed through the life of a child – Pu Yi, the boy emperor, in one case and Ruyi, the future successor to the "throne" of the Pang clan, in the other. Both children are held captive in a privileged environment that is represented, with fascination, as out of sync with modern times. Like the little Pu Yi, Ruyi is full of mischief. In an early scene, she has to be chased out of the ancestral parlor where girls are not allowed; the doors the elders close in order to shut her inside her quarters are, in terms of cinematographic angles, a clear imitation of the high imperial gates that shut Pu Yi in the Forbidden City.

Like Pu Yi also, Ruyi ascends to power by accident, when a proper male heir has failed to appear at the necessary moment. When she becomes the head of the Pang clan, Ruyi, once again reminding us of Pu Yi, introduces unprecedented policies that cause great consternation. Her order to retire her father's concubines, an act which is reminiscent of Pu Yi's historic retiring of the eunuchs of the palace, is shown to be a rather futile attempt at household reform. (The scene in which the concubines leave the family estate is visually reminiscent of the one in Bertolucci's film in which the royal family, led by the grown emperor, is forced to leave the forbidden city.) Above all, being cloistered in the prison-like world of her family town, Ruyi is ignorant of and longing for the new, modernized world outside. The arrival of Zhongliang from Shanghai, then, is not unlike the arrival of Reginald Johnston, Pu Yi's Scottish tutor, who brings Western education to the young emperor, including the fashionable item of a bicycle – an important detail which Chen does not neglect to include in his story.

The point of mentioning some of the borrowings Chen has obviously made from other films is not to accuse him of lack of originality. Rather, it is to emphasize that like writing, filmmaking, too, is conditioned by the utterances of others, the references others made in and of the past. In the case of film, of course, the more accurate word to use is "gazes," and what I mentioned as "allusions" a moment ago should be understood not simply as the content of the story but also as *ways of gazing* that have been inscribed in previous films. For a contemporary Chinese director making a film about modern China, the questions are especially complex: if making a film about one's own culture is a certain kind of homecoming, how does one go about mediating between the desire for portraying that "home" exactly as one thinks one knows it and the allure of multiple images that are already made of it by others and seen by millions more? In the light of the thematics of place, then, the older films of Li, Bertolucci, and others must be regarded as so many versions of a *topos* in its dual resonance as geography and as knowledge. Capturing the physical place, modern China, on film, these directors' works have also become sites of learning – visual archives on which directors such as Chen draw for their own work of imaging China. As these others' gazes beckon in their orientalist, exoticizing, or meticulously historical modes, the homecoming that is filmmaking inevitably becomes a process of citation and review, and – even as one produces a new collage of perspectives – of being (re)seduced with the sights/sites of others.

To return to the question of "authenticity" I raised at the beginning, it is virtually impossible for a director such as Chen to be "authentic" – if by "authenticity" we mean the quality of being "bona fide" to the point of containing no impurities, no traces of others. Once this is understood, we will see that, paradoxically, the impossibility of being authentic is exactly the reason Chen's work can be so provocative. Not-being-authentic here translates into a remarkable filmic *self-consciousness*, reflecting and refracting the ways modern China has been looked at by others, Chinese and non-Chinese, in the past century and a half.

The final image of homesickness

And yet, despite offering a self-conscious statement of what filmmaking amounts to in the postcolonial age by incorporating into his own film others' gazes and perspectives, Chen seems unable to overcome a familiar kind of emotion in relation to home – nostalgia. He expresses this emotion as he has often done in his previous works, through children. For his concluding image, Chen inserts an early scene from the childhood years of Ruyi, Duanwu, and Zhongliang: Ruyi and Duanwu are playing and running with their backs to the audience; Zhongliang, slightly older, is coming from the opposite direction facing us. As Ruyi and Duanwu turn their heads, the three children are looking at us at the same time. This moment is frozen as the final still. The gazes of the three children are a reminder of an exclamation made earlier by Zhongliang: "How nice it would be," he says, "if only we didn't have to grow up!" In terms of theorizations of the gaze, this *visual* conclusion confirms the ontological-representational relation that can, according to Slavoj Zizek, be asserted between nostalgia and children. Zizek argues that in the nostalgic mode, what is fascinating is not so much the displayed scene as "a certain gaze, the gaze of the 'other,' of the hypothetical, mythic spectator" who was still able to "take it seriously." "The innocent, naïve gaze of the other that fascinates us in nostalgia," he writes, "is in the last resort always the gaze of the child."

In terms of place, meanwhile, what the gaze of the child (as explained by Zizek) signifies is the longing for a *utopia*, a non-place, a place that does not exist. In the context of *Temptress Moon*, this is borne out by the fact that the three children were, even as children, never allowed to be innocent, naïve, or happy; childhood for them was not idyllic but filled with abuse and loneliness. In spite of the knowledge that his film has presented, however, the ending Chen supplies can only be read as a deliberate erasure of such knowledge. By invoking (and fetishizing) the gaze of the child, Chen forces certain narrative elements which have hitherto run quietly parallel to one another to crystallize and converge. The final image makes it possible to articulate these elements for the first time as *tendencies of idealization* that are present throughout the story from the beginning. And what is being idealized, whether by way of plot, characterization, or final screen image, is the non-existent. Like Zhongliang's journey toward Beijing, and like his designs on Ruyi, the invocation of childhood is a maneuver that is doomed to fail. The enlightened, revolutionary capital city of modern China, the pure virgin woman in the countryside, and the still, innocent gazes of children all turn out to be unreachable places. Yet precisely because they are unreachable, they seem all the more "authentic," all the more to be longed for. We thus have the vicious circle of a cultural complex in which idealism leads, as it always does, to homesickness, and vice versa.

Ironically, the implications of Chen's concluding image bring him much closer to the critics who accuse him of forsaking the "authentic" China. In their reluctance to give up what is irretrievably lost, be it a hypothetical childhood or a mythical Chineseness, the director and his critics are finally united as perpetrators of the seductions of a certain kind of homecoming, a well-trodden path familiar to all. As they probably know only too well, such paths lead nowhere. But that, it should be added, is also probably why their homesickness persists.

Notes

1 This is a problematic the politics of which I have considered in detail in Chow, 1995; see in particular Part II, Chapter Four.
2 Story by Chen and Wang Anyi; filmscript by Shu Qi. Please bear in mind that in the Chinese language, *fengyue*, literally "wind, moon," is a euphemism for eroticism or matters of sex.
3 This chapter is based on the version of the film *Temptress Moon* I saw in Hong Kong in the summer of 1996. Unfortunately, some of the scenes have been edited and cut from the North American version.
4 This reference to Diderot has, of course, been made famous by Foucault, pp. 77–80.

5 For an authoritative discussion of the problematic of seduction in psychoanalysis, see Laplanche, Chapter 3: "Foundations: Towards a General Theory of Seduction," pp. 89–151.

6 Lee Edelman commented thoughtfully that Zhongliang cannot reach Beijing because he has, literally from the outset, been "shanghaied." Hence, for Zhongliang, Beijing remains nothing more than a fantasy. This is evident in a revealing scene in which he interrogates Ruyi about her ignorance of the outside world. In his pretentious attempt to educate her, he describes Beijing in lyrical, revolutionary, but entirely bookish terms – as a place where the sky is blue, the walls are high, the girl students all have short hair and wear long black skirts, and so forth. While he has thus succeeded in seducing Ruyi with his professed enlightenment, he is painfully aware that he is, in effect, performing his own lack.

7 In *Farewell My Concubine*, Chen takes pains to show the process in which Cheng Dieyi "becomes" the character of the concubine in the opera of the same title. While a boy-apprentice in the Beijing opera troupe with which his mother left him, Dieyi is for a long time unable to accept his role as a woman and unable to speak his lines correctly. Because of this failure, he is severely punished, and he tries to run away. He would have successfully escaped, but on his way he unexpectedly comes across a street performance of none other than the opera *Farewell My Concubine*. Completely absorbed and moved, he changes his mind and returns to the troupe. From then on, he accepts, performs, and identifies with his assigned role – and fate – of "concubine" to the end.

8 For instance, the typical scenario in some of Lu Xun's short stories is that of a male narrator emotionally shocked by a spectacle of social injustice, regarding which he feels impotent; in spite of his sympathies for the victim(s), such a narrator usually takes flight in one form or another. Likewise, in Ba Jin's *Jia* (*The Family*), the predominant narrative action is placed in the characters who, feeling indignant at the corrupt nature of the feudalist patriarchal family system, attempt to rebel and take leave. Readers acquainted with modern Chinese literature are asked to see a more detailed discussion of this connection with May Fourth writings in Chow, 1997, also on *Temptress Moon*, which complements the present discussion. Insofar as Chan associates home and countryside with backwardness, he is modernist in his authorial perspective, a perspective that is different from the sentimental idealization/romanticization of the countryside as the place of simple and eternal truths that also runs throughout modern and contemporary Chinese literary culture. A recent example of this latter tendency is found in Zhang Yimou's 1995 film *Shanghai Triad*, in which the point-of-view character, a child, fascinated by Shanghai, nonetheless sees truth at the end through his experience in the countryside.

9 This can perhaps be described by way of the phrase "motion and emotion" (first used by Wim Wenders); see Tony Rayns's brief discussion, which is based on some of the rushes rather than on the finished film. The North American version of the film, because it has been heavily edited with many abrupt shifts of scenes, comes across as even more discontinuous and discomforting than the version shown in Hong Kong and Taiwan. In "Xiandai, houxiandai, huaijiu," I offer a related discussion of the effects generated by Chen's use of motion in terms of *melodrama*.

10 For more elaborate discussions of the status of women in Chen's other films, see the relevant sections in Chow, 1995.

11 This is one of a series of films made by Li on the late Qing during the 1970s and 1980s. Others include *Chuilian tingzheng*, *Xi tai hou*, *Qing guo qing cheng*, *Ying tai xi xue*, and *Huo long*. Li, a director who left mainland China in the 1950s, worked both in Taiwan and Hong Kong. He died in 1996 in the midst of making a film in Beijing. Li first became well-known in the 1960s with films he made for Shaw Brothers Ltd (in Hong Kong) and for his own company Guo Lian (in Taiwan). When box office trends no longer favored the styles of his early works, he made a series of pornographic films in order to stay in the business, and it was due to the success of these pornographic films that he received funding for his major historical films featuring the late Qing. One of his pornographic films was

entitled *Feng yue bao jian* (Precious lessons in matters of sex), which plays on the Chinese term "feng yue," which, as I pointed out, is a euphemism for "matters of sex." Since Li's film, I believe, pornographic films have often been referred to as "Feng yue pian" in Chinese. Is it a coincidence that Chen adopted "Feng yue" as the title of his film?

12 Rayns offers the following account: "In Beijing in 1993, while he was still searching for a scriptwriter for *Temptress Moon* and trying to deal with the Film Bureau's demands for cuts in *Farewell My Concubine*, Chen joked to me that he would definitely set his next film in 1920 – a year before the Chinese Communist Party held its first (underground) congress in Shanghai. That way, he implied, his scenario couldn't possibly be accused of misrepresenting the Party's role. So much for jokes in present-day China: the film is indeed set in 1920 ...," p. 13.

References

Ba Jin, *Jia* (1931). Hong Kong: Tiandi tushu, 1985.

Chow, Rey, *Primitive Passions: Visuality, Sexuality, Ethnicity, and Contemporary Chinese Cinema*. New York: Columbia University Press, 1995.

Chow, Rey, "Bulunbulei de youhuo – mantan Chen Kaige dianyang *Feng yue* zhong aiming." In Jiang Yinying (ed.) *Identity Difference and Subjectivity*. Comparative Liteerature Institute: Fujen University/Lixu Publishing, 1997, pp. 217–36.

Edelman, Lee, Comment (on Rey Chow's paper), delivered at the Annual Conference of *Narrative*, University of Florida, Gainesville, April, 1997.

Foucault, Michel, *The History of Sexuality*, Vol. 1 (1976). Translated by Robert Hurley. New York: Vintage, 1980.

George, Rosemary Marangoly, "Traveling Light: Of Immigration, Invisible Suitcases, and Gunny Sacks." *Differences: A Journal of Feminist Cultural Studies* 4.2 (Summer, 1992), pp. 72–99.

Laplanche, Jean, *New Foundations for Psychoanalysis* (1987). Translated by David Macey. Cambridge, MA: Basil Blackwell, 1989.

Rayns, Tony, "Motion and Emotion." *Sight and Sound* (March, 1996), pp. 11–13.

Zizek, Slavoj, *Looking Awry: An Introduction to Jacques Lacan through Popular Culture*. Cambridge, MA: MIT Press, 1991.

Part V
Receiving/retrieving Third (World) Cinema
Alternative approaches to spectator studies and critical history

One of the principal condemnations of the Third Cinema approach resulted from its insistent address to a unitary spectator who is at once disingenuous (requiring lessons in class consciousness and postcolonial development) and sophisticated (capable of appreciating an otherwise rarified oppositional aesthetics). Moreover, the suggestion that Third Cinema must resist the illusionistic proclivities of classical narrative harkened back to the Formalist position of art arising from a process of estrangement or defamiliarization. Not unexpectedly, the audiences who responded to the aesthetics of Third Cinema were already familiar with its political motivations. Thus, Third Cinema's critical reception and reception at film festivals could seldom be mapped onto the same experiential terrain as those of audiences at popular venues.

The two chapters that comprise this section deal with spectator subject positions and forms of popular reception on the one hand and with broader questions of critical history on the other. Both, however, address the lacunae of Third Cinema theory. Hamid Naficy, who has made important contributions to our understanding of transnational and exilic cinemas (and of Iranian cinema in particular), here deals with issues of spectator positioning in ways that are both amusing and moving. Indeed, his contribution may well be the most sophisticated study of concordant (hailing) and competing (haggling) subjectivities undertaken for reception studies pertaining to any cinema. What Naficy argues provocatively is that hailing and haggling are less the province of textual address (i.e. First Cinema hailing its obedient spectator in an Althusserian interpellative manner, as spectator theorists of the 1970s have posited, and Third Cinema haggling with its more participatory spectator), than of the concrete conditions of spectatorship themselves. Is an exiled Iranian spectator of Iranian cinema identical to other Iranian spectators or closer in perceptual terms to Western spectators looking from the "outside" at Iranian films? How is critical judgment itself shaped by the critic's own subject position? How stable or unitary is that subject position when the critic might well be polycultural?

At the opposite end of the critical spectrum from such introspection we find Wimal Dissanayake's perspectivalism. Dissanayake, who has already written a great deal about Asian Cinemas and about Indian cinema in particular, here endeavors to show that the key questions raised by India's vast popular cinemas address many of the most contested terrains of cultural studies – from debunking Habermas's notion of the erosion of the *bourgeois* public sphere by mass media to the role of historical residue and folk tradition in patterns of popular reception. Most crucially, Dissanayake charts the ground-work of sociologists, political scientists, media theorists, art historians and cultural historians who have jointly endeavored to deepen our understanding of the most culturally pervasive of cinemas, an approach which cannot be ignored by Third Cinema theorists and which could well enrich our understanding of spectators' responses to the many, varied manifestations of Third Cinema.

8 Theorizing "Third World" film spectatorship

The case of Iran and Iranian cinema

Hamid Naficy

> At home, I had lived most intensely in the cinema. ... In those dark halls, I had dreamed of a life elsewhere. Now, in the place that for all those years had been the "elsewhere," no further dream was possible.[1]

This chapter is about cinematic spectatorship in the Third World, specifically in Iran, and more generally about transnational spectatorship of films by Third World populations in film festivals. It seeks to problematize the master narratives of crosscultural cinematic discourses through self-narrativization. I use autobiography in order to avoid the problems which occur in most ethnographic encounters, that is, the effacement of the anthropologist, filmmaker, and film theorist from the text, which can result in denying the essential dynamics of the encounter and in producing a static picture of the people described. "It is this *picture* frozen within the ethnographic text, that becomes the 'culture' of the people" (Crapanzano 1980, p. ix). Indeed, crosscultural cinematic contacts have a polysemy and a dynamics which are rarely revealed in the neutral "invisible writing" of theoreticians and historians of crosscultural and global cinema (invisible, therefore, as in the non self-reflexive Classic Hollywood cinema style). I am not using autobiography nostalgically here, as a return to childhood and to a prelapsarian universe. Rather, I am using it as a searchlight to illuminate not only the essential interiority and multiple subjectivities of film spectatorship but also its undeniable but undertheorized social and collective dimensions, especially when films cross national and cultural boundaries. To accomplish this task, I rely not only on personal accounts of film viewing but also on audience ethnography, social history, and film theory. I speculate and theorize about the interpellative (hailing) effects of the film texts at the same time that I challenge these effects by invoking historical and cultural practices that seem counterinterpellative (haggling). If, as Teshome Gabriel states, Third Cinema highlights contexts and not individual heroes (1989, p. 60), then this essay is an example of an extension of Third Cinema theory in its emphasis on the social contexts of reception, albeit in directions which the originators of Third Cinema may not have envisaged.

There is, of course, the issue of the physical and discursive "location" of the author. Over forty years have elapsed between my first experience with cinema in Iran and this writing about it from a position in exile in the United States. Discursively, too, much film making and film theory separates my writing here from my early naïve film viewing there. To problematize, even dramatize, these issues of (dis)location, and to express the splitting effect of both cinema and of exile on the subjectivities of the so-called Third World spectators, in writing this essay I consciously alternate between using first person and third person pronouns. Many Third World filmmakers – at least the first generation – were wooed to cinema by Western films and a large percentage of them received their filmmaking training in Europe, the United States, and the Soviet Union. However, because of their awareness of unequal and unjust colonial and neocolonial relationships, many of them upon returning to their homelands made films critical of the West and attempted to create their national and individual cinema identities in contradistinction to Western cinema. This essay attempts to theorize, through my own experience, this alienating identification that cinema, along with other institutions of modernization, set into motion – a form of identification that problematizes the received notions of direct and hermetic cultural imperialism. Finally, since my project is to examine Third World film spectatorship, I will emphasize the primary site of this activity, the moviehouse.

Reading novels, watching films

My relation to the West and to Western movies was convoluted and multi-layered. It began early and it remained private, familial, social, national, and political all at once. I grew up avidly reading Persian and Western literature and I tried to see as many film adaptations as possible. Indeed, I was perhaps first drawn to cinema through its connection with literature, a connection which resonated reciprocally: it seemed to validate both the original novel and the experience of the cinema. At the same time, both literature and cinema vividly embodied the Western Other with whom I would have to come to terms.

I remember the young man, as I then was, spending the summer of 1960 (Persian year 1339) reading all the great novels that he could get his hands on. He read over 30 of them and saw many film adaptations. One warm spring night in April 1959, he took his Agfa 35mm still camera to the open air theater, *Sinema Mayak*, which was showing Leo Tolstoi's *War and Peace* (1956). He wanted to take color snapshots of the film as it was being shown. Unsure of how the ushers would react to the camera (it was unusual to carry cameras to theaters), he hid it under his jacket. When large close-ups of Pierre and Natasha (played by Henry Fonda and Audrey Hepburn) appeared, he discreetly took timed pictures, holding his breath to reduce the shaking of his hands. Captivated by the great novel, I had spent weeks reading, nurturing, and annotating it – noting in my diary, with a combination of awe and arrogance: "the breadth and the style of the book is utterly amazing. I am trying to understand it as fully as possible because it is worth it" (2/22/1339). He recalled years later that holding color slides of that movie, especially of Audrey Hepburn, had felt like holding a piece of a dream – a condensed image – consisting of Russia (site of the story) and of America (site of the film's production).

At nights, sometimes, I would put myself to sleep by going over scenes of the movies I had just seen. Narrative recall comforted me. One time, as he was falling asleep he remembered scenes from Victor Hugo's *Les Misérables* (1956), starring Jean Gabin. What a moving story! Two years earlier I had spent a part of my summer vacation with my parents in Khunsar, a cool, mountainous region, reading *Les Misérables* during the long afternoon siesta. Everyone would take a one or two hour nap. All was quiet but for the murmuring of the brook nearby rolling and falling over and around rocks. Lying down on my back on the floor, I voraciously consumed the Hugo tale, often crying at the trials of Cozette, Marius, and Jean Valjean. I was so taken with Hugo's style that I filled half a notebook with quotations from the book and wrote in my journal: "This is an amazing and compelling novel. It contains a world of emotions: love, kindness, humanity, conscience, justice, self-sacrifice. … It is really a great masterpiece." The memories of reading the novel and watching the movie commingled with the oncoming dreams. These cinematic memories and dreams also enlivened his otherwise drab and lonely waking hours, as he noted in his diary: "In my life these memories and dreams are all that satisfy me" (2/22/1339). Yes, it seems I was buying into the world foreign dream factories were offering.

The Soviet film affecting me the most was the romantic war movie directed by Mikhail Kalatozov, *The Cranes are Flying* (1957). The heroism of the Russian people and the lost romance of the protagonists so moved him that he wrote an unprecedented four page plot summary in his diary (10/15/1337). The film's war scenes and the haunting face of the lead actress, Tatyana Samoilova, were forever etched into his mind. Now, over four decades later, when I read over the plot summary, I am struck by that image of the cranes flying in the sky, the cranes Tatyana looked at in the end in order to remember her lost love, Boris, killed in the war. Now, when I remember that image, I am reminded of my own loss – my country, lost to exile. Such is the power of symmetry, memory!

Hailing the spectators, haggling with the movie

While as a boy I loved Western literature and thrived on it, as I grew my history of involvement with the West became more complex and ambivalent. My first "tangible" impression of North America was provided by my father who in 1953 had gone to the United States to attend Harvard University's medical school. In one of his letters home, he had inserted a two inch patch of his skin, which had peeled off after a long day's stay at the beach in Boston.

This piece of skin, this thin, transparent parchment, became a charismatic talisman: it captured me and my imagination and transported me to Boston harbor, a place I would visit years later. Holding the skin in my hand I felt close to him. In retrospect, I see that this skin was symbolically significant in another sense that only Iranians can fully appreciate. There is a Persian saying about a task or a person being so difficult as to skin you alive. In one sense, that skin-message was my father's way of symbolically communicating to us both the hardship and the pleasure of his first stay in the US. In another sense, that peeled piece of skin could be taken as a metaphor for what American foreign policy was doing to Iran at the time, that is, skinning Iran alive by supporting a coup against Mohammad Mosaddeq, a popularly elected prime minister.[3]

Then, within six months, my father returned bringing with him one of those slide viewers which displays a series of 3-D slides mounted on a round disk. Here was America, not mediated by means of the 35mm movie frames I used to buy as a child from street vendors or by my father's skin, but by means of crisp color slides in stereo – showing the United States' magnificent landscapes. Viewing those clean paved roads gracefully winding through snow-clad Yellowstone national park or Niagara Falls with visitors wearing yellow raincoats to protect them against the mist of the enormous cataract, he felt a deep yearning to be there, to feel and touch them. These images which stimulated synaesthetic pleasure, were more than any other factor responsible not only for planting in my mind the idea of traveling to the United States, but also for influencing my views of that country. While politically I abhorred the American foreign policy for violating my country's sovereignty, he was being wooed to America in the privacy of my own home, by my own father, in a most unconscious manner, and by the most seemingly innocuous agents – color pictures of natural beauty.

Until recently, many structuralist and poststructuralist theorists of cinema borrowing ideas from Louis Althusser, Antonio Gramsci, and Jacques Lacan, among others, postulated that cinema is an ideological state apparatus (ISA) that works to recruit subjects from among individual spectators by means of interpellation (Althusser), the hegemonic work of ideology (Gramsci), and the psychoanalytic process of the mirror-phase (Lacan). Althusser's simple example most clearly crystallizes what is meant: in the street a policeman calls, "hey, you there!" By turning to respond, in that very moment that we swivel on our heels, we have become his subject. Cinema is purported to operate in a similar fashion: ideologically inscribed in hegemony, it acquires the free consent of the spectators as its subjects. Such a formulation posits interpellation as a monolithic, universal, and unilinear process, discouraging escape and resistance. But, if the Althusserian street scene is viewed from the point of view of the subjects, especially in their varying social contexts, we find that the authority-subject relation is often subverted. Similarly, on a social scale, there are cracks, ruptures, inconsistencies, and contradictions, not only among the various ISAs but also within individual ISAs, which make resistance to and subversion of unilinear interpellation possible. Acting like a mirror during the mirror-phase, film creates split subjectivity, not a homogeneous subject at ease but one in dis-ease (dare I say, a diseased subject). As a result, in addition to "hailing" there is much "haggling" in cinematic spectatorship. Yes! Those glorious fictional films and innocent pictures of natural beauty were addressing me personally, and I turned and faced them. I became their subject, I was hailed. I became he. But, the I and the he haggled with each other, for they did not form a unitary subject at ease. There are many ways in which both hailing and haggling between self and other, real and fictional, and indigenous and foreign take place in the moviehouse.

I will examine these by turning to the context of the movies, the sociology and ethnography of their reception, the oral culture's spectatorial routines, and the margins of film history to create a composite narrative about the evolution of film spectatorship in Iran. While my first recollection of film watching is one of intense and anxious emotional reaction caused by narrative suspense, my identification with the diegesis was not total due to the social context of the reception. The moviehouse was a long, narrow, tunnel-like hall with high ceiling that was filled with people, smoke, and noise. This was a modest theater, located near our house, on Southern Chahar Bagh Street. Before a film began and during obligatory intermissions, amidst the clamor of the young male audience (I don't remember any women), a voice could be heard barely audible above the general hubbub, calling: "Coca Cola, Fanta, cigarettes, seeds, mixed nuts, snacks." It came from a young, disheveled boy carrying a wooden tray full of goods. In the early days of cinema, spectators not only sat in front of the screen but also in the back and, in the open-air theaters, on rooftops. Those who could not afford the price of a regular seat in front of the screen would be given an empty oil can behind the screen to sit on. Women were separated from the men by a curtain or by a divider erected in the middle of the theater. Even without these, women usually sat on one side and men on the other. When the lights finally dimmed, the national anthem was played over a scratchy loudspeaker. Everyone had to rise. The film, typically black and white, flickered on, the shaft of light coming from the projection booth, dancing amidst the smoke and the stench of the hall. In earlier days, some Tehran theaters sold hot food, especially steamy sheep tripe, lamb meat, and bread, which the audience ate while watching the movie (an early version of odorama!). Food was not apparently the sole source of smell since, at times, moviegoers, or their impatient children, who did not want to miss the movie, urinated on the floor instead of leaving the hall for the restroom. Shusha Guppy relates a story about this practice and the way the theater managers and spectators haggled over it:

> In desperation, the management projected a plea on the screen before each showing: "Gentlemen are requested to kindly refrain from relieving themselves inside this cinema," or simply, "Please do not urinate here but use lavatories outside." When polite language failed to produce the

expected result, harsher words were used: "God's curse on the son-of-a-whore who pisses in this cinema!" or, "Whoever pisses in this place is the son and brother and husband of whores! He himself is a bugger!" No good. Finally, it was thought that the image would succeed where words had proved ineffectual – a drawing of a huge equine penis was projected with the caption: "This will bugger any son of a whore who dares to piss here, and will then take care of his wife, mother and sister as well!" The audience just laughed, and turned the insult back on to the management by drawing similar niceties on the walls of the cinema. Eventually a solution was found: a little ditch was dug all around the auditorium which carried away any liquid from the floor to the sewer.

(Guppy 1988, p. 167)

No sooner had the movie started than someone, who in all likelihood had previously seen it, would begin to tell the story out loud moments ahead of the action: "Now *artisteh* (the artist, meaning, the male hero) is going to knock down *dozdeh* (the thief, metaphorically, the bad guy)." Another would intone, "Look, his car is going to go off the cliff," and so on. Some people in the audience objected loudly to the foretelling of the story, as it ruined the drama for them. Others, however, found it helpful since sound movies were not dubbed into the Persian at first and few people could understand the original language anyway. To help comprehension, local distributors began inserting at ten-minute intervals full-screen captions in Persian, which explained the action.

But these summarizing intertitles did not solve the problem for the majority who were illiterate. That is why students were in demand as intermediaries between the native population and the Western text, a role which they were to fulfill on a more significant scale in years to come. Outside the theaters, men who could not read would solicit young student-types to read the intertitles for them in exchange for a free ticket.[4] The students proved doubly useful once inside: other non-literate people would try to situate themselves within earshot distance of them to benefit from their service. The asynchronous chorus of young boys reading the titles aloud, however, aroused the ire of those who could read. As a result, there was always a vocal conflict and some-times fist fights between the two groups. You could hear the protesters shouting, "Quiet Mr! Shut up! Shut up!"

There was at the time a performance art of "reciting" or "reading" the curtain that was ingeniously adapted to film exhibitions. Curtain reciters or readers (*pardeh khan*) would hang a curtain in an outdoor plaza on which was painted massive scenes of Shii or Persian mythological and historical tales and great battles. Standing in front of the painting, the reciter would point with a stick to the various scenes, explaining and dramatizing with great showmanship the depicted stories, highlighting the moral or religious lessons to be drawn. During the silent era, a group of enterprising interpreters (called *dilmaj*), syncretically adapted this traditional practice to cinema as did their Japanese counterparts (called *benshis*) in an even longer-lasting tradition. Usually, they would pace in the aisles in the dark, reading out the intertitles. At times, however, they would stand next to the film screen (called "curtain" in Persian) and as the film was projected, they would point with a long stick to the figures on the screen – often warning the spectators of the coming action. At first, their power to foretell the plot was chalked off to their prescience!

When Western language talkies were first introduced to Iran in the early 1930s, naïve audiences unaccustomed to speech in cinema conjectured that sound films involved trickery and ventriloquism by skilled actors who were hiding behind the screen (Naficy 1981a, p. 42). Perhaps they thought so because they distrusted cinema (because of its illusionism), Western entertainment (because of its immoral influences), and the entrepreneurial local exhibitors (because of their shady practices).

The intervention of screen readers and student translators in the reception of the movies was in a sense subversive to the original intention of the film-makers. Since these intermediaries had to translate the intertitles, the subtitles, or the foreign language dialogue in real time, they often resorted to colorful Persian stock expressions, which indigenized and enriched the film experience. This subversive potentiality carried over into the sound era as well, especially when film dubbing became a big business. Since Iranian movies were usually not filmed in sync during production, skillful and versatile voice-over artists dubbed the actors' voices in postproduction. It can be safely said that approximately two dozen voice actors dubbed the majority of Iranian *and* foreign films shown in the country. Audiences drew special pleasure from hearing John Wayne and Jerry Lewis use expressions that Iranian tough guys or comedians used. Such intertextuality hybridized the diegeses and the characters who inhabited them. Also, because each voice-over artist often dubbed the voices of a number of different characters, strange cross-over resonances and dissonances would be set up between voices and characters, which could serve to confuse the mirror-phase identification with individual characters. The dubbing process involved narrative and structural changes as well. The names of characters, lines of dialog, elements of plot, characters' relationships, and even the order of sequences would sometimes undergo changes to make the films both palatable to local tastes and agreeable to the state's political and religious censors. Through drastic manipulation during dubbing, sometimes, a Western tragedy would be turned into an Iranian comedy (Mehrabi 1984, p. 439).[5]

Adding to the disruptive atmosphere of moviehouses and their counter-hailing potential was the loud cracking of watermelon, pumpkin, and sunflower seeds, which constantly interrupted the quiet moments of the film.[6] Moreover, in the early days, if the town notables and neighborhood tough guys (*lutis*) arrived late, often the projectionist would stop the film in mid-stream in their honor and resume the screening only after they were seated (Mehrabi 1984, p. 420). Audiences' oral interaction with the diegesis, too, heightened the contentiousness of the viewing experience. People would not hesitate to tell the actors on the screen what they should do next: "Oh, watch out, he is behind you;" "Yeah, punch him hard in the stomach, hit him, hit him." I remember watching *Samson and Delilah* (1949) from the balcony of a theater. When Victor Mature as Samson stood in the doorway to push the pillars apart, eventually destroying the temple, everyone urged him on and applauded wildly. I still remember the spectators' outstretched arms waving above their heads in the eerie, blue light of the projector in the smoke-filled hall.

The West has often fetishized its non-Western other, at first as a Noble Savage (White 1978). But, we struck back! As teenagers we counterhailed the West by fetishizing its movie stars, their names, and the world they stood for, not as icons of savagery but as emblems of civilization and modernity. Some of us took pride in our ability simply to pronounce the stars' names. In fact, the more difficult, the better. Naming them was to identify them, identify with them, and make them part of oneself – competencies to be flaunted. For example, my high school friend Hosain Kalbasi, took special pride and pleasure in his ability to pronounce the names of foreign stars out loud during our favorite pastime, strolling in the streets. In a style reminiscent of the "how, now, brown cow" school of pronunciation, he would move with great relish all those facial muscles unused when speaking Persian, in order to reproduce the stars' names accurately, such as, Eddy Duchin, Silvana Mangano, Dorothy Lamour, Sophia Loren, Gina Lolobrigida, Edward G. Robinson, Victor Mature, and Montgomery Clift. Passersby would throw looks of surprise and indignation at this group of young *flâneurs*, causing us to laugh heartily at upsetting them.

Other youngsters appropriated various identity markers of the stars, leading to such trends as "Douglasi mustache" (patterned after Douglas Fairbanks Jr's mustache), "Corneli hair style" (emulating Cornel Wilde's bouffant hair style), Charles Boyer's romantic glances, and Dorothy Lamour's posing.[7] This sort of fetishism was highly complex, for it was not only a form of idealization of American culture and the West but also of resisting them through their objectification. Idealizing them was also a way of undermining the traditional patriarchal and Islamic order at home, resulting in much criticism from cultural conservatives (Naficy 1981b, p. 351). As teenagers, we idealized the modern world that the West offered us. Cinemas were seen as signs of "progress" and "civilization" and as sites for secular worship rivaling that of the mosque. The metonymic association of cinema with secular worship was well understood and vehemently objected to by the clerical establishment. For example, Mojtaba Navab-Safavi, a leader of Feda'iyan-e Eslam, a fundamentalist group operating in the 1940s, chose a powerful and graphic metaphor to condemn the cinema's interpellative powers. He called cinema, along with other Western imports (romantic novels and music), a "smelting furnace," which could melt away all the wholesome values and virtues of a Muslim society (Navab-Safavi 1978, p. 4).

The strategies recounted so far, by which Iranian audiences interrupted, talked back to, translated, dubbed, fetishized, objectified, and haggled with the movies and the movie stars, transformed the cinema's "work" from one of hailing to haggling. By thus engaging with the movies, the spectators were no longer just their *consumers* but also the *producers* of their meanings. Making and watching the movies joined together in a "single signifying practice" (Barthes 1977, p. 162). However, these strategies, emerged largely spontaneously, often unconsciously, and sometimes as part of the natural process of development and experimentation which accompanies any new invention or discovery. To be sure, there were overt forms of resistance as well. The majority of the moviegoers were of the lower classes. The upper classes disparaged and shunned cinema, particularly locally made films, probably because they attracted the lower classes. The religious lay and elite as well as the secular elite also opposed cinema on religious and moral grounds. The penalty for intransigence was great. For example, my then teenage uncles (Reza and Hosain), who were under the guardianship of their older, religiously inclined brother Karim, received severe beatings for sneaking in to the movies.[8]

Despite the fragmentation of audiences along class lines during my teens (the lower classes usually went to see Egyptian, Indian, and Persian song and dance melodramas, while the educated and the upper classes frequented foreign "art" films), moviehouses became a site for resisting the state's repressive apparatus. Resisting and accommodating the state went beyond tampering with the film during dubbing; it extended into the sites of exhibition. Soon after Reza Shah came to power in the mid-1920s, for example, the government began requiring theater managers to play the national anthem before each film, in honor of which spectators had to rise to their feet. Although enforced during his rule, from the mid-1940s, audiences began to resist this state interjection into their entertainment by remaining seated. The government wavered on enforcing its policy. For a long time it tolerated this sort of passive resistance, then tried to enforce the policy by punishing the non-conformists and finally abandoned it altogether in the late 1960s after it was found to be a political liability.

Despite such interjections moviehouses acted as safe meeting places for political activists. In order to escape the gaze of Reza Shah's police and secret service, for example, leftists chose theaters as meeting places where, in darkness and anonymity, they could exchange words, notes, books, and packages. Bozorg Alavi's famous novel *Cheshmhayash* (*Her Eyes*), about the life of an anti-Shah painter, contains several episodes in which its leftist protagonists meet clandestinely in theaters. The notion of safety derived from anonymity turned theaters into sites for resisting cultural and religious conventions as well. Many young couples who could not be seen walking the streets together or meeting openly in cafes and restaurants, found the safe darkness of theaters conducive to experiencing rare and thus deliciously charged moments of privacy and intimacy. I remember watching in rapture Elia Kazan's *Splendor in the Grass* (1961), my girlfriend Zhina's hand in mine at the Moulin Rouge theater in Jolfa, the Armenian district of my home town.

Immediately after the revolution of 1979, which ousted the Shah, audiences used the safety of numbers in theaters to voice their opposition to the Islamist government. For example, during the American "hostage crisis," Ayatollah Khomeini had made a particularly colorful and vainglorious speech, threatening to "slap America across the face and appoint a new government" in Iran. A few days after that speech, in an Isfahan theater the electricity went out half-way through a film. Before the lights were turned back on, a clever spectator's voice was heard above the din of the audience, imitating and mocking that particular remark, by saying with great bravado: "I will slap the projectionist across the face. I will appoint a new projectionist," causing a great deal of audience applause.

Engaging with USIA films

The Western films exported to the Third World are usually commercial and fictional products that appear to be apolitical – even though as I have demonstrated they perform significant ideological work. However, the American government through the United States Information Agency (USIA) produced a massive number of manifestly political and "pedagogic" works such as non-fiction and instructional films that were distributed to many Third World countries, including Iran, in the early 1950s. It was a tumultuous time for the Cold War rivalry of the United States and the Soviet Union. The fall of Prime Minister Mosaddeq had intensified the Cold War tensions, causing the US government to launch an official policy to win the hearts and minds of the non-Communist world. This task was assigned to USIA, which President Truman created in August 1953, in order to:

> Tell all people throughout the world the truth about the official aims and acts of the U.S., to expose and counter hostile efforts to distort those aims and acts and to present a broad and accurate *picture* of the life and culture of the American people.
>
> (Naficy 1984: p. 190, emphasis added)

Taking a cue from Truman's formulation, this policy involved increased marketing of American motion pictures to the Third World and production and distribution of documentaries targeted at specific countries, primarily those in "danger" of conversion to Communism. In the case of Iran, which shared a long border with the Soviet Union, this meant showing American-made films to school children and to rural populations by means of mobile film vans and to the general public in commercial cinemas. All in all USIA showed over 800 films dubbed into Persian, over half of which were the Persian language newsreel *Akhbar-e Iran* (*Iran News*), created specifically for the Iranian market. These dealt with more topical and political issues such as the Point 4 program, the military and development programs in Iran (often involving the US), the activities of the Shah and the royal family, earthquakes, and a variety of human interest stories from the US, the remainder being principally concerned with improving primitive health, nutrition and agricultural methods.⁹

Like many students of my generation, I was a subject of this experiment in influencing hearts and minds. As an elementary school student in an experimental "model" school, planned and funded by the Point 4 program (administered by USIA), I was exposed to many of these films on a regular basis. Every Thursday afternoon (the day before the Iranian weekend), a green mobile film unit would drive into our school yard. A middle-aged man wearing a suit and a tie, who acted as both driver and projectionist, would emerge to set up his portable screen and 16mm Bell and Howell projector in our small recreation rooms. Powered by the generator inside the mobile unit, the projector opened a new world to us. Films were taken seriously enough in my school for teachers to require students to review them in writing. I still have a book of my reviews written in 1953 (1332), when I was in the fourth grade. It contains reviews of 16 films, most of which were shot in Iran and dealt with improving health and hygiene practices. A fourth of them were documentaries about life in the United States.

At first glance, what comes through my reviews and plot summaries is that the USIA films are closed texts. The world of the village is shown to be disturbed by a disease, such as tuberculosis or dysentery, but soon stability and calm is restored thanks to an external agent. The closedness of these texts, however, is somewhat illusory since on further analysis, their wider political connotations become apparent. It seems to me that at the heart of the US policy of technological transfer and development aid for the Third World since the 1950s, was this notion of homogenization and synchronicity of the world within Western consumerist ideology. This is a shift from the earlier policy of diachronicity, promulgated by colonists, which tended to keep the developed and the underdeveloped worlds apart. The emerging form of post-industrial capitalism sought synchronicity in the interest of creating global markets. Therefore, "underdevelopment," as a non-synchronous category, fell outside that ideology and that circuit of power relations, and was therefore considered a threat. It had to be controlled, countered, and contained.

The USIA films seemed designed to produce such a global synchronicity by isolating the problems and their solutions. For example, in these films the wider health, agricultural, economical, and political problems besetting Iran were generally not discussed. Problems were often fragmented and separated from their socio-political roots and contexts. Thus isolated, both the problems and the solutions were universalized and the threat of non-synchronicity was contained. All problems were knowable and soluble by means of Western technology and know-how.

The diegesis of these films was peopled with a central character (usually a young boy such as Said who suffers from tuberculosis) and a central authority figure (such as Doctor Khoshqadam, who treats him). The chief authorities dispensing well-being and prosperity were Point 4 development agents and physicians. These figures invoked and legitimized by proxy the power, knowledge, competence, authority, and, indeed, the right of both the Iranian government (by whom they were employed) and the entire Western economic and industrial apparatus (which trained and sponsored them) to solve indigenous local problems. The packaging of USIA films underscored their politics, for interspersed with the films shot in Iran were movies filmed in the United States, which offered a rival ideal model.

My reviews of these films, written at age ten, are strictly plot summaries. Why? I do not remember the terms under which we were given the review assignments, but I take the absence of evaluative judgment on my part to be a significant strategy, subconsciously applied, which transcends my own shyness. I take these absences to be a deliberate form of resisting, a refusal to make that 180 degree turn and be hailed as the subject of the West. To confine my interaction with the films to pure plot description was to rob them of their life force and effectivity. This apparent distance was not disengagement, but an active form of engagement. Some may take the absence of evaluative criticism to be an indication of my agreement with the films, but in this I tend to side with Jean Baudrillard (1985, p. 588) who suggests that such responses may in fact be a form of "refusal by over-acceptance," that is, a form of haggling. The same process was at work when as teenagers we objectified and over-exaggerated the looks, poses, and gestures of Western movie stars. By these means we were in a sense returning the interpellating gaze.

These forms of spectator counterhailing constituted a kind of crosscultural haggling with the West and with the Shah's government. Nevertheless, the bargaining tended to favor the West, for Westernization was overdetermined in most social spheres.[10] But as the anti-Shah revolution gained momentum in the late 1970s, the balance shifted in the opposite direction. Theaters became not only a site of resistance to and defiance of the government, but also a metonym for Western values, which were now in disfavor. That is why they became such direct targets of revolutionary ire, resulting in the demolition and torching of nearly a third (i.e. over 180) moviehouses nationwide (Naficy 1992, p. 178).

Making films in the West

My long-term relationship with the West, mediated at great length and from long-distance by means of cinema, finally became intimate and first-hand. Upon graduating from high school, the young man went to England to continue his studies. While there, films continued to be a major source of his knowledge of the West and a valuable aid in teaching him English. Watching films also had a healing effect on his profound loneliness. Every Friday evening, I would go to the movies, the most gripping and memorable of which was *The Mind Benders* (1963), starring Dirk Bogarde. In retrospect, I consider this film to be a metaphor of my own life as a foreigner. Here I was, an 18-year-old boy who had never flown in an airplane and had never ventured out of my country alone. Now, in a single stroke he was severed from the warmth of a large, extended family and planted abroad – a single, solitary seedling, adrift in a foreign land and surrounded by a reserved people and an unfamiliar language and culture. He was numbed by the experience of it all like the hero of *The Mind Benders*, a scientist played by Bogarde who underwent experiments to determine the effects of total isolation on his psyche. The absence of input made the scientist vulnerable to indoctrination, leading to psychosis. He considered the film significant enough to write about it in the journal I am reading (dated 5/5/1963). His analysis of why I was taken by the film is expressed in a removed, philosophical tone, which ends with the following question: "is it possible for humans to tolerate total isolation?"

In England, I was overwhelmed by input from the new society. But without realizing it I carried out an experiment similar to the one that Bogarde underwent, whereby I isolated myself as a means of re-programming myself to better adapt to the culture of the other. This took the form of solitary acts: reading, studying, going to the movies, and taking long walks in the countryside. Like the film, however, isolation made me more vulnerable to interpellation by the British culture. My journal of this period is filled with agonized poetry, my own or quoted from others, testifying to the cost of this experiment: depression, low self-esteem, and a sense of total isolation. Soon, I found a way out by moving to the United States to begin my formal studies in film and television production.

Yet, barely a month after arriving in Los Angeles, a sense of desolation and rage overtook him and he found solace in Stephen Crane's horrific poetry and Jean Paul Sartre's depressing existentialist philosophy. He copied many of Crane's poems and many passages from Sartre's *Nausea* in my journal. On 4/26/1964, for example, he filled an entire page with the word "nausea," repeated over and over, in a fashion chillingly reminiscent of Jack's possessed writing in Stanley Kubrick's *The Shining* (1980): "All work and no play makes Jack a dull boy." Last night, reading over these diary pages for the first time in many years, hair rose on the back of my neck. And tonight, while screening the film to my students in my film authorship seminar, I realized the similarity between my exilic panic then and Jack's unhinging in the Overlook Hotel.

Up to this point, I had been a consumer of the movies – with the exception of his childhood experiments with a primitive cartoon-strip projector. Now he began to study and make films professionally as a means of talking back to both here and there, and of ripping through my Iranian teenage angst, my English foreigner's isolation, and my American exilic trauma. The self-othering trajectory, begun long ago with photography and film spectatorship in Iran, was being complicated now from this position of exile. The distance that had once separated me from the diegetic world of America and had made that world all the more alluring, was dissolving with transplantation. The "elsewhere" was now "here." Me, myself, I, he – all of me – were here in the West at once, no distance separated us. But, unity, wholeness and ease were illusive, and, besides, a switch was taking place. Another elsewhere, another other, was now looming large. I am speaking of home, against which he had begun to define me anew.

One of his video projects at UCLA's M.F.A. program in film production, entitled *REM* (*Rapid Eye Movement*, 1969), inscribed some of these anxieties about wholeness, partiality and dis-ease. This surreal video, which was largely conceived during dreamtime, involved a teenage boy and girl on a quest in a mountainous, desolate land. The futility of their external quest was reflected in their limited interpersonal relationship, symbolized by their dialog during the thirty-minute video, which consisted of appropriately inflected repetition of a single word, "toilet." In one scene, they are on all fours in tattered clothing circling each other like two beasts and viciously barking the two-syllable word at each other. At the end, the young man finds in a dry creek-bed a television set, which shows an image of him discovering the set. At that point, the image on the TV cuts to a whole brain that is placed outside a skull on a table. A hand, indeed my own hand, reaches into the frame and proceeds to mash and kneed the brain like so much dough. Was he smashing my brains, or was it the foreign culture doing it? Was this a literalization of the self-othering that had begun long ago, with my first exposure to photography, Western literature, cinema, and color slides of American national parks? Whatever the impetus for and interpretation of these dissociative images, cinematic self-othering would become a major academic concern of his (cf. Naficy 2000) in the years to come.

Something else, some new type of othering was also going on, however; one that resulted from being in exile. Both *REM* and my thesis project, a computer-animated video called *Salamander Syncope* (1971), in their choice of titles pointed to, and in their content and form embraced, one of the frequent responses of the exiles to the trauma of deterritorialization: paralysis and fracturing. Only years later in the course of writing books on exile cultures and identities (Naficy 1993, 2001) and of revising this essay would he become fully aware of these early manifestations of my concern with exilic self-othering. It was indeed by making films and writing books that he attempted to understand and express my agonized and agonistic life in exile. These acts of self-definition countered years of spectatorial self-othering and hailing by modernity and by Western films. Now, however, a new reversed form of spectatorship was to begin, with other consequences.

Exilic film festivals in the West

This involved watching Iranian films in Europe and the United States instead of viewing Western films in Iran. It also involved organizing and curating film festivals that showcased Iranian, Third World, and exilic and diasporic films. Such forms of spectatorship and exhibition resulted in complex and highly slippery subjectivities that are open to all sorts of intercultural and translational haggling. For example, in June 1995 while conducting research in Paris for a book on Iranian cinema, I attended a private screening of Mohsen Makhmalbaf's *A Time to Love* (*Nowbat-e Asheai*, 1991) at MK2 Productions, which was considering the film for distribution. Made by one of the best-known new directors to emerge from Iran since the revolution of 1979, the film had been banned in Iran for its love theme, bold treatment of a love triangle. My friend Azadeh Kian and I were the only spectators in the comfortably appointed screening room. Makhmalbaf, who lives in Iran, had shot the film in Turkey (perhaps partly to avoid Iranian censors) with all the film's dialogue in Turkish, a language I did not know beyond certain words. The film was subtitled, but in French, which at times passed too fast for my understanding, especially since I was trying to take notes. On these occasions, I would nudge Azadeh who would whisper the Persian translation into my ears. Trying to keep up with her translation and with the ongoing film and its subtitles, I was forced to take notes hurriedly in English and Persian, whichever served the moment best. Thus, watching this single film involved multiple acts of translation across four cultures and languages. This chain of linguistic and cultural signification pointed to the radical shifts that had occurred in the globalization of cinema since my childhood. In those days, cinema screens were monopolized by the West, particularly by American films, and Third World people were more consumers of these films than producers of their own narratives. But now we were making and exhibiting our films, not only in our own countries but also across national boundaries, and we were finding receptive audiences, not only in film festivals but also in commercial venues. Significantly, what occurred in that screening room involved not only watching but also reading, hearing, translating, and writing a film – all of which are part of the spectatorial activities and competencies needed for these new globalized Third World and diasporized cinemas, what I have elsewhere called "accented films" (Naficy 1999).

Film festivals are prime sites for intensified national and transnational translations and mistranslations, as well as hailing and haggling over acts of representation. He understood this to his bones, when in 1990 I organized at UCLA the first major film festival of Iranian films in the United States, featuring a large number of postrevolutionary films and introducing the new works of such veterans as Abbas Kiarostami, Bahram Baizai, Amir Naderi and Dariush Mehrjui, as well as post-revolutionary works by Mohsen Makhmalbaf, Rakhshan Benetemad, Said Ebrahimifar and Abdolfazil Jalili. For almost a decade, the anti-Iranian politics and policies in the US and the Islamic Republic's hostility towards both the American government and the Iranians abroad had discouraged importation of postrevolutionary films. As a result, this cinema was largely unknown and unavailable here even though Iranian films had begun to receive high praise at international festivals elsewhere. The UCLA event and the ensuing controversy helped change all that.

The planned festival came under vociferous criticism by some exiles, particularly by extreme rightist and leftist media producers and filmmakers, who alleged that it would whitewash the Islamist government's human rights violations. Some exiled opponents of the government, particularly filmmaker and actor Parviz Sayyad, called festival organizers, including myself, members of the pro-government "cultural militia in exile" (Sayyad 1996, p. 55) and "celebrators of fascism" (p. 57). He mobilized sexual metaphors, in the style of the clerics he detested, to accuse festival organizers of "flattery" (p. 77), "flirting with" (p. 36), and "going to bed with" (p. 10) the oppressive Islamist regime. Our aims, according to him, were political: to "purify" the government (p. 54), "conceal" its evil deeds and human rights violations (p. 55), help it "re-gain its lost prestige" (p. 132), "neutralize all opposition movements" against it (p. 31), and, finally, "deceive" the foreigners about those deeds and violations (p. 82). Sayyad and his cohorts called for a total boycott of Iranian film festivals abroad.

The man who took snapshots of films and knew loneliness also knew most of the protesting filmmakers, had worked with some of them before, and had even promoted their films in academic circles, including those of Sayyad. Their protest and what became personal attacks were very painful to him, particularly as I was not at all interested in promoting the Islamist regime and had published criticism of its cultural politics and treatment of artists. Rather, my purpose was to encourage those who were making high quality films under difficult conditions and widespread censorship inside Iran by exposing their films to both Iranian and international audiences. To honor them and to provide a forum for discussing filmmaking under the Islamic Republic, I had invited two well-known auteurs, Abbas Kiarostami and Dariush Mehrjui, to be the festival guests.

Festival spectators were in turn impressed and the Iranians among them were touched by the films from the homeland and they embraced the festival enthusiastically. They flocked to the theater in large numbers, from as far away as New York City, Washington, DC, and Houston, and at times stood in line for over eight hours to obtain tickets. The atmosphere was festive but somewhat tense because of the presence of well-known exiled entertainers holding placards and protest signs. It was there that Kiarostami walked up to Sayyad and sardonically offered to take his place in the protest line to free him to go inside to see the films that he was objecting to, sight unseen. Needless to say he did not accept the invitation, although other protesters later attended some screenings.

What Kiarostami and Mehrjui told the audiences inside imparted an understanding about the intense ideological battle over cinema that was raging inside Iran. It became clear to them that the filmmakers there were no pawns of the government; nor were they collaborators in its ideological projects. What the festival accomplished was to create an image of Iran as a complex living culture and society, not one that was totally silenced, subjugated, or ruined by the backward ruling mullahs, as the festival opponents claimed. Filmmakers and audiences in Iran through various haggling strategies had found ways of expressing themselves despite the clerical domination of the

ISAs. Even some government officials connected with film supported this nascent post-revolutionary cinema. So, to the extent that this festival as a site of cultural translation and transaction showed that the Islamist regime was not monolithic, it permitted a more realistic and nuanced representation of the dynamics of culture and society in Iran. These counterhegemonic functions brought to light by the festival more than made up for the pain that the orchestrated misinformation and personal attacks of the politicized exiles had caused.

Their vehemence suggested that the debate was not so much over Iranian politics as it was over exilic politics. Many artists in were perhaps envious because while their careers had languished or had been ruined by exile, those of their counterparts such as Kiarostami and Mehrjui were flourishing even under heavy censorship. The exiles also wished to maintain the comforting psychological barriers that they themselves had created by their fetishized and frozen representations of Iran as a ruined land filled with victimized people. The intense audience involvement with the movies, however, indicated that the films had succeeded in breaking through those barriers, unleashing the threat that heretofore had been kept in check – that of the homeland unfettered by repressions and distortions of exilic politics. The result of such a break-through was that spectators, many of them tearful upon exiting the theater, began to contemplate the unthinkable: the possibility of reconciliation, even return (Naficy 1993, p. 170). A similar cinematic reconciliation, the opposite of cinematic self-othering, occurred in him as I completed my film studies PhD that same spring and for the first time since the revolution returned home for a brief cathartic visit.

Like other film festivals, the UCLA event not only created awareness and facilitated debate and exchange of ideas about filmmakers, films, and censorship mechanisms, but also served the important function of creating interest for the new films among Western film critics, distributors and exhibitors. Several of the festival films were picked up for US commercial distribution, and festivals of Iranian cinema gradually became a regular, annual event in many cities in the United States and Europe.[11] In 1992, the Toronto International Film Festival called Iranian cinema "one of the pre-eminent national cinemas in the world today" (Festival catalog, p. 8). No filmmaker received more critical and popular acclaim abroad than Kiarostami, whose picture appeared on the cover of the July-August 1995 issue of *Cahiers du cinéma* (no. 493) above the caption which declared simply: "Kiarostami le magnifique." Inside, nearly fifty pages were devoted to his works. In due course the films of the majority of the directors who had contributed to the festival gained international recognition and distribution.

I had been othered by my experience as a film spectator. But it is part of the polysemy of cinema that I was able to use that agent of my othering in my reconstructive project of selfing. Indeed, making films, teaching and writing about films, and organizing film festivals were his strategies for my self-understanding, self-narrativization, and self-fashioning both at home and in exile. These strategies were in the final analysis forms of sublation, which resolved my non-Western and Western contradictions into a newly formed hybridized unity. It involved identifying with the West, idealizing it, fetishizing it, consuming it, becoming subject to and consumed by it, resisting and subverting it, and finally contributing to its remaking. It was a heterologic process by which I, me, myself, and he gradually – but not permanently or unproblematically – came to map onto one another, creating a partial and multiple subject who was simultaneously both here and there.

Notes

1   Naipaul, V.S., "The Enigma of Arrival" (1986), p. 41.
2   This essay is a considerably revised version of Naficy 1996.
3   The political context of the time was this: around the time my father left Iran, the nationalist and popular politician Mohammad Mosaddeq had become prime minister. He launched a series of reforms, chief among them, curbing the power of the royal family and nationalizing the British oil assets in Iran. These and other policies caused a great deal of political havoc both at home and abroad. While the Americans, interested in stemming the British monopoly in Iranian politics and economy, first supported Mosaddeq, they soon turned against him fearing a communist takeover in Iran. The confluence of British and American interests resulted in a coup in the summer of 1953, which led to Mosaddeq's ouster and his arrest and the return of the Shah to power. Intellectuals particularly felt betrayed by the US. The memory of this betrayal was to play a role in the anti-Americanism of the 1979 revolution and the subsequent "hostage crisis."
4   This situation may have attracted homosexuals who were rumored to frequent the moviehouses.
5   After the Islamic revolution of 1979, dubbing became more of a politico-religious instrument, consciously and openly employed to remove or alter offensive Western influences and women's representations. For details, see Naficy 1992, 1994.
6   Iranians' appetite for seeds is so great that a journal estimated that in 1984 alone a total of 200 million tumans worth of seeds had been consumed in Iranian theaters ($25,000,000 then). See "Ja'i Bara-ye Masraf-e Tannaqolat va Tanvir-e Afkar," *Mahnameh-ye Sinema'i-ye Film* 3:31 (Azar 1364/November 1985), p. 4.
7   This is reminiscent of the citizens of Abidjan, Ivory Coast, who in Jean Rouch's film *I, A Black* (*Moi Un Noir*, 1957) frequent a bar named Chicago and adopt the name and identity markers of famous movie stars, such as Edward G. Robinson and Dorothy Lamour. See my interview with Rouch (Naficy 1979).
8   Parental worry about cinema was partially justified in so far as popular forms of entertainment in Iran like in many other countries involved practices some of which were considered by mainstream culture to be immoral and unethical.
9   For a description of the production and distribution of USIA films made in Iran, including *Iran News*, and a full list of the films, see Issari 1989 and Naficy 1984.
10   For theorization of how cinema and Westernization were overdetermined in Iran, see Naficy 2000.
11   Facets Multimedia in Chicago and http://www.IranianMovies.com/ are two mail-order sources of videos of Iranian cinema.

References

Barthes, Roland (1977) *Image/Music/Text* (Stephen Heath, trans.), New York: Hill and Wang.

Baudrillard, Jean (1985) "The Masses: The Implosion of the Social in the Media," *New Literary History* 3 (Spring), pp. 577–89.

Crapanzano, Vincent (1980) *Tuhami: Portrait of a Moroccan*, Chicago: University of Chicago Press.

Gabriel, Teshome H. (1989) "Third Cinema as Guardian of Popular Memory," in Jim Pines and Paul Willemen (eds) *Questions of Third Cinema*, London: BFI.

Guppy, Shusha (1988) *The Blindfold Horse: Memories of a Persian Childhood*, Boston: Beacon Press.

Issari, Mohammad Ali (1989) *Cinema in Iran, 1900-1979*, New York: Scarecrow Press.

Mehrabi, Masud (1984/1363). *Tarikhe- Sinema-ve Iran az Aghaz ta 1357*, Tehran: Entesharat-e Film.

Naficy, Hamid (1979) "Jean Rouch: A Personal Perspective," *Quarterly Review of Film Studies* (Summer), pp. 339–61.

Naficy, Hamid (1981a) "Iranian Documentaries," *Jump Cut* No. 26, pp. 41–4.

Naficy, Hamid (1981b) "Cinema as a Political Instrument," in Michael Bonine and Nikki Keddie (eds) *Modern Iran: The Dialectic of Continuity and Change*, Albany, NY: SUNY Press, pp. 341–59.

Naficy, Hamid (1984) *Iran Media Index*, Westport, CT: Greenwood Press.

Naficy, Hamid (1992) "Islamizing Film Culture," in Samih Farsoun and Mehrdad Mashayekhi (eds) *Iran: Political Culture in the Islamic Republic*, London: Routledge, pp. 173–208.

Naficy, Hamid (1993) *The Making of Exile Cultures: Iranian Television in Los Angeles*, Minneapolis: University of Minnesota Press.

Naficy, Hamid (1994) "Veiled Visions/Powerful Presences: Women in Post-revolutionary Iranian Cinema," in Mahnaz Afkhami and Erika Friedl, (eds) *In the Eye of the Storm: Women in Postrevolutionary Iran*, London and New York: I.B. Taurus and Syracuse University Press, pp. 131–50.

Naficy, Hamid (1996) "Theorizing 'Third World' Film Spectatorship," *Wide Angle* 18:4 (October, 1996), pp. 3–26.

Naficy, Hamid (1999) "Between Rocks and Hard Places: the Interstitial Mode of Production in Exilic Cinema," in Hamid Naficy (ed.) *Home, Exile, Homeland: Film, Media, and the Politics of Place*, London and New York: Routledge, pp. 125–47.

Naficy, Hamid (2000) "Self-Othering: A Postcolonial Discourse on Cinematic First Contact," in Fawzia Afzal-Khan and Kalpana Seshadri-Crooks (eds) *The Pre-Occupation of Post-Colonial Studies*, Durham, NC: Duke University Press.

Naficy, Hamid (2001) *An Accented Cinema: Exilic and Diasporic Filmmaking*, Princeton: Princeton University Press.

Naipaul, V.S. (1986) "The Enigma of Arrival," *New Yorker* (August 11), p. 41.

Navab-Safavi, Mojtaba (1978/1357) *Jame'eh va Hokumat-e Eslami*, Qom: Entesharat-e Hejrat.

Sayyad, Parviz (1996) *Rah-e Doshvar-e Sinema-ye dar Tab'id*, Los Angeles: Parsian.

White, Hayden (1978) "The Noble Savage theme as Fetish," in *Topics of Discourse: Essays in Cultural Criticism*, Baltimore: Johns Hopkins University Press, pp. 183–96.

9 Rethinking Indian popular cinema

Towards newer frames of understanding

Wimal Dissanayake

Cultural coordinates

Few cinemas have been as much maligned and subject to critical derision as the popular commercial cinema of India. The widely used and negatively-charged term "Bollywood" indexes one significant aspect of this complex discursive field. India continues to be the largest film-producing country in the world with an annual output of over 700 films. A few years ago the figure was as high as 900. And nearly 90 percent of these films belong to what critics term the popular cinema as opposed to the artistic cinema as exemplified in the works of such auteurs as Satyajit Ray, Mrinal Sen and Adoor Gopalkrishnan. Popular cinema is still a dominant force in India providing a useful site for the negotiation of cultural meaning and values and inviting the vast mass of movie-goers to participate in the ongoing conversation of cultural modernities. Consequently, the domain of popular cinema is one that merits close study and analysis.

Until about two decades ago, Indian popular cinema was dismissed out of hand by film scholars, film critics and intellectuals in general as unworthy of serious academic attention. It was often characterized as being meretricious, escapist, mindless drivel and totally irrelevant to the understanding of Indian society and culture. Only a few voices chose to challenge the might of conventional wisdom and offer dissenting views, seeking to point out the discursive significance of popular-commercial cinema as an instance of modern cultural production imbricated with a plurality of important and contentious issues related to ideology, power, cultural modernity, nationality and state formation. However, during the last two decades or so the scholarly tide has changed and there has been a significant attempt to study popular cinema with the seriousness it deserves and to locate it within wider discursive fields and regimes of signification. The efforts of such scholars as Ashis Nandy, Geeta Kapur, Ashish Rajadhyaksha, Ravi Vasudevan, Madhava Prasad, Sumita Chakravarty, Sara Dickey, and M.S.S. Pandian, to name but a few, are extremely significant in this regard.[1] These scholars approach popular cinema with distinctive perspectives and vantage points; however, they are united by a deep conviction that Indian popular cinema needs to be studied and examined very seriously. Indeed, with something now approaching critical maturity in the field, the time has come to examine the various pathways that have been cleared in order to gain a deeper understanding of Indian popular cinema and to identify some significant gaps and potentially fruitful lines of inquiry that yet need to be pursued.

The popular cinema of India can be understood most productively within the discursive boundaries of cultural modernity. Modernity, as commentators like Marshall Berman have pointed out, is a highly complex phenomenon that touches on all aspects of human existence, ushering in profound changes in society and in cultural perceptions.[2] For purposes of analysis we can identify four main and intersecting discourses related to modernity. The first is the socio-economic discourse that calls attention to such phenomena as urbanization, industrialization, massification, expansion of transport, proliferation of technology and the emergence of consumer culture. The second, is the cognitive discourse that seeks to focus attention on questions of rationality, with particular emphasis on instrumental rationality. Indeed, instrumental rationality is valorized as the preferred mode of cognition through which human society is comprehended and constructed. The third discourse relates to the political dimensions of modernity. It directs our attention to the spread of secularism, and the challenges to traditional norms of conduct, the nature of polity and subjectivity. Fourth, there is the discourse of experientiality and phenomenological participation in modernity foregrounding issues of new perspectives on society demanded by the rapidly evolving contexts of living and sensory experience. The writings of such eminent social and cultural analysts as Georg Simmel, Walter Benjamin and Siegfried Kracauer are extremely important in this regard.[3] While all four of these interconnected and interanimating discourses are relevant to the understanding of Indian popular cinema, it is the sensory and experiential dimension that is most significant. It draws attention to the discourse of cinema, newer perspectives and frames of intelligibility and the transformations that are incessantly taking place within the texture of urban experience. In any analysis of the commercial cinema of India and its evolution, this dimension invites closer study.

As we probe the sensory and experiential aspect of modernity, we need to focus on issues of tempo, fragmentation, chaos, and over-stimulation brought about by the images, the various cultural dislocations engendered by the changes in the living environment. These are vitally imbricated with the appeal and the social meaning of Indian popular cinema. As Berman remarked, what is interesting about modernity is the complex ways in which human beings become both objects and subjects of the modernizing process.[4] And popular cinema in India reflects the ways in which Indian movie-goers become both objects and subjects of the processes of cultural modernization. Georg Simmel, in an insightful essay titled "The Metropolis and the Mental Life," written over a century ago, observed that, the rapid crowding of changing images, the sharp discontinuities in the grasp of a single glance and the unexpectedness of on rushing impression; these are the psychological conditions which the metropolis creates with each crossing of the street. With the tempo and multiplicity of economic, occupational and social life, the city sets up a deep contrast with small town and rural life with reference to the sensory foundations of psychic life.[5]

The deeper currents inflecting the commercial cinematic discourse, as in most other Asian countries, have to be understood in terms of the dynamics of cultural modernization. Contrary to notions of progress maintained by modernization theorists of the 1950s, modernity is multifaceted and multivalent and the process of modernization is by no means unilinear. It is evident that modernization is a global condition that reshapes our understanding of self and society, time and space, past and present in culturally specific ways. Modernity is not reducible solely to the imperatives of the economic, although they are extremely important in the way in which they inflect our thinking. Its relationship to cultural formations is vital and demands focused attention. Its interaction with tradition is not one of simple opposition; it engages tradition at different levels of apprehension, promoting revaluations and urging relocations of tradition. Cultures are, of course, not timeless entities but products of history, politics, and geography. They are sites in which meanings relevant to everyday life are constantly made, unmade and remade. Popular cinema in India has to be understood in relation to the dynamics of modernization as they impinge on the cultural consciousness of Indian people. Ashis Nandy observes that popular cinema provides the vast mass of movie-goers with the cultural categories with which to make sense of their lives. In this regard his invocation of the image of the slum as a way of troping Indian popular cinema is extremely suggestive:

> The popular cinema is the slum's point of view of Indian politics and society and, for that matter, the world. There is in both of them the same stress on lower-middle-class sensibilities and on the informal, not-terribly-tacit theories of politics and society the class uses and the same ability to shock the haute bourgeoisie with the distinctiveness, vigor and crudity of their theories.[7]

Nandy points out that urban slums consist of people who are deracinated and partially decultured, having most often been first or second generation economic migrants to the cities. They are people who have moved away from tradition and have been compelled to loosen their bonds to community and caste. This is, of course, not to suggest that slums have no access to cultural traditions. As Nandy observes, "often the resistance of culture is seen in the most dramatic fashion in the urban slum."[8]

According to Nandy, two processes are central to a deep understanding of their resilience. First, the slum recreates the remembered village in a new guise and resurrects the old community ties in new forms. He says that slums may even have their own representation of classicism. It is, of course, not classicism as textualized by ancient expositors of a Sanskritic age. It is what classicism is when adapted and transformed to suit the imperatives of a mass market. Second, according to Nandy, slum dwellers create their own culture out of the welter of experiences available to them. How diverse time periods and cultures are telescoped and how diverse communities, ethnicities and worldviews are amalgamated and interanimated is vital to a proper understanding of urban slum culture. He goes on to say that,

> Both processes are conspicuous in the popular film – the remembered village and the compacted heterogeneity between strange neighbors. That is why the popular film ideally has to have everything – from the classical to the folk, from the sublime to the ridiculous, from the terribly modern to the incorrigibly traditional, from plots within plots that never get resolved to the cameo roles and stereotypical characters that never get developed.[9]

The urban slums and popular-commercial films in India are direct outcomes of modernity. Nandy's deployment of the slum as a trope for popular cinema opens up interesting lines of inquiry that could be pursued productively.

In order to understand the nature and significance of Indian popular cinema we need to examine its genealogy. In this regard, certain formative influences present themselves as being significant and far-reaching in their power of inflection: the ancient epics that form the basis of Hindu religious belief, the vibrant, European-influenced Parsi theater of the nineteenth and early twentieth century, the classical cinema of Hollywood, and lastly the MTV music video.

From its inception Indian cinema drew upon the epics *Ramayana* and *Mahabaratha*, which were an animating force of classical poetry, drama, art and sculpture. This influence can be explored in terms of thematics, narrativity, ideology and communication. From its inception up until today, the two epics have continued to furnish Indian filmmakers with themes and storylines. The very first surviving Indian feature film, *Raja Harischandra*, made in 1913, was based on the *Ramayana*. Since then hundreds of films have drawn on the *Ramayana* and the *Mahabaratha* for plots. In addition, thematics related to motherhood, femininity, patrimony and revenge, as enunciated in films like *Mother India*, *Awaara*, and *Zanzeer*, find repeated and emphatic articulation in poplar cinema.

It is only by paying close attention to the structure of narrativity in Indian popular cinema that we can begin to understand its uniqueness as a cinematic discourse. Although, as I shall indicate later, Indian cinema was hugely influenced by Hollywood, the art of narration with its endless circularities, digressions and detours, and plots within plots remained characteristically Indian. Once again, the influence of the two epics is readily apparent. Instead of the linear and logical and psychologized narratives that we find in Hollywood cinema, the mainstream Indian cinema offers us a different order of diegesis that can be understood most productively in terms of the narrative discourses enunciated in the *Ramayana* and *Mahabaratha*.[10]

In discussing the nature and significance of Indian popular cinema the question of popular ideology (an ideology influenced by the traditional theologies of India's epic cycles) rewards close scrutiny. Despite various attempts at social critique, calling attention to economic and political disparities, as well as social injustices, the popular cinema in India is by and large committed to the maintenance of the status quo. When we take into consideration the nature of the economics of film production and the distribution mechanisms, this can hardly come as a surprise. The pivotal idea informing the two epics is one of safeguarding the existing social order and valorizing its axiological basis. As Vijay Mishra insightfully points out, as a result of the fact that the *Ramayana* and the *Mahabaratha* were ideological instruments employed for the expansion of the structures of belief approved by the ruling classes, there is also a significant way in which the popular Indian cinema legitimizes its own existence through a re-inscription of its values into those of the two revered epics.[11]

In terms of communication too, the vital interconnection between the epics and commercial cinema is clear. As Mishra has observed, the epics which were transmitted orally were inextricably linked to ritual and folklore. Being an integral aspect of Indian culture, they found statement in diverse ways and forms in local narratives. What this oral communication precipitated was the severance of links with an original, ur-text, becoming, instead, a plurality of narratives and texts. However, the shape and form of the individual accretions did not basically challenge or subvert the guiding rules of the major narrative, which remained vital and fixed. Each presentation was distinctive and was defined only in relation to the larger narrative. This line of thinking is fully consistent with Mishra's view that,

> Bombay films too are moments of a grand narrative; each individual movie is a play or the discursive practice which makes up the other, unseen movie as one massive unit. In short, the Bombay film is one massive system with a series (incomplete) of specific actualization.[12]

Hence, we can say that the two epics, the *Ramayana* and the *Mahabaratha*, have played, and continue to play, a significant role in the structuration of popular-commercial cinema in India.

With this in mind, it is appropriate to focus attention on the classical Sanskrit theater as a formative influence on popular films. Sanskrit theater constitutes one of the richest legacies of classical Indian culture. It was highly stylized and its preferred mode of presentation was episodic, placing great emphasis on the idea of the spectacle. In it, music and dance came together in an exquisite union to create a complex artistic unity. The classical Indian theater was guided by clear injunctions related to the selection of plots, heroes and heroines, use of language and the structuring of the narrative discourse. Poetry was deemed an integral part of the theatrical experience. Indeed, from the very earliest times, drama was regarded as a branch of poetry (*drishya kavya*). Poetry was utilized in the service of commenting on morals, enhancing emotions, and conjuring up vividly in the minds of the spectators the background of action of the drama. Mime and dance constituted vital elements of the Sanskrit theater. Indeed, the Sanskrit word "*natya*," meaning drama, is derived from the root "*nrit*" (to dance).

We can identify several features of classical Indian theater which have had an important bearing on the construction of popular cinema in India. Classical Indian plays were spectacular dance-dramas, with relatively loose narrative requirements, in contrast to the tightly organized plays in the West. They were non-naturalistic and stylized, and invited an imaginative participation from the audiences. As much of the force and vitality of the classical theater was derived from traditional and conventionalized vocabulary of dramatic statement, the more one was familiar with the conventions, the easier it was for one to participate in the experience presented on stage. These plays can be described as heroic romantic comedies with a pronounced lyricism. The ultimate aim of the classical Indian playwright was the generation of a dominant aesthetic emotion (*rasa*) in the audience. Classical Indian theater flourished as a form of court entertainment; hence, its informing ideology was one of keeping intact and reinforcing the existing social order. Throughout my discussion of the classical Indian theater, I have chosen to use the past tense because, for all intents and purposes, Sanskrit theater ceased to exist as a living tradition since about the twelfth century. Hence, the question naturally arises, how can we identify this theater as a formative influence on popular cinema if it has been dead for the past eight centuries? It is here that the regional folk dramas of India assume a great significance.

After about the tenth century, Sanskrit theater began to decline owing to a number of factors. Concurrently, several dramatic forms emerged or matured in the various regions of India, which albeit of a comparatively unrefined and inelegant nature preserved and embodied some of the central features of the classical theatrical tradition. The Yatra of Bengal, Ram Lila and Krisna Lila of Uttar Pradesh, Bhavai of Gujerat, Bhagavata Mela of Tanjore, Terukkuttu of Tamilnadu, Vithinatakam of Andhra Pradesh and Yakshagana of Karnataka are the most prominent among them. These various regional folk dramas, basically the work of untutored folk artists, as opposed to their highly refined and learned forebears, contain one important feature, namely, that in varying degrees of reliability they incarnate in living form some of the more deeply encoded inscriptions of classical Indian drama. An examination of the central features of these folk plays makes it evident that they have been influenced by and carry over the styles and techniques of Sanskrit theater, but because the folk theater is only one of many influences the melodramas of popular cinema may seem distractingly heterogeneous to those unfamiliar with their conventions. Nevertheless, in their deployment of humor, music, dance, the structure of the narratives, the informing melodramatic imagination, the folk dramas of India have clearly had a deep impact on the makers of popular commercial cinema.

In our inquiry into the genealogy of popular cinema, the next important cultural force that we need to explore is the Parsi theater that came into existence after the nineteenth century. The Parsis, who formed a rich and gifted community, in part because of the unavailability of a deep-rooted cultural tradition of their own in the Indian soil, took up drama both in Gujarati and in Hindustani. During the nineteenth century, even at the height of the British empire, the Parsis had succeeded in gaining a wide reputation as resourceful playwrights and versatile technicians, influencing theatrical traditions throughout India; Parsi theatrical companies toured the country performing before packed audiences. Some of the more notable among them, like the Elphinstone Dramatic Company of Bombay, visited neighboring countries like Sri Lanka (then Ceylon) and played to enthralled audiences. The Parsi playwrights excelled in both social and period dramas. Stylistically, these plays displayed an odd mixture of realism and fantasy, narrative and spectacle, music and dance, lively dialogues and ingenious stagecraft, all amalgamated within the accepted narrative discursivities of melodrama. These Parsi plays with their lilting songs, crude humor, bons mots, sensationalism, and dazzling stagecraft, were aimed at appealing to the vast mass of theater-goers. The normal run of adjectives used by sophisticated critics to characterize these plays are "hybrid," "vulgar," "sensational" and "melodramatic." These plays bear an uncanny resemblance to the generality of commercially-oriented films made in India. If the folk theater was based in rural areas and sought to present the lexicon of traditionally inherited theatrical articulation, the Parsi plays indexed an urban theater exposed to Western styles, sensibilities, and a semiotics of commodified desire and entertainment. In terms of thematics, visuality, cultural inscription, narrative discourse and modes of presentation, Parsi theater and commercial cinema share much common ground.

In discussing the genealogy of contemporary popular Indian cinema, the next important cultural force that invites close attention is Hollywood cinema. The influence of Hollywood on the makers of popular cinema in India is both deep and pervasive. Indian filmmakers were greatly impressed by Hollywood films and actors and actresses, and sought to adapt the codes and conventions of Hollywood cinema to suit local tastes, sensibilities and conventions. Indian film directors found the technical resources that their Hollywood counterparts had at their disposal most attractive and sought to imitate them and create an Indian world of magic and make-believe. The glamour associated with the star system and the commercial attractions of the studio system were quickly adopted. Makers of commercial cinema in India, very often, took directly from Hollywood films storylines, character types, memorable sequences, and reshaped them to suit local sensibilities. Moreover, some of the Indian filmmakers paid tribute to their favorites. For example, Raj Kapoor was an admirer of Charlie Chaplin, Harold Lloyd, Laurel and Hardy, Buster Keaton and the Marx Brothers. It was Chaplin who appeared to have stirred his deepest comic imagination. In a number of celebrated films, he was able to indigenize the screen persona of Charlie Chaplin in a way that appealed to a large segment of the audience.

Most of all, Indian film directors and producers were greatly fascinated by the enticements and possibilities of the musicals. Hollywood musicals stood at a very interesting angle to the idea of performance in the classical and folk theater as well as that of the Parsi theater. The heyday of Hollywood musicals was from about the 1930s to the early 1950s. It is evident that a large number of these musicals had as their chosen subject matter the world of entertainment itself. The narratives of these films were largely conventional, even predictable, while the songs and spectacle cleared a representational space in which both the characters and the audiences could indulge in flights of fancy. It was through the instrumentalities of the plot that the apparent disparity between the narrative and spectacle were reconciled. This, of course, is not a trait discernible in commercial films made in India.

While drawing liberally on the Hollywood musicals, the popular cinemas of India sought to pursue a different strategy; the storyline was not employed to heal the division between narrative and spectacle. Instead, song and dance sequences were and are used as natural and logical articulations of situations and feelings emanating from the dynamics of day to day life. The Hollywood musicals claimed to sustain the facade of reality by legitimating the spectacle, as for example in *Singing in the Rain*, directed by Stanley Donen, where singing and dancing were lavishly employed because the story was about singing and dancing. The filmmakers of India, on the contrary, in endeavoring to enhance the element of fantasy through music, dance and spectacle, created the impression that songs and dances were the natural outcome of emotional statement in the given situation. However, this did not necessarily mean that the plot and the song and dance sequences had to inhabit the same continuous narrative space.

Makers of popular films in India also sought to adopt pathways that differed significantly from some of the conventions and preferred modalities of presentation valorized by Hollywood filmmakers. One of the fundamental tenets of Hollywood filmmaking, for example, is the need to cover up the artifice, the constructedness of firm articulations of narrative. All aspects of film production were perceived as being ancillary to the projection of a realistic and psychologically convincing narrative. As a result, camera angles were largely at eye level; lighting was unobtrusive; framing was aimed at focusing attention on the central action of a given sequence; cuts were made at logical junctures in the unfolding of the narrative: these devices served to foster an illusion of reality and to promote ready identification of audiences with characters appearing on the screen. Popular Indian cinema, on the other hand, grew out of somewhat different roots; there was never a deeply felt desire to conform to the "invisible style" pursued by Hollywood. Hence, while makers of commercial films in India were fascinated by Hollywood and sought to imitate its products in certain ways, they also chose to ignore some others.[13]

Among extraneous (or internal) influences, music videos are a comparatively newer force that has begun to inflect popular cinema in India. During the past two decades with the growing exposure of Indian audiences to MTV disseminated through national and international channels, Indian filmmakers have seen in it a rich resource for stylistic innovation. The pace of the films, the quick cutting, newer forms of presenting dance sequences, and the camera angles that one now sees in Indian films are a direct result of MTV. Mani Ratnam's films or box-office hits like *Satya* or *Kuch Kuch Hota Hai* bear testimony to this new trend. One reason for the mass appeal of cinema has always been the clever mixture of entertainment and technology. Hence it is hardly surprising that modern film directors in India associated with popular cinema are seeking to establish newer connections between technology and entertainment and so set in motion newer circuits of desire and pleasure.

There are a number of interesting points that need to be made regarding these formative influences. First, it is clear that these forces never congealed, as did the system of classical Hollywood narrative, into a neat unity reinforcing each other. Instead, they retained their identities and distinctiveness and followed their own path, giving popular cinema its characteristic amorphousness. This also resulted in the dominance of "force" over "form" in the Deleuzian sense.[14] Second, these diverse influences are filtered through an evolving and modernizing consciousness and the interpretations put on particularly the more ancient influences take on a hybridized emphasis. Third, the meaning and relevance of these forces changes in accordance with the newer social and cultural discourses that come into play thereby investing Indian popular cinema with a timeliness that is vital to elicit popular participation. Hence, as we explore the genealogy of popular cinema in India, what we find is not a smooth confluence of diverse forces leading to an elegant unity but a problematic coexistence of different influences within the evolving matrix of cultural modernity. Any attempt to rethink popular cinema in India must take into consideration the saliency of this phenomenon.

Given the heterogeneous and polyphonic pattern of influence and cultural exchange, it is perhaps important to isolate the most significant clusters of thinking on Indian popular cinema. The classical approach that has been favored by film critics historically, has been liberal humanism. The work of a writer like Chidananda Dasgupta, an important critic, filmmaker and proponent of an Indian art cinema, exemplifies the dominant traits associated with this approach. In 1948 he co-founded the Calcutta Film Society which played a significant role in the cultivation of cinematic taste. He has written on popular cinema from his distinct vantage point comparing it to the norms and expectations of art cinema. It is Dasgupta's considered judgment that the kind of chauvinism and cultural nationalism that has surfaced in recent times in India is directly attributable to the harmful influence of popular cinema with its mythicizations of the past and the underlying Hindu chauvinism.

In his book titled, *The Painted Face*, Dasgupta has sought to trace a direct relationship between the politics in Andhra Pradesh and Tamilnadu and the power of popular cinema. Like some of the theorists associated with the Frankfurt School, Dasgupta subscribed to the notion that the audiences for popular films are non-discriminating, gullible and constitute an undifferentiated, monolithic group. However, both theoretical and empirical studies of spectatorship have clearly established the fact that popular audiences are discriminating, and that they read films differently in keeping with their backgrounds, interests, and inclinations. Nevertheless, Dasgupta's approach to film and film audiences is still the most dominant approach to film analysis in India, with its valorization of cinematic realism.[15]

More recently, there are those who have begun to advocate a more psychologically based approach to Indian commercial cinema and locate it within wider regimes of cultural politics and social transformations, situating popular cinema at the intersection of diverse contemporary discursivities. The work of Ashis Nandy is extremely important in this regard. He was one of the earliest among contemporary intellectuals in India to recognize the importance of popular cinema as a window that opens onto the wider culture. Nandy is a leading intellectual who has written illuminatingly on such topics as nationalism, modernity, selfhood, science, development and rationality. Hence his essays on Indian popular cinema are informed by a deep interest in cultural psychology and Indian politics.

Unlike Dasgupta, Nandy sees a certain value in commercial cinema. According to him, it allows us to understand "from below" the dynamics of cultural changes and political transformations taking place in India. He is critical of the unthinking acceptance of enlightenment legacies of rationality, secularism and modernization and sees in popular cinema cultural trends, discourses of community, ethical values and modes of resistance to the homogenizing propensities of modernization. Nandy has remarked that,

> The commercial cinema in India does tend to reaffirm the values that are being increasingly marginalized in public life by the language of the modernizing middle classes, values such as community ties, consensual non-contractual human relations, primacy of maternity over conjugality, priority of the mythic over the historical. But even such indirect criticism of middle class values is cast not in the language of social criticism but in that of playful, melodramatic spectacles.[16]

What is interesting to note about Nandy's work on cinema is that while his younger contemporaries are deeply preoccupied with high theory associated with modern film studies and cultural studies as a way of making sense of Indian cinema, Nandy keeps a safe distance from overarching theoretical positions and was in some ways the precursor of the style of contemporary cultural studies. He avoids the vocabularies of analysis, the tools of exposition put into circulation by poststructuralists, postmodernists and cinepsychologists placing value on intelligibility.

Simultaneously, the neo-modernist writings of film scholars and film critics like Ashish Rajadhyaksha and Geeta Kapur have proved exceedingly important in understanding the deeper currents that inform and inflect the cinematic discourse of India. Rajadhyaksha, Kapur and like-minded critics who are associated with the influential *Journal of Arts and Ideas* have played a crucial role in opening up fruitful lines of inquiry into questions of tradition and modernity, narrative discourse, regimes of visuality, and the commodification of art and spectatorial pleasure in relation to popular cinema. Kapur's essay on the film *Jai Santoshi Ma* and Rajadhyaksha's essay on Phalke are exemplary in this regard.[17]

In his insightful essay on "The Phalke Era," Ashish Rajadhyaksha considers the nature of neo-traditionalism as a way of understanding and exploring the complex ways in which traditional forms of cultural articulation and performativities were inflected by the newly introduced technologies associated with the films. Rajadhyaksha has uncovered the ways in which filmic narrativity grew out of culturally rooted narrative discourses and performativities, thereby focusing in an interesting way on questions of visuality and regimes of signification, spectatorship and pleasure. He pays particular attention to the notion of the frame. Commenting on an observation made by André Bazin regarding the frame being centripetal and the screen centrifugal, Rajadhyaksha says that,

> in Phalke's films, the frame functions neither centripetally nor centrifugally but as a holding constant. Its defining tangibility is to the viewer's gaze rather like a cane to a blind person, locating spaces as the gaze feels itself plotting out the universe of the imaginary.[18]

Commenting on another classic of Indian cinema *Sant Tukaram*, he points out how in Indian visual arts the frame has very rarely been employed in the Western sense of container. Instead, what we find is the use of framing to produce narratives, to modulate the rhythms and work as a representational strategy.

Reception studies too, have started to play their part, and currently there are a number of scholars who have focused on the idea of active spectatorship, the purposeful participation of the audiences in negotiating meaning. Far from neglecting the agency and active participation of the audiences in negotiating meaning, these critics focus on the vital interactions between filmic texts and spectators. In *Cinema and the Urban Poor in South India*, Sara Dickey has explored the complex ways in which movie-goers attribute meaning and significance to films and relate to actors.[19] Likewise, in *Sholay – A Cultural Reading*, Malti Sahai and I sought to focus on the active participation of audiences in creating meaning out of cinematic texts.[20] This approach signified an understandable reaction against the kind of liberal humanist film criticism that was very powerful in the 1970s. Initially, journals such as *Screen* were instrumental in disseminating this particular viewpoint. Drawing on the writings of Lacan and Althusser these scholars sought to focus on the production of the textual subject and largely ignored the empirical subject who was located at a particular historical conjuncture. The embodied viewing subject was redefined in relation to the poststructural discourse of the subject. He or she was seen as a product of discourse, an effect of the signifying system. Indeed the critics who were unhappy with this approach underlined the need to focus on the historically situated, empirically observable viewing subjects who were at once distinct individuals and members of an audience. This was a salutary move in that it served to call attention to the agency of spectatorship and a rejection of audiences perceived as undifferentiated masses.

Even among those more inclined to classical film theory, there is a very exciting body of writing that has emerged during the last fifteen years or so that can be broadly described as dealing with issues of cinema and cultural politics: the work of scholars like Ravi Vasudevan, Sumita Chakravarty, Madhava Prasad, Lalitha Gopalan, Vivek Dhareshwar, and Tejaswini Niranjana, to name only the most prominent among them in this regard. Although they do not adopt a uniform approach to cinema and analysis of cinema – and there are significant differences among their respective approaches – one can see in their writing a common orientation towards the study of cinema in India, with a particular emphasis on the intersections of politics of culture and narrativity. Their works have contributed significantly to the rethinking of popular cinema among academics, if not among educated movie-goers in general.

Vasudevan, for instance, has explored the territory of Indian melodrama and the discourse of cultural modernity with great prescience. By discussing the Hindi social films of the1950s as instantiations of popular culture, he has brought out the complexities of popular cinema and the various layers of meaning that we need to uncover if we are to attain a proper understanding of it. He points out the diverse ways in which the idea of the popular was constructed in critical discussions of cinema in the 1940s and 1950s. What distinguishes Vasudevan's analysis from others with a similar interest is his skill in close readings of films, paying particular attention to issues of narrativity, spectacle, and representational strategies, and modes of address associated with the Hindi film. He has sought to demonstrate the "ways in which diverse systems of representation" were brought into a conversation with each other and how this phenomenon with "a narrative manipulation of characters' social position offered a certain mobility to the spectator's imaginary identity."[21] Vasudevan combines close readings of popular films with analyses of larger social transformations, indicating popular cinema to be an extremely important field of sociological investigation.

M. Madhava Prasad has elected to focus on the distinguishing features of popular cinema, paying close attention to the question of narrativity and the complex ways in which diverse historical, economic, social, and cultural forces have sought to shape and inflect popular cinema in India. Prasad foregrounds the notion that Indian cinema has deep roots in modern society and that it both reflects and reshapes the changing contours of the ideological and the political in the Indian sub-continent. In his investigations, Prasad has paid particular attention to the manifold inter-relationships between cinema and the imperatives of capitalism, the state as a force shaping filmic narration, and gender relations as a terrain in which contestations of meaning are played out. His sophisticated analyses of popular films open up important avenues of inquiry leading to the plurality of interconnections between cinematic narration, capitalism and state formation.[22] Likewise, Sumita Chakravarty, in her book *National Identity in Indian Popular Cinema 1947–1987*, examines cinema as an important site of ideological inscription, a repository of cultural knowledge and a negotiation of social meaning. Her focus is on the diverse ways in which national identity is articulated in popular cinema, on the interplay between the global and the local, the national and the transnational, in the shaping of popular cinema in India.[23] Along with her landmark contribution to the scholarship of the sociology of Indian cinema, we can also place the recent writings of Tejaswini Niranjana, Vivek Dhareshwar, Lalitha Gopalan, and Ranjani Mazumdar who have succeeded in bringing about newer perspectives and modes of analysis of the once despised popular cinema of India.

Fields of inquiry

Clearly, the appreciation of the nature and significance of popular cinema has changed considerably during the past fifteen years. A newer generation of film scholars, schooled in Euro-American film theory, have succeeded in bringing about a re-assessment of Indian commercial cinema. While recognizing the importance and advantages of these efforts one must also remain alert to the possible dangers lurking in them. One such danger is the uncritical application of Western theory in evaluating Indian cinema. This is not to valorize any cultural essentialism or enforce a strict division between East and West, but rather to emphasize the necessity of interrogating the fashionable Euro-American theories through the political and cultural specificities of Indian cinema. Without such a stance, there is a real possibility of a newer Orientalism taking over film studies in India. As Paul Willemen observes, reading Indian films through British or American film studies frameworks may in fact be more "like a cultural cross-border raid" or "an attempt to annex another culture by requesting it to conform to the raiders' cultural practices," than a critical contribution.[24]

To accomplish the task of cultivating indigenous frames of reference without falling into the equally perilous trap of essentialism or cultural exceptionalism is not an easy undertaking. It demands great powers of acuity, local knowledge and situated understandings. In order to move towards more productive forms of cross-cultural and comparative film theorizations, we need to take in to cognizance the contemporary relevance of traditional aesthetic conceptualities, ranging from *rasa* and *dhvani* theories to conventions in the visual arts. This is one way of creating more locally based vocabularies of cinematic redescription rather than slavishly deploying the Western lexicon.

As we seek to rethink Indian popular cinema, we also need to pay very close attention to the concept of a national film culture. Historians of Indian cinema have tried to delineate the emergence of a national film culture in terms of totalizing concepts such as nationhood, authenticity and indigenousness. However, in more recent times the idea that it is more fruitful to talk of popular cinemas rather than one popular cinema has met with increasing approbation. This is partly due to the fact that today it is not only the Bombay-Hindi cinema that matters; during the past two decades popular cinemas associated with the southern states of Andhra Pradesh, Tamilnadu and Kerala have emerged to claim large segments of the viewing public. What is interesting to observe in this regard is not only the distinctive identities of these regional popular cinemas but also the constant interactions that take place between and among them. Rather than being confined to specific geolinguistic spaces these popular films seem to cross borders through dubbing, thereby influencing other regional cinemas. This phenomenon is not confined to the South where there are common linguistic characteristics but takes place between the North and the South as well. Mani Ratnam's films have been dubbed into Hindi and have enjoyed a wide popularity. In the light of these interesting developments one needs to examine afresh the concept of "national" film culture in terms of regional identities as well as interactions and reconfigurations among them.

In our continuing attempts to rethink Indian popular cinema and work towards formulating newer frames of understanding we need to focus on what I think are a number of important areas of study. These foci are only suggestive and by no means exhaustive. The first is the concept of the public sphere. In his book, *The Structural Transformation of the Public Sphere*, which has exercised a profound influence on both humanists and social scientists, Jurgen Habermas delineates a set of forces and institutions that took shape in the late seventeenth and eighteenth centuries in Europe and which were pivotal to understanding democratic discourse and oppositionality. He designated this as the bourgeois public sphere. What was noteworthy about this public sphere from the point of view of Habermas was the potentiality it unleashed for separating out the political discourse from both the state and civil society and urging an interrogatory gaze on both domains. Habermas explicates the ways in which the public sphere differentiated itself from the state and the civil society in terms of the important role played by newspapers, journals, literary salons, coffee houses and works of fiction.[25]

Habermas was of the opinion that the liberal bourgeois public sphere that emerged displaying an adversarial relationship to the state, began to decline as a consequence of the rise of mass media. However, Alexander Kluge, Oskar Negt and later Miriam Hansen succeeded in pointing out the importance of cinema as a vital adjunct of the public sphere.[26] With these perceptive studies in mind, we need to pay due attention to the fact that the public spheres took different shapes and forms in different cultures. In the case of India, the idea of cultural performativity and mass participation outside the confines of the written or published word was crucial to understanding the significance of the public sphere. Hence, even more than elsewhere, in India cinema becomes an important cultural institution associated with the public sphere.

All the more so because of the nature of British colonialism in India. Dadasaheb Phalke, the father of Indian cinema, as he is generally referred to, saw cinema as an important mode of stimulating public opinion. He was active in the Swadeshi movement opposed to British imperialism and recognized the value of films in furthering that cause. For him cinema was not just entertainment; he was deeply conscious, as is reflected in his writings, of indigenizing the newly acquired art of cinematography and combining it with local modes of aesthetic understanding and evaluation. Similarly, when we examine the surviving early Indian films, we see a preoccupation with vital social issues of the day. For example between the period 1934–9 a number of significant films like *Chandali, Dharmatma, Bala Yogini, Lakshmi*, and *Thyagabhoomi* all dealt with the issue of untouchability. *Achut Kanya* made in 1936 remains an often-cited example of contestation of caste hierarchy in popular cinema.

No clearer illustration of its role in the public sphere can be seen than cinema's overt participation in Indian politics. One has only to see the ups and downs of the DMK in Madras to realize the importance of this observation. The DMK which has played so vital a role in politics in the state of Tamilnadu has to be understood in terms of cinema. A film like *Parasakthi*, with its unconcealed antipathy to the Congress Party and the authority exercised by the Brahmin caste, exemplifies this trend. Films such as *Parasakthi, Velaikari* and *Oor Iravau* made direct interventions into politics. The well-known politicians C.N. Annadurai and M. Karunanidhi were script-writers who succeeded in injecting their politics into cinema. In many of these films the deployment of party symbols and playful use of names of party leaders in dialogue and song were a common occurrence. In certain films such as *Panam* and *Thangaratnam* the narrative was interwoven with documentary footage dealing with party meetings.[27]

A second area of investigation that demands close and sustained attention is the interplay between globalism and localism. Indian cinema furnishes us with a convincing and particularly long-standing example of this interplay. It foregrounds, in interesting ways, issues of cultural modernity, nationhood, secularism, capitalism, consumerism, ethnicity, citizenship, cosmopolitanism and collective agency. Cinema originated in India, as indeed in all other Asian countries, as a result of the complicated dynamics of globalization. One of the defining features of the contemporary world is the increasingly ramified interplay between the local and the global. Clearly, this process has been in operation for centuries, but the velocity of it has risen sharply in the past five decades. This interaction has generated remarkable transformations in the spaces of politics, economics, and culture as newer forms of capital, largely originating in the West, began to imprint their local traces and inflect in unanticipated ways historically sedimented practices. How the symbolic forms and modalities of association of Western capitalism are transformed, localized, and legitimized in most countries in relation to their historical narratives and changing lifeworlds is at the heart of the discourse of localism. And this discourse is in vital intrication with the cinema of India.[28]

A useful way of coming to grips with the local global dialectic is through an examination of the production of newer localities. When we interrogate the intersecting narratives of the global and the local, what we are seeking to do is to focus on the production of the local and its ever changing contours in response to the demands of the global. The local is hardly static; its boundaries, both spatial and temporal, are subject to incessant change. It is characterized by a nexus of power plays, agonistic interests, pluralized histories, struggles over polysemous signs, and asymmetrical exchanges. The local is for ever transforming itself and reinventing itself as it strains to reach beyond itself and engage the translocal. What is interesting about cinema is that it foregrounds and gives figurality to these complicated processes in compellingly interesting ways. When we examine popular cinema in India from the work of Phalke to that of Ramesh Sippy and Manmohan Desai, we begin to realize the importance of this interplay between the global and the local. What is interesting about cinema is that it makes available to us semioticized space for the articulation of the global imaginary and its formation within the discursive practices of the local.

A study of contemporary Indian modalities of film production, distribution, and exhibition as well as the circles of spectatorship underlines this. Apart from the state-run Doordarshan, satellite channels such as Rupert Murdoch's STAR network, and Subhash Chandra's Zee Television are having a significant impact on the tastes and sensibilities of Indian movie-goers. These transnational influences naturally serve to influence styles, techniques, regimes of signification and visualities of Indian cinema. As a consequence of the proliferation of mass media, the world is shrinking as never before and this very shrinkage has had the effect of generating local narratives with great vigor, opening up newer constituencies of spectators, most notably among the diasporic communities of Indians in the United Kingdom, United States, Canada, and Australia as well as those who trace their origins to India and who live in countries like South Africa and in the Caribbean. Interestingly, the expansion of this transnational audience for Indian popular cinema is influencing its choice of themes and experiences as well.[29]

The interplay between the local and the global and its newer manifestations influence the cinematic discourse at all levels. Let us for example, consider the textualization of the city in Indian cinema. Cinema had its origins as an urban art form and it continues to be a prime shaper of the urbanization of consciousness. The interplay between the local and the global has significantly affected the representation of urban experiences in films. As a consequence of the interanimation of the local and the global, cities like Bombay or Calcutta not only represent themselves but also clear a space for other global cities to make their presence felt. It is almost as if Foucauldian heterotopias are in operation. To represent Bombay is also to partially represent Los Angeles.

These transformations have deep implications for the production of newer libidinal economies and spectatorial subjectivities in Indian commercial cinema. Hence we need to take multi-faceted approaches to the dynamics of the local/ global interactions as we seek to understand the newer reconfigurations of popular cinema.

A third area of investigation that demands attention is the textual poetics of popular Indian cinema. Until recent times, Indian cinema was judged according to the norms and conventions of realism. European art cinema, most notably neo-realistic films, were seen as useful yardsticks. The art cinema in India was realistic and was judged worthy of serious analysis while the popular cinema, which was largely non-realistic, was regarded as counterfeit. However, in recent years, once it was established that realism is just one more convention in cinema and that there are other ways of assessing films, the straitjacket of realism began to be loosened. Concurrently, the long-held notion that Indian cinema was the Other of the West began to lose force and critics realized the importance of understanding the aesthetics of Indian cinema from within its own discursive frameworks.

Some useful work concerning recent trends has already been undertaken by cultural analysts like Ashish Rajadhyaksha, Geeta Kapur and Anuradha Kapur, focused on traditional Indian aesthetic forms as means of mapping some of the representational strategies of popular cinema. Geeta Kapur, for instance, suggests a reassessment of the frontality of Indian popular films:

> Frontality of the word, the image, the design, the formative act, yield forms of direct address; flat, diagrammatic, and simply profiled figures; a figure-ground pattern with only notational perspective; repetition of motifs in terms of "ritual play"; and a decorative *mise-en-scène*.[30]

Similarly, Anuradha Kapur makes the observation that,

> Frontality of the performer vis-à-vis the spectator … enables among other things the relationship of erotic complicity. Now frontality has several meanings in the open theatres of earlier times, but perhaps a set of altogether different meanings come about with the construction of proscenium theatres, which is where Parsi companies performed. In open theatres frontality of the performer indicated a specific relationship between the viewer and the actor, turning the body towards the spectator is a sign that there is in this relationship no dissembling between the two; the actor looks at the audience and the audience looks at the actor; both exist – as actor and audience – because of this candid contact.[31]

In the Parsi theater, while the narrative unfolds in a unilinear way, the performance of the actors and actresses who make no attempt to conceal the fact that they are performing subverts that unilinearity. One can see this in some of the early Indian popular films as well. The frontality of the performer, then, introduces a creative tension and ambiguity between narrative and performance.

Similarly, the concept of *darshana*, which has religious connotations in Hinduism, is significant in terms of the idea of the gaze. As Prasad points out, the structure of spectation in which the spectator occupies an isolated, individualized position of voyeurism coupled with an anchoring identification with a figure in the narrative is specific to Western popular cinema and a small tendency within Indian cinema. Turning to the Hindi feudal family romance we find that its organization of the look differs from the above model in not being governed by a pre-modern institutionalized structure of spectation embodied in the tradition of darshana, which in its most widely employed sense refers to a relation of perception within the public traditions of Hindu worship, especially temples, but also in public appearances of monarchs and other elevated figures.[32]

Some commentators on popular cinema in India have focused on the concept of *rasa* which calls attention to the dominant emotion associated with each sequence in a play or a film. However, in terms of filmic communication, there is another aspect that merits analysis, namely, the conferral of agency on the spectator. The *rasa* concept, as developed by Bharata Muni, Abhinavagupta and other theorists, focuses on the spectator and how he or she generates emotion in relation to the theatrical experience. This focus on the listener, the reader, the spectator is a distinguishing characteristic of classical Indian models of communication as is clearly evidenced in works like Bhartrhari's *Vakyapadiya*. These distinct aesthetic norms represent pathways that have not been traversed adequately.

At the same time we need to examine the various ingredients that go to form Indian popular cinema as a way of assessing their aesthetic significance. Indian popular cinema is a total cinema that is guided by a poetics of excess, in which narrative, spectacle, humor, action, song and dance combine in a loose union to present a cinematic experience whose very constructedness is foregrounded. In seeking to construct a poetics of Indian cinema it is of the utmost significance that we pay close attention to the signifying potentialities of each of these ingredients and the way in which they both construct and contest familiar discourses.

Let us for example consider the central importance of dance sequences in Indian popular cinema – a subject that has received scant attention among film scholars. All popular films contain dance sequences, and critics have often described them derisively as extraneous additions calculated to appeal to the vast mass of movie-goers. Some see in them the display of eroticism otherwise not possible in Indian cinema. It seems to me that dance sequences perform a far more vital role than these still prevalent observations would have us believe. They are a vital part of the meaning of popular films, introducing important creative ambiguities and tensions and calling attention to the creation of new scopic regimes.[33]

Dance sequences in Indian films raise a number of significant questions related to narrative construction and signifying practices. What is the relationship between narrative, spectacle and performance as concretized in dance? In what ways do dance sequences signify and inflect categories of gender identity? What is the nature and status of the kinesthetic semiotics given articulation through dance? How do the performing bodies enact their own difference from themselves? How do the bodies in dance sequences supplement and subvert the bodies in non-dance sequences in films? How does dance display the institutionalized codes of visual representation? How do foreign-inspired dances, as for example those inspired by Michael Jackson, both construct and contest indigenous forms? How do they widen the authority of spectatorial regimes?

The dance sequences in popular-commercial films introduce interesting ambivalences of feeling and thought. For example, in the unfolding of the narrative the lead woman character may be portrayed as submissive, traditional, innocent, and coy while her dance sequences allow her a greater freedom and to celebrate her body and acquire a sense of agency. Dance is important not only in films like *Chandralekha* and *Janaj Janak Payal Baje* which deal with dance but also in Raj Kapoor's now classic romantic films as well as in action films like *Sholay*, *Bombay* and *Satya*. In popular films, female characters are often delineated as stereotypes, earning the opprobrium of critics. However, in the dance performances the internal contradictions, the self-divided nature of stereotypes are foregrounded, generating both assurance and anxiety. Two areas of particular interest in dance sequences are the parameters of performative space and the complicated relationship between the performer and the spectator.

Dance numbers in Indian popular cinema bear an interesting relationship to the world. They have the world as their referent but also succeed in creating their own autonomous world. The interaction between these two worlds opens up productive lines of inquiry. The conventions, cultural codes, that are inscribed on the bodies in motion offer us a useful bridge on which to move from one world to another. The dances contained in Indian films enable us to question such categories as gender identity, masculinity and femininity, regimes of visuality, and the carnal consciousness of the body. Thus dance sequences, which are de rigueur in Indian popular films, are the key to comprehending the totalities of popular reception.

Another area of investigation that one could profitably explore is the ethnographic study of Indian popular cinema from a socio-historical optic. During the last one and a half decades or so, there has been a rise in theoretically sophisticated close readings of popular films in the light of the newer theorizations put into circulation by Western film scholars. Concomitantly, there has been a desire to apply the analytical tools and vocabularies of redescription associated with Western high theory. This is indeed a salutary development. However, there is a deeply felt need to supplement these theorizations with carefully constructed empirical and historical research. This is not a call to retreat into a naive empiricism or positivism but to fortify through social analysis the interesting theoretical lines of inquiry that have already been opened up. The work of scholars like Steve Hughes is highly significant in this regard. His forays into cinematic discourse, governmental interventions and the formations of film audiences in Madras are exemplary in that they provide us with useful models of the type of historical and empirical research sorely needed in the domain of Indian film studies which have long been prey to vast over-generalizations. Indeed, in order to acquire a deeper understanding of the nature and significance of popular cinema as industry, as entertainment, as ideology, as technology, one has to engage in archival research conducted along the lines pursued by Hughes, M.S.S. Pandian and Prem Chowdhury, a practice already discernible in contemporary American and European film scholarship as well.

Still another little-charted terrain, the complex relationship between popular cinema and the political culture of India, has to be explored in greater depth as a means of constructing the newer frames of understanding I have proposed. In discussing the salience of the public sphere in relation to cinema in India I pointed out that from the very beginning there was a vital connection between cinema and politics, as was seen in Phalke's use of the resources of cinema to further the cause of the Swadeshi movement. We need more analyses of cinematic works in relation to the contours of political culture. Vivek Dhareshwar and Tejaswini Niranjana have offered an insightful reading of the film *Kaadalan* with reference to the body, violence and political discourse.[34] Moreover, issues of nationalism, secularism, state and capitalism are imbricated in complex ways in the current discourse of political culture in India. Interestingly, the ambivalences, the fissures, the faultlines associated with the discourse of political culture are reinscribed in the texts of popular films like Mani Ratnam's *Bombay* and *Roja*. Hence, as a means of re-examining and re-situating cinema in the evolving political culture of India, one has to explore these entanglements as they find statement in popular films.

As a preliminary example let us consider the concept of community. Rustom Bharucha makes the observation that cinema is probably one of the most contested cultural sites in India today, and one in which secularism is being narrativized with an increasingly communal subtext. The interconnection between notions of secularism, nationalism, and community is one that invites close scrutiny in terms of its reinscriptions in popular cinema.[35] Political scientists like Partha Chatterjee have expressed the view that the concept of community, with all its fuzziness, has not disappeared from the popular political discourse.[36] On the contrary, with the ever greater intrusion of the state into the inner recesses of social life, it assumes greater and greater importance as a means of understanding the relationship of the state to popular culture. Commercially oriented cinema in India, from its very beginning, has either directly or obliquely addressed the concept of community. How filmmakers rewrote this concept in their respective texts, and how the inscriptions changed over time is an area of analysis that is likely to prove extremely valuable.

Nationalism, on the other hand, usually takes established paths based on imagined communitarian ideals. The glorification of the past is an outcome of the imperatives and anxieties of modernity. It is hardly surprising that cinema, which is a metonym of modernity, has played a crucial role in the recrudescence of cultural nationalism. However, the equation between popular cinema and cultural nationalism is complex and multivalent. As Dipesh Chakrabarty and others remarked, the rise of fascistically oriented movements of ethnic nationalism in India has resulted in an understandable reaction against the critiques of modernity and enlightenment rationality formulated and disseminated by some modern political analysts. However, he cautions us against simple equations and elisions of thought. He says that,

> we short-change ourselves intellectually when we attempt to understand the current ethnic conflicts in India through a grid that has liberalism and fascism locked into an unremitting binary opposition to each other, as though they belong to entirely different and uncontested histories.[37]

Hence we need to bring into play the discourse of politics and the discourse of popular cinema in more complexly imagined ways with the intention of deepening our understanding of both politics and cinema.

Furthermore, as a consequence of the interface between the global and the local we witness a simultaneous process of transnationalization and deterritorialization of consciousness leading to new communitarian cultural imaginaries. While traditional and pre-modern notions of community linger in the collective consciousness of the people, they are grafted onto more decentered, contested and hybridized forms of community. These issues need to be brought into our mappings and analyses of the contextual relevance and cultural knowledge generated by commercially oriented cinema. Whether it be the overtly patriotic films of Manoj Kumar or a seemingly progressive filmmaker like Mani Ratnam or the parody of communalism in *Amar, Akbar, Anthony* or a popular family entertainment like *Hum Aapke Hain Koun*, we see the reinscription of these issues in interesting ways.

The social transformations underway remind us that we need to direct our attention to the relation between cinema and consumer culture. What the idea of consumer culture points to is the fact that social values, social practices, the cultural imaginary, notions of identity and citizenship are defined in terms of consumption and the power of the market. Identity is a function of commodity consumption and not the other way around as we are normally predisposed to think. The power of consumer culture has deep implications for the re-understanding and re-location of Indian popular cinema in that cinema mirrors, promotes, and contests the changing face of consumer culture in India. As it is on the basis of culturally grounded modalities of consumption that we tend to produce and reproduce social relations, cultural practices and guiding values, how popular cinema operates within a rapidly changing consumer culture becomes an increasing urgent subject for investigation. When charting the relationship between consumer culture and popular cinema, the way it is represented and contested, how it becomes a condition of possibility for cinema, its role in promoting consumer culture, the cultural discourses that popular films give rise to through posters, advertising, merchandise, video cassettes, calendars, public appearances of actors and actresses, and other consumerist tie-ins become important areas of cultural inquiry.

Finally, the whole area of spectator participation and the nature of the filmic experience deserves closer scrutiny. Largely as a result of the kind of theorizing that was popular in the 1970s, the mechanisms of the signifying system and the concomitant production of textual subjectivities were privileged over historical viewing subjects. Yet, anyone familiar with the audience partici-pation in Indian popular cinema would realize that instead of positing a universal modality of spectatorship, it is important to examine the culturally-grounded nature of spectatorship and spectatorial agency. For example, in popular Indian cinema the viewing subjects see themselves as active participants in the creation of meaning. Their very overt behavior testifies to this proclivity. The audiences applaud, exclaim passages of dialogue, join the singing, laugh and weep and offer comments both critical and laudatory and turn the filmic experience into a performance like a folk-play. Moreover, it is customary for audiences, if they like the film, to see it many times; the ability to exclaim passages of dialogue and join in the singing and offer anticipatory comments being an outcome of this prior familiarity. What this suggests is that in comparison, say, with Western audiences, there is a distinct character to the nature of audience participation in popular films in India. This aspect needs to be investigated, going beyond the all too familiar Western psychoanalytical concepts that tend to valorize the textual production of undifferentiated subjects.[38]

In the process of elucidating some of the governing discursive features of India popular cinema I have underlined certain areas of investigation that would enable us to deepen our understanding of this phenomenon. Clearly, one can identify more areas for exploration. What I have sought to do is to emphasize the need to rethink Indian popular cinema and work our way towards the construction of newer forms of understanding and analysis, and I have charted the critical shifts directing us to a complex field worthy of serious and sustained exploration. Indian popular cinema, in a significant sense, is what theorists and critics make it out to be; it is not a cinema that Third Cinema critics can afford to ignore.

Notes

1 See for instance:
   Ashis Nandy, *The Savage Freud and Other Essays on Possible and Retrievable Selves*, New Jersey: Princeton University Press, 1995 and *The Secret Politics of Our Desires*, London: Zed, 1998.
   Geeta Kapur, "Mythic Material in Indian Cinema," *Journal of Arts and Ideas*, Vols 14–15, 1987, pp. 79–107.

Ashish Rajadhyaksha, "The Phalke Era: Conflict of Traditional Form and Modern Technology," *Journal of Arts and Ideas*, Vols 14–15, 1987, pp. 47–78.

Ravi Vasudevan, *Making Meaning in Indian Cinema*, New Delhi: Oxford University Press, 2000.

M. Madhava Prasad, *Ideology of the Hindi Film: A Historical Reconstruction*, New Delhi: Oxford University Press, 1998.

Sumita Chakravarty, *National Identity in Indian Popular Cinema, 1947–1987*, Austin: University of Texas Press, 1993.

Sara Dickey, *Cinema and the Urban Poor in South India*, Cambridge: Cambridge University Press, 1985.

M.S.S. Pandian, *The Image Trap*, New Delhi: Sage, 1992.

2   Marshall Berman, *All That is Solid Melts Into the Air: The Experience of Modernity*, London: Verso, 1983.

3   Georg Simmel, "The Metropolis and the Mental Life," in K. Wolff (ed.) *The Sociology of Georg Simmel*, London: Collier-Macmillan, 1950.

Walter Benjamin, *Selected Writings, Volume I*, ed. Marcus Bullock and Michael Jennings, Cambridge: Harvard University Press, 1966.

Siegfried Kracauer, *The Mass Ornament*, Cambridge, Harvard University Press, 1995.

4   Marshall Berman, op. cit., p. 49.

5   Georg Simmel, op. cit., p. 6.

6   Ashis Nandy, *Secret Politics*, p. 29.

7   Ibid., p. 27.

8   Ibid., p. 29.

9   Ibid., p. 31.

10 See, for instance, K. Moti Gokulsing and Wimal Dissanayake, *Indian Popular Cinema: A Narrative of Cultural Change*, New Delhi: Orient Longman, 1998.

11 Vijay Mishra, "Towards a Theoretical Critique of Bombay Cinema," *Screen*, Vol. 6, No. 3/4, 1985, pp. 133–46.

12 Ibid., p. 138.

13 The relationship between Indian popular films and Hollywood is not one of simple influence. Indian filmmakers very often appropriated the axiomatics of Hollywood cinema, and made use of it for culture-specific purposes. In the process they both extended the discursivities of Hollywood cinema and also subverted them.

14 Gilles Deleuze, *Cinema 2: The Time-Image*, Minneapolis: University of Minnesota Press, 1989. He identifies two types of images, the subjective and time images. In the subjective images the perspective of a person who is involved in a given interaction determines the meaning, while in the time images, the composition of shots yields a commentary that undercuts the subjective perspective referred to earlier. Certainly, when we examine the ramifications of the ideas of spectacle and performance in Indian popular cinema, it is the time-image with its implications of what Deleuze terms a "crystalline regime" that invites closer attention.

15 Chidananda Dasgupta, *The Painted Face: Studies in Indian Popular Cinema*, New Delhi: Orient Longman, 1991. Taste, of course, is an interesting and complex concept. Pierre Bourdieu remarks that in matters of taste, more than anywhere else, all determinations need to be construed as negation and that tastes are first and foremost distastes. See, for example, *Distinction: A Social Critique Of The Judgement Of Taste* (Richard Nice, trans.), Cambridge, MA: Harvard University Press, 1984.

16 Ashis Nandy, *Secret Politics*, p. 29.

17 Geeta Kapur, op. cit. and Ashish Rajadhyaksha, op. cit.

18 Rajadhyaksha, ibid.

19 Sara Dickey, op. cit.

20 Wimal Dissanayake and Malti Sahai, *Sholay – A Cultural Reading*, New Delhi: Wiley Eastern, 1992.

21 Ravi Vasudevan, op. cit., p.99.

22 M. Madhava Prasad, op. cit.
23 Sumita Chakravarty, op. cit.
24 Paul Willemen, *Looks and Frictions: Essays in Cultural Studies and Film Theory*, Bloomington: Indiana University Press, 1994.
25 Jurgen Habermas, *The Structural Transformation of the Public Sphere*, Cambridge: MIT Press, 1992.
26 Oskar Negt and Alexander Kluge, *The Public Sphere and Experience*, Minneapolis: University of Minnesota Press, 1993. Miriam Hansen, "Early Cinema, Late Cinema: Permutations of the Public Sphere," *Screen*, Winter, 1993, p. 47.
27 The relationship between cinema and political culture is a many-sided one. It is also a question of reading closely various filmic texts with a cultural politics in mind. Let us, for example, consider the interplay between women and the discourse of nationhood as enunciated in popular cinema. The trope of motherhood is constantly invoked as a means of generating patriotism and love for the nation even as women are marginalized and confined to the private sphere. It is also interesting to observe how Hindu women from the upper middle class are presented as spaces in which the ideas of nationhood are imbricated with Hinduism. This is indeed a common occurrence in the popular cinema of India.
28 For a more sustained discussion of these issues see Rob Wilson and Wimal Dissanayake (eds) *Global/Local: The Cultural Production of the Transnational Imaginary*, Durham: Duke University Press, 1992.
29 See, for instance, Ackbar Abbas, *The Politics of Disappearance*, Minneapolis: University of Minnesota Press, 1995.
30 Geeta Kapur, *When Was Modernism?* New Delhi: Tulika Press, 2000, p. 249.
31 Anuradha Kapur, "The Representation of Gods and Heroes," *Journal of Arts and Ideas*, Vol. 23–4, p. 92.
32 M. Madhava Prasad, op. cit., p. 78.
33 Dance figures very prominently in a variety of practices in traditional Indian culture. In the case of theater, there was a heavy emphasis placed on gesture and bodily movement. Classical Sanskrit dramaturgists identified four main modes of conveying meaning in the theater. They are speech (*vachika abhinaya*), gesture (*angika abhinaya*), facial expression (*satvika abhinaya*) and costuming (*aharaya abhinaya*). As we can see, three of these four modes deal with the body and bodily motions. Interestingly, cinema itself developed from technology intended to capture the flow of bodily motion.
34 I refer, in particular, to Vivek Dhareshwar and Tejaswini Niranjana, "Kaadalan and the Politics of Resignification: Fashion, Violence and the Body," *Journal of Arts and Ideas*, Vol. 29, 1996, pp. 5–26. The idea of violence has been central to narrative discourse from the early beginnings of Indian popular cinema. Until recent times males were at the center of the violence. However, a number of contemporary films like *Pratighat, Sherni, Commando, Kali Ganga, Khon Bhari Mang* and *Police Lock-up* have violent female protagonists, raising a number of significant issues related to questions of gender identity, female agency, and the challenges to the patriarchal social order.
35 Bharucha, Rustom, *In The Name Of The Secular*, Delhi: Oxford University Press, 1991.
36 Partha Chatterjee, *The Nation and Its Fragments*, Princeton: Princeton University Press, 1993.
37 Dipesh Chakrabarty, "Modernity and Ethnicity in India," in J. Macguire, P. Reeses and H. Brastead (eds) *The Politics Of Violence*, London: Sage, 1996.
38 It has to be noted that cinema has emerged in India as an efficacious site in which audiences are interpellated as consumers, investing them with consumer identities. This relates vitally to the commodification of everyday life that invites close analysis. Cultural critics and philosophers like Georg Simmel, Gyorgy Lukács, Pierre Bourdieu and Michel de Certeau have sought to penetrate the rust of commodity form in order to comprehend the meanings and significance embedded in everydayness.

Index